# HOW TO HELP AN ELEPHANT MAKE A U-TURN

# HOW TO HELP AN ELEPHANT MAKE A U-TURN

### A New Approach to Leadership and Transformational Change

# G.K. JAYARAM

MAVEN
RUPA

Published in Maven by
Rupa Publications India Pvt. Ltd 2015
7/16, Ansari Road, Daryaganj
New Delhi 110002

*Sales Centres:*
Allahabad Bengaluru Chennai
Hyderabad Jaipur Kathmandu
Kolkata Mumbai

Copyright © G.K. Jayaram 2015

While every effort has been made to trace copyright holders and obtain permission, this has not been possible in all cases; any omissions brought to our attention will be remedied in future editions.

The views and opinions expressed in this book are the author's own and the facts are as reported by him/her which have been verified to the extent possible, and the publishers are not in any way liable for the same.

All rights reserved.
No part of this publication may be reproduced, transmitted, or stored in a retrieval system, in any form or by any means, electronic, mechanical, photocopying, recording or otherwise, without the prior permission of the publisher.

ISBN: 978-81-291-3564-3

First impression 2015

10 9 8 7 6 5 4 3 2 1

The moral right of the author has been asserted.

Printed and bound in India by Replika Press Pvt. Ltd.

This book is sold subject to the condition that it shall not, by way of trade or otherwise, be lent, resold, hired out, or otherwise circulated, without the publisher's prior consent, in any form of binding or cover other than that in which it is published.

# CONTENTS

*Foreword* — vii
*Introduction* — ix
*Author's Note* — xix

1  Why Is Leadership the Most Critical and Urgent Need of Our Age? — 1
2  Developing a Transcendent Leader — 23
3  Three Generic Models for Change Thinking — 120
4  The Management of Transformational Change — 145
5  Leadership Development—How? — 214

*Notes* — 253
*Acknowledgments* — 261

# FOREWORD

Over the years I have enjoyed many conversations about leaders and leadership with my old friend, G.K. Jayaram. Though all our impassioned discussions, in various capacities—as a friend, as the first Chairman of Infosys, as the person I first turned to when thinking of the Infosys Leadership Institute—Jayaram has, for me, been the quintessential friend, philosopher and guide. I take great pleasure in inviting you to participate in, what I believe, is yet another very meaningful conversation, albeit in book form.

Leadership is a much overused word and many things to many people. As Jayaram, points out, the need of the day is to bring about change. Progress is positive change. It requires that people accept new ideas, new dreams, new people and new challenges. This means that people have higher levels of aspiration, hope, energy, confidence and enthusiasm. A leader's main task is to bring about change, to create enthusiasm for change. That is why we need leadership. That is why we need transcendent leadership, as Jayaram so eloquently argues.

At the core of this task of change lies a vision and, more importantly, values. A vision has to be built on sound, eternal and context-invariant values to sustain the enthusiasm and energy of people over a long time. A value system is a protocol for behaviour in a community, where the community and the individual progress on a sustainable basis. As with people, my belief is that a company's value system is its guiding light in hours of darkness, confusion, self-doubt and dilemma. More importantly, putting the interest of the community above one's personal interest will eventually lead to the betterment of the individual. So when Jayaram talks about integrity of vision or purpose, and integrity of values, he highlights the very core of leadership.

His '3+5 Transcendent Leadership' model provides a recipe for rehabilitating lost leadership qualities and rejuvenating societies. Transcendent leadership is built on the foundation of the 3 Is—integrity, intensity, imagination—and the 5 pillars of empathy, self-awareness, interpersonal wisdom, community wisdom and global wisdom.

This book shares the concepts, models and best global practices to help create leaders who will respond to the challenges of the twin revolutions—the revolution of rising expectations in emerging countries (and indeed globally for the poor) and the spiralling of reduced expectations in the developed nations.

Let me conclude by suggesting that the best way to read this book is to treat it like a conversation. Read a few pages, turn them over in your mind, and think about what it means before you move on; form your own views and most importantly, act on them. This is food for thought, not a snack to eat standing up. I hope you will enjoy it as much as I did.

N.R. Narayana Murthy<br>
Chairman Emeritus, Infosys<br>
October 2014

# INTRODUCTION

## The Elephant and I

It all started with my father, one of my favourite people, and elephants, one of my favourite animals. We were probably the only family I have ever known who had elephants as pets. To be precise, we had two adults and one baby elephant. My father was a forest ranger and in India the perks of this job, meagre and sparse as they were, included prominently taking care of the gentle giants of the forest. Throughout our childhood, we lived deep in lush green forests in the middle of nowhere with our nearest neighbour miles away. If your father is a stockbroker, he might talk to you about Wall Street; if he is a lawyer, he might talk to you about cases; if he is a forest ranger in South India during the British Raj, he talks to you about elephants.

During the course of a lazy evening, my father asked me a question that stuck in my mind forever: 'What do you do when a wild elephant chases you through the forest?' I am sure many people have lain awake at night pondering this question—it certainly intrigued me.

I answered, 'I don't know, Dad. What do you do?'

'Well, son, first of all, you run,' said my father, 'but don't underestimate the elephant and its speed just because it's so huge. An elephant, when it's charging, can actually run at 25 mph. So the way to escape the thundering giant is to run making broad U-turns when you are in front of it—its greatest strength is also its greatest limitation.'

You see, on the one hand, even though it is so huge, an elephant can run at a speed of 25 mph (I have since heard that African elephants can run at 35 mph. Is this a case of intercontinental species-sibling rivalry? Or is it process improvement?), but on the other hand, because it is so huge, when you make a broad U-turn, it has to come almost to a standstill before it can change direction. And it is there that you, nimble-footed human, have the advantage over this mammoth creature.

There. Now you know how to survive an elephant chase.

Consider another situation: an elephant—one that you care for deeply—is not trying to chase you down, but is running towards danger. It needs to change direction swiftly, not only for its own survival, but maybe also yours. This book is about helping such 'elephants'—our societies, businesses, corporations and organizations of every size and kind that are unable to easily change course. Can they do so themselves? Or do they need nimble-footed people to lead them? Where do you find such leaders?

'Not another book on leadership, please!' you groan. But I ask—if we know all there is to know about leadership, then why are seeing increasing cynicism about our leaders in every sphere of human activity, whether it is business or politics or religion? We see massive leadership failures all around us which demand urgent action—the citizenry and the powerful elite alike need to reflect and debate upon the reasons for these failures. Instead, most of these incidents are swept under the carpet or, worse, they are whitewashed with cover-ups.

Admit it. There may be libraries full of books with 'leadership' in their titles, but the world's organizations are still indelibly flawed. We have either not learnt to use that knowledge to make the world a better place, or all that knowledge has not been entirely useful in the real world. So here is my humble contribution: a book which discusses how we can choose, nurture, develop and perpetuate leaders who will help these elephants make U-turns.

Since 1968, I have worked with various organizations around the world. I wanted to create a book which reflected my experiences. I invited 50 leaders from diverse fields to let me listen to their thoughts on a variety of issues relating to leadership. The result was an interesting, often arresting, array of experiences and insights. The 50 were not chosen by a random sample. The sample was not statistically significant, and I did not balance for age (a third each of black, salt-and-pepper and grey? Nah) or industry (poultry at one end and astrophysics at the other? Not really). The primary criterion for choosing these chairpersons, professors, entrepreneurs, consultants and CEOs was for their ability to reflect upon their lives in general and on leadership in particular. I did attempt to ensure that women leaders are adequately represented in the book, since the number of women at the top continues to be small due to a long history of discrimination in the workplace, which is changing ever so slowly now. Despite the effort, men outnumber women in my pantheon of leaders by 3:1 (as the civil-rights marchers once sang in America, 'We shall overcome...someday', and that day will dawn only when equal rights amendments are passed in India and across the world by the male legislators who have successfully resisted it so far).

Some of these chosen leaders are deductive thinkers: they start from lofty principles and then dip to ground-level realities. Others are inductive: they present empirical data first and then draw inferences from them. But they are all 'amphibians' to different degrees, capable of being in water and on the bank, seamlessly traversing the grounds between the abstract and the concrete.

Throughout the book, I have inserted excerpts from these 50 interviews as and where relevant. While the thoughts and sentiments quoted from the interviews are faithfully reported (some verbatim, some edited for clarity), the interpretations are my responsibility and I absolve my kind and gracious interviewees of all responsibility. In other words, the flowers belong to them but the garland is mine and I have placed their thoughts where I feel they belong.

## The Interviewees

N.R. Narayana Murthy—Co-Founder and Chairman Emeritus, Infosys
Kiran Mazumdar-Shaw—Chairman and CEO, Biocon
Rohini Nilekani—Founder and Chairperson, Arghyam
K.V. Kamath—Chairman, Infosys, and Non-Executive Chairman, ICICI Bank
Chanda Kocchar—Managing Director and CEO, ICICI Bank
Binny Bansal—Co-Founder and COO, Flipkart
Sachin Bansal—Co-Founder and CEO, Flipkart
Subroto Bagchi—Chairman, Mindtree
Vinita Bali—Managing Director and CEO, Britannia Industries
S.D. Shibulal—Co-Founder, Infosys
T.V. Mohandas Pai—Chairman, Manipal Global Education

Sanjay Anandaram—Co-Founder, JumpStartUp
Kishan Ananthram—Chairman, IonIdea (USA)
Brindala Ananthram—President and CEO, IonIdea (USA)
M.J. Aravind—Senior Corporate Executive, VC
Sudip Banerjee—Ex-CEO, L&T Infotech, and Ex-President, Wipro
Dharen Chadha—Ex-Global Strategic Planning Director, J Walter Thompson (JWT)
K. Dinesh—Co-Founder, Infosys
Chetan Elvis—Partner and Marketing Director, Mahiti Infotech
Devapriyo Ghose—Leadership Development Consultant
Kris Gopalakrishnan—Co-Founder, Infosys
Anal Jain—senior executive in in international and Indian IT firms
K. Jairaj—Former Additional Chief Secretary, Government of Karnataka
Ashok Kamath—Managing Trustee, Akshara Foundation, and Ex-CEO, Analog Devices India
Rishikesh Krishnan—Professor (Corporate Strategy and Policy), Indian Institute of Management, Bangalore (IIMB)
Rajiv Kuchhal—former Infosys employee and former COO, On-mobile
Jacob Kurian—Partner, New Silk Route; and former employee, Tata Unisys, Titan
Anjan Lahiri—CEO, It Services, Mindtree
Michael Lee-Chin—Chairman, Portland Holdings (Canada)
Haragopal M—former Senior Vice President, Infosys, and Global Head, Finacle
Vijay Mahajan—Chairman, BASIX
Dr Vivek Mansingh—Chairman, AxisCades; former Head, Dell India; Cisco, India
Prof. Ashok Mishra—Chairman-India, Intellectual Ventures, ex-Director, IIT, Mumbai
Daljit Mirchandani—Ex-Chairman, Ingersoll-Rand
Deependra Moitra—Independent Consultant
Terry Moodley—President, Standard Bank; and Head of Personal and Business Banking, Standard Bank (South Africa)
Jacqueline Novogratz—Founder and CEO, Acumen Fund (USA)
Madan A. Padaki—Co-Founder and Director, MeritTrac
Mali Mahalingam—Executive Vice President & Global Chief People Officer,

Symphony Services Corporation
Sanjay Purohit—CEO and MD, EdgeVerve Systems Ltd, An Infosys Company
S.K. Raman—Chief Operating Officer, Kemwell
Ramesh Ramanathan—Co-Founder, Janaagaraha
Swati Ramanathan—Co-Founder, Janaagaraha
Sreekanth S, Rameshaiah—Executive Director, Mahiti Infotech
K. Ramkumar—Executive Director, ICICI Bank
Anu Rao—Ombudsman, Professional Effectiveness Coach, Mediator, Consultant
Hema Ravichandar—Ex-Senior Vice President, HRD, Infosys Ravichandar—CMD, Feedback Business Consulting Services Pvt. Limited, India
Manish Sabharwal—Co-Founder and Chairman, Team Lease Services
Sharad Sharma—Ex-Head (Research and Development), Yahoo India
Trilochan Sastry—Professor and Ex-Dean (Academics), Indian Institute of Management
R. Sriram—Co-Founder, Next Practice Retail; and Co-Founder, Crosswords
V. Ganapathy Subramanian—Head of Strategic Planning, Infosys
Rishikesha Krishnan—Director & Professor of Strategy at Indian Institute of Management, Indore

## How to Read This Book

As you read through this book, I implore you to talk to me in your mind, react, debate and even fall asleep at times; please take off on your own private journeys if you feel the need, but do always return refreshed and ready to engage with me again. We will reflect on the issues that bind you and me and the world around us into one big family, happy or unhappy. I will at times be descriptive, at others prescriptive, without being restrictive, let alone proscriptive, about your autonomy to differ from me. All that I ask is that you reflect on my experiences and engage with my proposed models for understanding our world. You are urged to form your own models and, if sufficiently intrigued, to act upon them.

The two areas where leaders have the power to influence the lives of every person on earth are politics and business. Hence, everything that is presented between these covers is addressed directly to leaders in the corporate and the political world. And, of course, it is also relevant to the rest of us who are in, one way or another, inextricably woven into the fabric of these two vital fields of human endeavour.

Now, here is a 'site map' of the book for those accustomed to browsing websites.

In what follows, I present a set of propositions which are the gist of this book. The rest of the book is an elaborate explanation and defence of the propositions stated here. I will attempt to 'sell' you the concept of transcendent leaders (TCLs), substantiated with examples. I want you to close this book saying, 'We need, want and can create transcendent leaders for our organization. I am to be one of them, and I know how to become one. My boss needs to be one, and every leader at every level of my company needs to be a transcendent leader. If I am not one and my boss is not one, I need to know how to recognize the gaps and work to fill them.' This is the beginning of leadership development, where you play the role of your own 'guru'.

**Thesis**

I would like to argue that TCLs create transformational change (TC) in their organizations, acting as both, a means of accomplishing such change and as a product of such change. These leaders create other transcendent and transformational leaders (TFLs) who carry on the transformational change.

What do these 'trans-words' mean? You may ask why I call leaders who create transformational change as transcendent leaders instead of transformational leaders, or why I do not call the change made by transcendent leaders as transcendent change. After all, Professor Amartya Sen called us 'argumentative Indians' and these questions are bound to arise in a curious mind. Transformational leadership is a process in which leaders and followers connect with each other to reach a higher level of morale and motivation. It is a mutually influencing, transforming group. I would like to argue that the TCL has a deeper understanding of her world and the larger universe to which her small world belongs. She not only connects with her followers, but she also engages deeply with her immediate surroundings and the larger universe, to evolve her vision, values and strategies. Transformational leadership is a part of transcendent leadership, but does not encompass it fully.

The chapters that follow will state, define, describe and defend with examples the following propositions:

1. We urgently, perhaps desperately, need a new kind of leader—TCLs.
2. TCLs are needed and can be found at every level of an organization from the boardroom to the shop floor, from the Chairman to the chief of the *safai karamcharis* (janitors). The TCL model is both non-exclusive and non-elitist. TCLs are you and me.
3. A TCL is a systems thinker. This means that a TCL believes that everything is interrelated and, hence, her every action is thought out with regard to the entire system she is part of. This means that she, as a leader at any level of the organization, executes the following set of actions for all the relevant internal and external domains influencing her organization, such as its people, those who fund it, its clients or consumers, those who lay down its laws and regulations and anyone who can help or hurt the system in a significant manner: She collects data, analyses impact, chooses a 'strategy' (as well as backup options) to change the system the transformational way, executes the strategy perfectly, evaluates the impact on all relevant domains, such as employees and customers, and finally repeats the cycle—the helix of change.
4. The central job for a TCL—the raison d'être—is to create and lead transformational change. Everything else is mere administration of status quo, which though important, does not require one to transcend but only to conserve.
5. Any transformational change requires many leaders, each possessing a different skill. A TCL develops systems and processes, but above all a culture that helps transform existing leaders into the right kind of leaders for each task of TC. For example, a particular TC might need different leaders to play the role of a general, colonel, major, captain, lieutenant or sergeant, but there could also be a situation where the same leader may have to play multiple roles according to the needs of the situation.
6. I propose that no one can make someone else a leader; each person makes herself a leader and another may help or hinder them. The

process of creating new kinds of leaders is a complex, multi-strategical process and ultimately it is a mere catalyst for the individual to develop or recreate oneself into the right kind of leader. No one person can create a TCL. The opportunity, the ambience, the knowledge and tools are provided by the organization, and those who can exploit the given opportunities to transform, or reinvent themselves into a combination of their desired roles and the organization's needed roles, become TCLs.

So how do you navigate through this book? How can you customize your use of it, assuming you find any use in it?

If you are interested in psychology and you want to check your mental model of an ideal leader against mine, flip to Chapter 2 and tear my ideas apart. If you wish to learn how to create an in-house leadership development institution, skip to the last chapter. If you are faced with a major change in your enterprise and are looking for a roadmap, skip to Chapter 5. Or else you could read this from beginning to end, as Sherlock Holmes said to Watson, 'omitting no details whatsoever, however trivial'. I promise a chuckle or two, and maybe an occasional insight. Every chapter attempts to answer the questions of 'what', 'how' and 'why'. This means that there is some local theory supporting each topic. After all, you are not buying a dishwasher and need just the operating manual. You need the deeper stuff, the 'why' underlying the 'what' and the 'how'.

The use of 'I' versus 'we' in a book such as this is always a dilemma. Since this is a conversation with you, and since I am the only one writing this book, it seems rather pompous, phony and downright silly to use the royal 'we' instead of the honest 'I'. If we were actually sitting together and talking, I wouldn't call myself 'we', would I? But the convention—the hallowed tradition, in fact—is to address you as though a whole bunch of us or His Royal Highnesses ('We are very pleased with the behaviour of the Indian colony') is condescending to speak to you. Regardless, I will try and be me and use the first person singular pronoun.

The use of 'he' versus 'she'. Take the following example: 'What does a leader do? He or she...' You see, all authors face this problem when they have to choose a gendered pronoun. Traditionally, most authors choose to use 'he' and claim that it is the convention and that 'he' is generic and includes 'she'. (Really? The last time I checked, all the 'hes' I knew were quite distinct from all the 'shes' I knew.) The second, and more awkward option, is to use 'he or she' every time. The third is to be thrifty and save many syllables by saying 's/he'. But there is one other option that appeals to me. Since the invention of the alphabet some 3,000 years ago, give or take a few hundred years, 'he' has had the starring role and has been the generic representative of all humanity, including the 51 per cent made up of women. So why not start the new millennium and continue for the next 3,000 years using 'she' as the generic symbol for all humanity? It will be historic justice and an equal opportunity for women to discriminate against men. Seems fair to me.

So then, here it goes!

## AUTHOR'S NOTE

Let me first say a few words, tell you a little about my writing style and about myself. I am fond of words, so this book has a lot of them. But I will ask you to imagine yourself at my home, sitting on a sofa, sipping a mellow drink of your choice. You are in a very generous mood, so you have graciously consented to let me speak to you through the evening.

As you will see, among the many things I like are, quotations and proverbs. Two of my favourite quotations are:

'Where you stand depends on where you sit.'—Nelson Mandela

'What Peter says about Paul says more about Peter than about Paul.' —Baruch Spinoza

So where have I sat? What does it say about me? Since all writing is autobiographical, let me tell you my side of the story as well (in brief; I'm not that immodest), and you can infer whatever you choose in light of this book. Everything I say in this book is filtered through my genes and my life's experiences. Where I sit is because of them, and what I say about the world will say a lot about me. My nature and my nurture, my heredity and my environment are the glasses through which I view the world. All writing is ultimately autobiographical—my biases, prejudices, dreams and dilemmas—all influence what I say here, so you are forewarned.

When you read this book, you will read it through your own unique 'glasses', your own context. You can no more help it than you can get out of your skin and get into mine. Neither of us can avoid any of this. To claim to be objective would be as spurious and laughable as me claiming to be a 6-feet 4-inch blue-eyed blonde Scandinavian (I am not; stop laughing, those of who have seen me). Hence, for full disclosure and for 'truth in advertising' (because everything we say is 'an advertisement of ourselves'), I give you at least the bare minimum of 'facts' about me. You can trace, rightly or wrongly, the origins of my views in my own origins and the journeys I have undertaken in my lifetime.

I am 70 years and 228 days old as I write this line. I pre-date Nehru's 'Tryst with Destiny', but not by much. I did not know who Gandhiji was on 30 January 1948. The first time I heard of this man, one of my two greatest future heroes, was when my pretty cousin, four years older than me, rushed in to the house shouting, 'Gandhi Thatha is dead!' She was crying and since I liked her, I too cried.

Now I cry for Gandhiji is truly dead in India. This book, trivial as it is, is a grateful tribute to the great man. My many brothers and sisters around the world are privileged to know that '...such a man as this one ever in flesh and blood walked upon this earth,' to quote Einstein, another great hero. I am proud to be born into the same species.

I had a mother who, I was told, was a petite beauty in her youth; she was still lovely when I was born, the tenth child, after seven of my little brothers and sisters had died. Poor little Amma! God knows what she went through, bearing and losing so many. When I was born after my two brothers survived (the seventh and the eight), they discovered a lump the size of a tennis ball on the top of my head (no doubt stylishly arranged). Appa and Amma and all my aunts and uncles said, 'Here is another one to be taken away.' My 80-year-old aunt tells me that my mother put the infant with the 'swollen head' on her lap and said, 'Maybe your luck will be better than mine, and this one will survive.' Between the two ladies they managed to convince the 'powers that be' to leave this child alone or else, and the rest is...an addition to what was then in 1941 a population of 31.87 crore or 318 million. (As an aside...India's population in 1941 was higher than the US' population on 31 December 2011.)

My mother never went to school because her father believed that girls did not need an education. ('There was a school right across the street in our small town,' my mother would lament. No offense, Grandpa, but what is it with my gender, I wonder.) She taught herself how to read Kannada, our language, and would read magazine stories in the afternoons and prayer books in the mornings and evenings. She was full of proverbs and I have inherited that fondness for 'words of wisdom' uttered by others. Beware, you will be the ones I will inflict these upon. (After all, why bother saying something yourself if someone else has said it better?) She was the one who brought us up, since father often had to go the forest, three to five days a week at times, and we had to live in the village of Jannapur so that we could go to school in the neighbouring town.

And my father! Appa walked for five days, as a 16-year-old, from his village to the big city to find a school. He dropped out of high school after the first year to find a job and to educate his younger brother. As a forester in the royal gardens, which were located up a hill, he bicycled daily to work. When I was born, we lived in the middle of virgin forests (the so-called Hebbe forests which went under a mountain of water when a dam was built on Bhadra River much later). Our home was built on stilts to discourage tigers from visiting us for breakfast.

The forest department gave Appa elephants—for elephants were the beasts of burden, the lorries and trucks of yesteryears—to work in the forests, dragging down trees and stacking up logs. We had two adult elephants and a baby elephant was born around the same time as I was. They named it 'Jayalakshmi', the female version of my name. We three boys would feed the elephants in the morning and then ride them through the Bhadra River to the forests with Appa. There was nothing to do there but play, drink milk (yes, there were no fast-food stalls) and daydream in the woods. I love elephants to this day.

('What happened to the lump,' did you ask? You didn't ask? You didn't even remember? Shame on you. I was a newborn. You would surely like to know what happened. Well, I'm told the lump disappeared over a period of 21 days. Nobody knows why. We used to have guests like that during my childhood. They came uninvited and they left unannounced. Of course, no one would dream of saying anything to them. It would be too rude. We just waited. We were silent spectators to this entry and exit of characters who was not in the script of our play at all. I think they did the same with the lump. The doctors pleaded helplessness, 'Can't operate on a newborn', and my family was fatalistic, 'If God so wills, it will live.' I am happy to report to you that the baby lived. I think it was a good thing, but then I'm biased).

Father was a man of few words—the average words spoken when you add his to mine comes out quite normal. He was not given to profound philosophical reflections on values and such, but everything I know and respect in life in terms of integrity—simple honesty, incorruptibility, hard work and courtesy—I learnt from this simple man.

A true story: My earliest memory is of a dark hall with high ceilings in our forest home at dusk. There was only a kerosene lamp which heightened the shadows and threw a stark circle of light around the lamp. I was probably 3 years old and was playing by myself in the hall. A man, stocky and clad in a dhoti and a shirt, came to the door. He was a family friend who worked for my father as a contractor and who brought in 'coolies' for work. (This is all hindsight knowledge; I knew nothing of all this obviously, except that the man was called Ammaberi and that he was kind and funny and that he rocked me on his generous paunch with uproarious laughter). My mother came out of the kitchen to the hall. The man saluted and extended a basket full of vegetables to my mother, who took it just as my father came out of his study.

What happened next is etched in my memory. Father took in the scene in a glance and walked up to Mother. Now, he doted on my mother. They were quite a pair. He, at 5 feet 8 inches and she, 10 inches shorter. It was said that it was a 'love marriage' in 1918, Father having dared to ask his father to ask her father for her hand. (This was facilitated by the fact that they lived in the same village.) He never ever raised his voice at her, but he said to her then, 'What is this, Sesha? Have I not told you not to take these things?' He then turned to the man, and his fury was something to behold for a 3-year-old. He flung the basket towards the man and all the vegetables flew across the room. He then screamed at him, 'How dare you come with such gifts to my home? People who see this will think Rangachar (my father's name) takes bribes and does favours. Get out of here this instant, and if I ever catch you bringing anything here again, your contract will be cancelled!' I heard him mutter to himself, 'What would people think? What would God think?'

I have never forgotten this episode. He has never preached to us and has never told us how to live. I just saw him living the values that I have come to learn are the ones that sustain a community, a society and the world. I could not have learnt in any better way.

I have a wife and two children without whom I would be barren and devoid of love. They are the home from which I come and to which I return, though they may not always know this and I may not tell them. (Love in the abstract is hard. You need to vest and invest love in something you can touch, feel and hold. That is why many humans worship idols.

God is hard to grasp; God as an idol, a picture, a talisman hung around your neck, is so much closer). This book has been reviewed critically and approved by them. For me, the 'meaning of life', as we shall speak of it later, is inextricably connected to having these three in my life.

Having been poor a third of my life, I have done a 'hop-skip-and-jump' onto 'a place in the sun' where, according to the *New York Times*, I am not poor anymore. Inside the affluent man sits a poor little Indian boy who cannot believe his good luck, nor can he bear the existence of irrational systems which impose bad luck on large numbers of people and blithely move on as accomplices before and after the fact.

Enough about me (reluctantly said)—is there ever enough about oneself? As Oscar Wilde said, the only love that is everlasting is self-love. However, since I am quite vain about my humility, I insist we move on from me to…my book.

I present basic propositions in each chapter and will try to convince you that these propositions are valid and true. As you read, you will find in each chapter sudden outbursts of theory, cases or examples. You can skip back and forth (or not), based on how you think and learn.

'There are two kinds of people in the world: those who divide people into two kinds and those who don't,' said the philosopher William James. I think there are two kinds of readers. First, there are those who as they buy (or borrow) a book, say to themselves or to anyone within earshot, 'I hope this has some damn practical stuff I can use. Not all that theory junk again.' This is the 'show me the money' or 'the proof of the pudding is in the eating' type of reader. Then there are those who say, as a French philosopher once said, 'It may work in practice, but does it work in theory?' My guilty secret? I am a theory junkie. I want to know not only *how* something works, but also *why* it works. And thus I fall into this second category of readers. My professor once told me a long time ago, 'Jaya, you don't *have* to start with the origins of the universe to arrive at what to have for breakfast.' But bear with me, and I hope you both shall be satisfied.

# 1

# WHY IS LEADERSHIP THE MOST CRITICAL AND URGENT NEED OF OUR AGE?

> *'…great men—so called—are but the labels that some serve to give a name to an event, and like labels, they have the least possible connection with the event itself. Every action of theirs that seems to them an act of their own free will, is in an historical sense not free at all, but in bondage to the whole course of previous history, and predestined from all eternity.'*
>
> —Leo Tolstoy, in *War and Peace*

Humankind has always had leaders, whether the majority wanted them or not. However, from the beginning of the second half of the twentieth century, we have seen an increasing *need* for leaders. The reasons are rich and specific:

- We have entered an age of faith where we have become overwhelmingly dependent on unseen institutions that provide us with essential products and services on which our very lives depend. We need good-to-great leaders to create and manage these institutions.
- We have entered an age of democracy where everyone, in theory at least, is considered equal. This is the first time in history that such a 'burden' has been placed on the shoulders of the common man, and the promise of equality often clashes with the universal tradition of feudalism and the habitual rule of the elite. Paradoxically, to evolve into a truly egalitarian and equitable society, we need great leaders who are chosen by us, and who will in turn help us grow into leaders in our own right, which is the true meaning of the 'promise of, and

belief in, equality' (PROBE).

+ While there have always been some among us who have dreamed the impossible dream, PROBE has inculcated in the common person a deep and pervasive hunger for opportunities to grow. Hope is born every day in millions of human hearts. In developing societies, this rising hunger translates into the 'revolution of rising expectations' (RORE). This, if not harnessed and transformed into constructive energy, will lead to class warfare and the destruction of societies. That is the task of great leaders—to manage the RORE.

+ Western societies and Japan gained great prosperity by exploiting democracy and the Industrial Revolution. The explosive growth and the growing ambition of the citizenry, which were both the parent and the progeny of this former RORE, has turned into a 'spiral of reduced expectations' (SORE). Dreams are fading and a sense of resignation and an acceptance of less are becoming the norm for the majority. Frustration has replaced hope for many. These societies are still rich, but the spirit which animated and produced the wealth is getting rapidly poorer. There is a need to rejuvenate these societies and provide them with a sense of constructive purpose. Hope needs rebirth; and for that, we need great leaders.

**The Age of Faith**

Here is a simple exercise to explain why I say we live in an age of faith. Take a piece of paper and write down every single activity you performed, from the moment your eyes opened this morning, till you got to work. (That is sufficient for now. If we need to go further, we will do so later). For each activity, identify what you had to use to do it and on whom you had to depend to achieve the best results. Now do the same for your great-grandparents (try and guess, if you're not sure). (The hourglass has been turned over. The sands of time are rapidly dropping. I hope you have answered the questions).

Did you do it? Mine read as:

WHY IS LEADERSHIP THE MOST CRITICAL AND URGENT NEED OF OUR AGE? ♦ 3

| Activity | Me | Great-grandfather/Mother |
|---|---|---|
| Woke up at 6:30 a.m. | Alarm clock | Circadian rhythm |
| Brushed my teeth | Toothbrush, toothpaste | Neem tree stick |
| Took a bath | Geyser/boiler to heat water, toilet soap, shampoo, etc. | Wood/coal fire to heat water shampoo—*sheekakai* tree |
| Breakfast | Bread from bakery, cereal | Food made from the produce of farm |
| Kissed my wife good morning | Lips | Not sure if they ever kissed. Never asked. |
| Drove to work | Japanese car | Walked to the farm/stayed at home |

Let's stop. Do you have anything very different? I would guess not, but if you do, let's keep it for later because I have a point to make.

We are supposed to be living in the age of reason. We have inherited 200 years of science and technology. We base our lives upon logic and reason. After all, that is what science is about, right? Look at the lists again. Everything I do from the moment I wake up to the moment I fall asleep is utterly dependant on totally unknown agencies in this age of globalization (not even individual human beings or local familiar shops). My toothpaste is made by a company which is a subsidiary of a famous American company (yes, same as yours). I have absolutely no idea where it was made, if it was made 'right', or if the latest research reports have declared it to be carcinogenic. Okay, if the latter was true, I would have read it in the newspaper, but I would just switch to a competitor's product. And how do I know that they wouldn't find *that* to be carcinogenic next year? By then I would have put it in my mouth for a whole year. Then why do I use it? I just believe in science and modern industry and government regulation and a host of such unseen 'gods' on which my life is entirely dependent.

But in the case of my great-grandma and grandpa, there were no such concerns. The neem tree was in their yard. If it had been carcinogenic, they would all have died generations ago. They did not; I am here, am I not? For most of their activities, they were dependent on no one but themselves (and maybe a village producer).

If we look at our activities during the rest of our day, the point becomes even more clear. Assuming we brave the hazards of the bath and breakfast, look at the drive out. I am dependent on the health of my car. Okay, let's assume I am a very careful owner who has it serviced every day. Let's assume my driving skills are excellent (my wife begs to differ). But what about the thousands of other drivers who are on the road with me at the same time? What about the health of their cars? What of their skills? What if they had scraped through their driving test yesterday and are driving shakily by my side today? What if the oncoming truck has a driver who has been declared at risk of an imminent cardiac arrest but is driving anyway? What of that lady who is speaking animatedly on her cell phone while ostensibly driving her SUV? What if...the probability of a disaster occurring is remarkably high.

And yet we believe that all will be well and we go through our lives with this faith. Yours and my great-grandparents' did not need any such faith. Their lives were far less interdependent. They had to take care of themselves for the most part. Yet, the myth is that theirs was the age of blind faith, replete with beliefs, and yes, even superstitions, whereas our age is seen as the quintessential age of reason.

Well, it is not, as we have seen. So what? What does this realization mean to us?

The American political scientist, Francis Fukuyama, stated our condition succinctly, '[...] a nation's well-being, as well as its ability to compete, is conditioned by a single, pervasive cultural characteristic: the level of trust inherent in the society.'[1]

As the 'volatility, uncertainty, complexity, ambiguity and interdependence' (VUCAI) of our society increases, so much so that these five factors have come to pervade and define the post-World War world, the need for trust in our institutions has become an imperative. We have no choice but to trust, because in the absence of trust, we cannot cope with the VUCAI. But such implicit and explicit trust mandates that we choose leaders who create institutions for us which are worthy of it. Since we are at the mercy of these myriad institutions (governments with their numerous functional departments, business corporations, education and health-care providers and every other structural component of a modern society), our very survival depends on our ability to understand, deeply and comprehensively, who we want as leaders and why. They will embody our dreams and help us make them realities. The wrong ones will lead us to nightmares from which we may never wake up. However, there are serious problems and deficiencies in the method we use to identify and choose leaders.

We have faith, blind faith, in our institutions, and not trust based on knowledge and reasoned wisdom. We have blind faith in all kinds of corporations and distant unseen governments (whose representatives we elect once in four or five years and see no more till the campaigning for the next elections start), with no clear system which outlines how we influence, evaluate or hire and fire them. In sharp contrast, we have little faith in each other, as neighbourhoods and communities. We see each other on the streets every day, transacting our lives, yet we don't care enough to find out more about our neighbours, to become acquainted with them, to share experiences and to get to know each other better. But, you might say, why bother? What will I get out of these trivial interactions? How will it help my life? We shall address that by and by.

Why do we have so much faith in these unseen institutions? Why don't we question them and make them deserve our faith? Do you know how ordinary 'they' are? 'They' are just like us, a little better, a little worse, but on the whole 'they'—political leaders, corporate magnates, religious gurus, sports icons, film stars—do put their pants on one leg at a time. And, as Nikita Khrushchev reportedly said, 'The Czar and I look the same in the bathtub' (Khrushchev was a real tubby fellow, so I assume the Czar would not have been amused by the comparison). By deifying our leaders, we put ourselves down. If we continue to do this for generations, then we will end up believing the hype and the press we helped create in the first place.

We need to learn a lot, especially about our leaders. We need to learn because we know so little about them, because we are so dependent on them for so much in our lives, and because they are like us—unreliable, dishonest and plain lazy at times.

## The Conditions for Change

Another reason for our urgent need for leaders now is because the current conditions are ripe for change. Change requires an optimum mix of hope and frustration. Until now, the world had been strictly divided between the hopeful and the frustrated, but recent developments have created the right conditions for change everywhere. The developing world is evolving and the developed world is devolving, making change inevitable. Whether this revolution is virtuous or violent will depend on the quality of our leaders. Let us begin with the reasons for hope.

> *Hope springs eternal in the human breast;*
> *Man never is, but always to be blest:*
> *The soul, uneasy and confin'd from home,*
> *Rests and expatiates in a life to come.*
>
> Alexander Pope,
> *An Essay on Man, Epistle I*, 1733

The poet had the emotion pegged right, but 'the life to come' in which hope resides is not in the hereafter in some unknown unseen heaven, as was the belief for most people since the dawn of history. It is right here on earth, and not in some distant future after we are dead and gone from this 'vale of tears', but right now or very soon.

We live in an age of equality, certainly in theory and partly in fact. Economic and democratic development has spread to much of the world, aided by the rapid increase in communication and information, raising the expectations of the poor and marginalized.

## The Age of Equality

What has been the greatest miracle in human history? Some of you may name technological miracles—they are truly marvels to behold—but nothing comes close to the miracle of the PROBE.

Never before in history has this been even remotely true. Never have so many, in so little time, come to hope for so much. Never has the promise been so prevalent. Most countries in the world have enshrined it in their Constitutions and have promised that all their citizens, each and every one of them, are equal and have inalienable rights. From the beginning of the twenty-first century, vast multitudes of people have actually come to believe that they have the right to be considered equal. Till even the mid-twentieth century, such a belief would have been scoffed at, ridiculed and, in fact, would have earned serious punishment in most societies. But the miracle of this secular 'faith' is here, and it is here to stay. The PROBE is held across the political spectrum, from those on the right and those on the left. Whether one wants more government or less government, whether one is a social or economic conservative or liberal, whether one is religious[2] or secular, the universal tenet of this faith is that the government is, and should for ever more be, 'Of the people, by the people and for the people.'

This is far from realization, though. There are deep divisions within most societies—and in some, equality is a mere slogan bandied about by cynical politicians to get and hold power. But notwithstanding these realities, it remains true that we've never before had those who rule us say, 'You are equal to us; actually, you are the boss and we serve at your command.' And never before have 'we, the people' actually believed it and behaved as though it were true.

We have been promised equality and that has created a need for leaders and institutions to deliver on this promise. But leaders have promised us great things before, and it would be easy to be cynical about this one as well. What makes our age different is the degree to which this promise has been met through two developments: democracy and globalization.

## Democracy

At one end of the spectrum of human existence, there is the individual. Individuals have never had such freedom in terms of equality offered in economic, social and every other human sphere of activity. This is a Revolution with a capital 'R' pertaining to the individual human being (ordinary people, just like you and me). On the other end of the spectrum, we have nations and societies which are now, willingly or unwillingly, part of a Democracy of Nations (DON—Dawn of DONs?).

Like every society and nation throughout history, we, the people, have been dependent on our leaders for the very survival, let alone the prosperity, of our individual and collective lives. What has changed in the new millennium is that this dependence has deepened and become all-pervasive. They, the leaders, are so many, and we elect them. The last 50 years stand out in 5,000 years of human civilization not because our leaders can influence our lives, but because we can influence theirs.

## The Flat World

It is a 'flat world' out there, they say. For the first time in history, there is hope of a level playing field for all nations and individuals (and all the clusters in between). This is an absolutely new evolutionary situation for us as a species.

Calling the twenty-first century the 'Asian Century', or recognizing the clout of the BRIC (Brazil, Russia, India and China) nations is merely the rising of DONs. What mutual deterrence did for nuclear weapons, commerce and demographic dividends 'an optimum mixture of frustration and hope' on the part of millions of human beings will do for the polity of nations. For the first time in history, societies can be almost equal, if not in military might and economic affluence, then at least in influencing and holding their own for a fair share of the earth's resources. This cannot happen without creating institutions that can regulate and negotiate these new situations. We need leaders who are capable of this feat.

## RORE in India

These two developments, democracy and globalization, have moved us towards a level political and economic playing field. This has given hope to the formerly hopeless, and has led to the phenomenon called RORE—as explained earlier. RORE is borne out of sudden hunger for more, a lot more.

> The revolution of rising expectations, a term first used to describe Asia's awakening in the early 1950s, is the single most powerful force yet unleashed for social development. It marks a stage in which individual members of society not only venture to dream or hope or work for higher levels of accomplishment, but in which those aspirations have coalesced into a conviction and expectation that

they will achieve, possess and enjoy more than their parents or they themselves have in the past.³

The last two decades have been, and the present continues to be, a rediscovery of India, both in its awesome and awful aspects.

A few decades ago, India's growth rate was dubbed the 'Hindu rate of growth'—a derisive term used to ridicule the low number—but now, India has one of the highest growth rates in the world. Many billionaires dot the country with conspicuous consumption patterns matched only by oil sheikhs in the Middle East.

We were brought up amid hand-wringing and hearing lamentations about the accursed population growth and dire predictions of a Malthusian catastrophe (disasters caused by unchecked population growth), but Malthus stands discredited. A Green Revolution has brought food surpluses and relief to places of despair. I now hear of the 'demographic dividend'—75 per cent of the Indian population is under 35—and the populations of Japan, America and even China will age before than that of India. India will soon overtake China and become the most populous nation in the world. Even sooner, it will emerge as the third largest economy after China and the US, outstripping a hapless Japan. It seems like only yesterday when Japan was considered the 'world conqueror' and it was often held up as a model of development, with lessons to emulate for the richest and the most productive nations in human history. O tempora! O mores!

RORE needs, in fact demands, that we as a society respond to these new aspirations and the unmet but intensely felt discontent of the masses, by innovating and looking for new solutions. These solutions are not primarily technological; plenty of these are available already and more arrive at our doorsteps every day. RORE calls for new models of ourselves ('How can I transform myself to respond to the RORE?') and of leadership ('How can we develop leaders with the intensity, integrity and intelligence to help create and nurture transformation?').

## The Side Effects of RORE

With all these reasons for hope, however, has come a profound sense of frustration. The promise of equality—both political and economic—has remained a promise for too many. As economies develop, there is a growing chasm between the rich and the poor, globally. In some economies, this difference has become so great that there has developed a clear divide between the top 1 per cent of the population and the remaining 99 per cent.

In economics and politics the scorecards of the leaders, in creating prosperity and equality for all, is dismal. President Obama, on 21 January 2012, in his inaugural address for his second term, spoke with feeling and deep realization about the malaise affecting the richest nation in human history, 'For we, the people, understand that our country cannot succeed when a shrinking few do very well and a growing many barely make it.'

What are the implications of this alarming trend?

Timothy Noah, a journalist, says, 'The gap between the rich and the poor has been growing for the past 30 years in most of the world's advanced economies, and especially in the United States.'[4]

Nobel Laureate Joseph E. Stiglitz says, 'The top 1 per cent have the best houses, the best education, the best doctors and the best lifestyles, but there is one thing that money doesn't seem to have bought: an understanding that their fate is bound up with how the other 99 per cent live. Throughout history, this is something that the top 1 per cent eventually do learn. Too late.'[5]

The *New York Times* commented on the repercussions that could be caused if this divide continues to expand unchecked, '[…] the ever widening inequality will undermine our democracy: Americans believe fervently in the value of social equality, and social equality is at risk when incomes become too dramatically unequal… Growing income inequality makes it especially difficult to maintain any spirit of *e pluribus unum*.'[6]

Noah's and Stiglitz's anxiety springs from the serious undermining of the PROBE. The greatest miracle in human history may be in imminent danger of a premature demise. Listen to Noah again, 'How much inequality can the republic stand before the social and political fabric frays? […] You'd have to be blind not to see that we are headed in the wrong direction, and we've been heading that way for too long […] The worst thing that we could do to the Great Divergence is get used to it.'[7]

Here is UNICEF's dire evaluation of the situation:

> […] we find a world in which the top 20 per cent of the population enjoys more than 70 per cent of total income […] It would take

more than 800 years for the bottom billion to achieve 10 per cent of global income under the current rate of change. Also disturbing is the prevalence of children and youth among the poorest income quintiles, as approximately 50 per cent are below the $2/day international poverty line.

Overall, the extreme inequality in the distribution of the world's income should make us question the current development model (development for whom?), which has accrued mostly to the wealthiest billion. Not only does inequality slow economic growth, but it results in health and social problems and generates political instability. Inequality is dysfunctional, and there is a grave need to place equity at the centre of the development agenda.[8]

India is no exception to this trend. According to a *Times of India* article, 'Inequality in earnings has doubled in India over the last two decades, making it the worst performer on this count of all emerging economies. The top 10% of wage earners now make 12 times more than the bottom 10%, up from a ratio of six in the 1990s.'[9]

This is a trend that has become prevalent even in other developed economies, such as Japan. An article in *The Economist* says:

> Shadowy figures—Japan's poor are so well hidden that they are hard to measure [...] The discovery of a dead family of three—an elderly man crippled by a bad back, his wife, and their 39 year-old son—has again drawn attention to its existence [...] Such stories are shocking. So, for many Japanese, are figures from the OECD that made Japan the sixth worst of 34 countries in terms of the share of the population living in poverty (America came in even lower).[10]

The increasing divide between the rich and the poor can lead to situations where the top 1 per cent refuse to take responsibility for their actions because of the power they wield. The global recession of the late 2000s was caused by the financial leaders of Wall Street whose greed led the global economy to the precipice of the destruction and indirectly effected the loss of the life savings of millions of middle class and poor. The leaders whose irresponsibility caused these losses were left free to enjoy the spoils of their ill-gotten wealth. This could have been possible only because of a flagrant failure of leadership in financial, political and regulatory institutions.

Politically, these financial failures have caused a great deal of international instability as well. The European Union is falling apart. Greece, Portugal and Spain are reeling under the impact of the recession and are unable to practise the fiscal discipline that the EU imposed.

'Suddenly, normally calm economists are talking about 1931, the year everything fell apart,' Paul Krugman wrote in the *New York Times* on 25 June 2012. 'The really crucial lesson of 1931, however, was about the dangers of policy abdication [...] And it's happening again, both in Europe and in America [...] The fact is that the Fed, like the European Central Bank, like the US Congress, like the government of Germany, has decided that avoiding economic disaster is somebody else's responsibility.'[11]

Meanwhile, on the other side of the world, India struggles to realize its newly heralded, recently glimpsed and as yet elusive growth. Even if the growth rate stabilizes and there is a high-level development, there is another, graver and more formidable challenge. How do we share this new found prosperity with 'we, the people'?

Going back in history, Sir M. Visvesvaraya, the *diwan* (minister for the king) of the large kingdom of Mysore in the 1930s, and the architect of the kingdom's modernization and development, once famously said, 'I do not want to redistribute poverty.' If the whole country is poor, one has to create wealth, or else it will be a redistribution of poverty. The problem for India in the coming decade, and its leaders specifically, will be quite the opposite. What if you create wealth, but have neither the political will nor the social consensus among the elite to redistribute it?

The so-called 'demographic dividend'—the 70 per cent of the population who have grown up with the promise and the belief in equality—will be teetering on the hope that we will be able to summon the collective will and the conscience to give them equality and justice for all in the face of affluence. And these youths will surely remember what Charles Dickens knew. 'In the little world in which children have their experience,' says Pip in Charles Dickens's *Great Expectations*, 'there is nothing so finely perceived and finely felt as injustice.' Our world is increasingly unjust to our children; billions of them will surely remember and rebel.

A generation ago, poverty was seen as the rule and affluence as the exception for most, but we now see the deepening of this division in the name of development. Shades of poverty, like the shades of brown faces in India, are too many to count. Though there is always someone else who is poorer by comparison, now there is a sharp break between the top 1 per cent and the bottom 99 per cent.

**Inequality of Power**

It would be a grievous error to mistake political leaders to be the centre of all power that makes or breaks our present world. The rise of corporations, once confined to a few nations (mostly the US and Western Europe) but increasingly multinational, have come to exercise enormous influence on the affairs of nation-states, either indirectly, through the control of politicians, or often directly through brazen campaign-financing to tilt the balance of electoral power.

In 2010, when the Citizen United case went to court, the US Supreme Court ruled that corporations, non-profit organizations and labour unions are free to spend on 'electioneering communication'. The verdict opened the floodgates for corporate funding of parties and candidates, and its impact will be seen in the years to come—the world's richest democracy had just made it easier to buy and sell elections. President Eisenhower, in his last address to the nation in 1961, warned of the influence of the military-industrial complex—where the arms industry, the US military and the US political system worked together, such that the industry was often given privileges and bureaucratic waivers in exchange for political funding. Since then, the 'industrial' part of this power equation has come into its own. It has grown even more powerful and even more unregulated. The great recession of 2008 was widely seen as the result of Wall Street going wild and of laxity in the regulation of the finance industry, which allowed executives to sacrifice the common good at the altar of personal, let alone corporate, greed. The principle of the 'greatest good for the greatest number' had been silently altered to 'the greatest good for the smallest number'. The American economy is barely emerging from the powerful destruction wrought by this financial tsunami. Europe is still reeling under the aftermath of this manmade, in fact, leader-made, catastrophe. Countries like Greece, Spain, Cyprus and many others may have suffered damages to their very social fabric. Recovery may be long and slow, if they recover at all.

These are massive leadership failures which behove urgent and deep reflection and debate among the citizenry and the powerful elite alike. Instead, most of these events are swept under the rug or, worse, whitewashed with cover-ups. The 'vital balance'—the Goldilocks effect—of which we will know more in Chapter 4, is sorely missing between the much-needed wealth- and job-generating machine called capitalism, and the checks and balances in society which should regulate and control the destructive impulses of the marketplace. 'Any man can bear adversity; give a man power and that will test his character,' said Abraham Lincoln. Commerce and politics bestow upon their leaders, through position and wealth, both formal and informal power. The value systems of these global leaders are tested by the access to power and they, with a few honourable exceptions, have 'fallen off the log' and have taken a lot of us with them. Instead of rescuing us from the ravages of VUCAI—volatility, uncertainty, complexity, ambiguity and interdependence—these leaders have intensified the impact. We need to massively rethink the kinds of leaders we must create before it is too late.

Perhaps the changes have been too fast. We, as a species, were unprepared for this dismantling of the status quo that has been thrust upon us by the forces of history. We are behind in the evolution of our personal values and capabilities, and we are woefully lacking in organizational structures and processes to match our democratic dreams—whether it is in politics, industry, civil society or religion. Take politics, for instance. Earlier we had the feudal model, where the king ruled over the nobility, and the nobility ruled over the peasants. Then came the global miracle. Democratic revolutions sprang up in every sphere of human activity within a nanosecond of human evolutionary time, forcing unprecedented social upheavals in the seventeenth century. Our leaders have tried to apply old rules to a new reality and look where it has landed us now. Politically, we have 'old wine in new bottles', with money as the most necessary prerequisite to gaining and holding power. In some fledgling (and not-so-fledgling) democracies, it is the combination of money and muscle power which ensures political power. Caste, class, creed—old divisions have usurped the ballot box and we are ruled by the same old emperors with new clothing and new slogans. Economically, the bubble bursts every decade or so, and those who are caught in the exploding bubble are dismissed as 'collateral damage'. The economic generals are immune to the consequences of their actions. Socially, we have achieved significant progress in undoing historical injustices and inequities based on gender, race, caste and religion, only to find that unconscionable economic inequalities continue to strangle the delicate throats of democracies, young and old. Basic human rights, as listed in the United Nations' Millennium Development Goals, remain a distant dream for most of humanity. Whatever progress we have made has been minimized by the persistence of economic inequality, which continues to disempower these historically marginalized groups.

The image that comes to mind is that of the comic strip character 'The Incredible Hulk' who, when angry, morphs into a giant and his garments tear apart because they had been made for an earlier, smaller body. In the case of society, as the aspirations of the people explode, infrastructure and leadership needs to accommodate this growing demand for opportunities or, like the Hulk's clothes, our social fabric too will rip. We are chaotic, and we are unjust to the majority of our fellow humans, and as yet we do not have a clue on how to make the transition from being a theoretical democracy to becoming a real one.

As for corporate leadership, not much has changed in terms of the method used to select the top management, but their power and influence have sharply increased. This is not because the present-day industrial magnates are more powerful than their predecessors in the nineteenth or twentieth centuries. In fact, the so-called 'robber barons' of the nineteenth century in the US were a law unto themselves for a time. The 'House of Morgan' was supposed to have owned the federal government for decades, having loaned enough money to sustain the running of the government. Though individually industrialists may have lost power, collectively, as a sector, they have grown immensely powerful. It is not the individual power of the great industrialists that we must pay attention to as much as the collective power of the industrial sector and its leadership, who are not accountable to anyone save their shareholders and a hand-picked board.

There is a lot that is not known about leaders, despite libraries being written about them. We have a historically urgent and unique responsibility and opportunity to understand the phenomenon of leadership. The rapid spread of democracy around the world has made us the beneficiaries and the victims of political and corporate leadership, with or without our control. What we do as a society to choose good leaders will differ sharply, based on how we want to assure PROBE for all. Democracy demands accountability from its leaders and citizens alike (at least in theory).

Imagine political and corporate leadership as jobs which require a candidate to graduate in order to take up the role. How would we design an educational programme that would ensure the transformation mandated by the new challenges of the PROBE? What would be the curriculum? Would the present incumbents pass? And who will create the leaders that adapt us, as a species, and as a culture, to the imperatives of the 'flat world'?

It is us, each one of us, the 'people'. If a nation is corrupt, if a democracy has become a government 'of the corrupt, by the corrupt, for the corrupt', we, the citizens of that democracy, are accomplices to it being so. Hence, you cannot start a discussion about our leaders or the creation of new institutions unless you are willing to confront yourself as a whole, a 'warts and all' human being, and ask, 'How do I rise to the challenges of this brand new evolutionary situation?' If each of us, or at least enough of us, do not respond to the Gandhian dictum, 'Be the change you want to see', nothing will change. We will be stuck wearing the garments of the 'primitive' nineteenth century, which would be unsuitable for the flat, egalitarian world where, for the first time in history, the ordinary human has come to rule.

## SORE in America

America is experiencing collective self-doubt at a societal level. It doubts itself and is getting sucked down into a SORE—spiral of reducing expectations. This self-doubt is reflected in the opinions of the intelligentsia and of those in leadership positions, whether in the right or the left of the political spectrum. Despite the difference in logic, they arrive at the same conclusions. Those on the left assert that the leadership has failed to create more opportunities and hence the people are deprived. On the other hand, those on the right insist that people are less enterprising and hence they suffer. Is it that we do not work because we cannot find jobs, or do we not work because we do not want to work? Either way, wherever you belong in this spectrum, SORE is the consequence.

Listed below are both liberal and conservative views, not so much to discuss their rightness or wrongness, but to emphasize that they both sense a collective SORE—a dream that recedes and a self-perception of weakness and decline.

- Nobel laureate Joseph E. Stiglitz, known for his leftist position, said, '…growing inequality is the flip side of something else: shrinking opportunity. Whenever we diminish equality of opportunity, it means that we are not using some of our most valuable assets—our people—in the most productive way possible…'[12]
- David Brooks, a well-known commentator on the right, in his column in the *New York Times*, said, 'Obama misunderstands this moment. The Progressive Era, New Deal and Great Society laws were enacted when America was still a young and growing nation. They were enacted in a nation that was vibrant, raw, under institutionalized and needed taming. We are no longer that nation. We are now a mature nation with an aging population. Far from being under institutionalized, we are bogged down with a bloated political system, a tangled tax code, a byzantine legal code and crushing debt. The task of reinvigorating a mature nation is fundamentally different from the task of civilizing a young and boisterous one.'[13]
- Adding to the characterization of America as a 'mature nation with an aging population…bogged down…bloated…tangled…byzantine… crushing', another acute observer of contemporary American society, Ross Douthat, a rightist, chimes in with different but equally compelling evidence of a society whose people aren't dreaming anymore, 'In a sense, the old utopians were prescient: we've gained a world where steady work is less necessary to human survival than ever before. But human flourishing is another matter. And it's our fulfilment, rather than the satisfaction of our appetites, that's threatened by the slow decline of work.'[14]

This lack of economic confidence should not be happening. Like in 1931, Western nations have the resources they need to avoid catastrophe, and indeed, to restore prosperity. Additionally, we have the advantage of knowing much more than our grandparents about economic depressions, their origins and possible solutions. But knowledge and resources are no good if those who possess them refuse to use them. And that's what seems to be happening. The fundamentals of the world economy aren't, in themselves, eroded enough to be all that scary; it's the almost universal abdication of responsibility that fills me, and many economists, with a growing sense of dread. This lack of leadership is heralding the death of the American dream and is presaging, if not already ushering in, a mellower, less ambitious, less productive society. If this is a premature obituary and if the American dream does come roaring back, it will be because the SORE met its match in the kind of leaders who can rekindle the spirit of a young, raw, nascent and vibrant nation, rearing to go for the brass ring once more.

**Frustration and Hope**

RORE and SORE are both born of two parents—hope and frustration. An optimal combination of these seemingly contrarian components can cause the birth of revolutions and can nurture them.

Frustration is born out of the failure of repeated attempts to deal with a problem or need. For most of humanity, these problems have been poverty, lack of opportunity for a decent livelihood and lack of access to health care and other basic necessities of life. To this is added hope, which is the feeling of adventure and singleness of purpose shared by a group of people who are about to embark on a project whose goal is "finally" to meet certain identified human needs.

The more radical the nature of the new idea, the greater or more intense is the depth of the frustration which caused its origin. For example, any major socio-political change or, for that matter, any revolution in any sphere of human life, has been caused by an intense frustration with the status quo. In the words of Ackoff, 'Collective action directed at redeveloping society can arise only out of desperation and hope. Desperation, in turn, arises out of deprivation and frustration: hope out of ideas that hold promise.'[15]

It is important to stress that the ingredients in the cauldron, the explosive mixture of frustration and hope, may be of any origin—they may be endemic to the culture and value system, or they may spring 'eternally in the human breast' as the poet Alexander Pope claimed. Neither frustration nor hope alone is capable of motivating or inducing the drive to transform the status quo. Frustration alone is not enough to compel a population to believe that a revolution is in order. On the other hand, hope alone does not propel us towards transformation. It is as though, on the one hand, one doesn't dare to hope for a revolutionary new system unless driven by frustration to feel that one has nothing to lose, and on the other hand, one doesn't dare to respond to frustration creatively unless fuelled by a powerful hope for something better.

To bring it to full fruition, this miracle of PROBE needs a level playing field. To assure freedom for all, we need a so-called 'flat world', where everyone has equal opportunity, as proposed by Thomas Friedman in his 2005 bestseller, *The World Is Flat*. The idea struck Friedman after a conversation with Nandan Nilekani, the former CEO of Infosys. A flat world is a world without global barriers to economic participation. According to Friedman, equality can come about only when the domestic barriers to political and economic participation are removed, a view espoused by enlightened economists and social activists and reflected in the phrase 'inclusive growth'. However, Friedman believed that technology and the free market will be instrumental in 'flattening' the world, a view that leftist economists such as Stiglitz strongly disagree with. Some tools for ushering in such a 'flat' world are partially here. Democratic revolutions and civil rights movements, birthed by historic forces, on behalf of every oppressed population in every society and facilitated by miraculous technologies, continue to this day. The 'new age of equality' is struggling to come out of the womb of history. The danger inherent in this climb is obvious: the RORE—once you have tasted a morsel you want the whole banquet, or else you feel deprived—is at work. And the higher you climb, the steeper the fall if you do not have the 'equipment'—the knowledge and skills—to climb all the way.

However, this dream—and it is still a dream for a majority of mankind even though a cherished one—cannot and will not come true unless we, the people, unlearn old habits and patterns of thinking, and learn again about leadership and followership. Yes, one cannot create great leaders unless we make ourselves great followers in the age of PROBE. Hence, while we speak only of leaders here, we must understand that they are just the tip of the iceberg, and that the remaining four-fifths of the iceberg under water are the followers who chose their leader wisely. The wise follower must nurture, critique, revere and revile as needed; he or she must retain the good and dispose of the bad, like the celestial swan in Sanskrit epics, which can separate water from adulterated milk by sipping the milk while spitting out the water, the so-called *hamsaksheeranyaya*— हंसक्षीरान्याय in Sanskrit.

The promise of equality stands at a historic crossroads because of two revolutions brewing within two of the largest democracies in the world. At the end of the first decade of the new millennium, we have two storms gathering in our midst. They are rising in the two largest democracies of the world—India and America—but will almost certainly affect every other nation, democratic or otherwise. The two revolutions are contrary in nature to each other: one is occurring in the growing, hungry populations of its society, and the other is playing out in the apparently stagnant and, if not actually declining, certainly complacent, parts of each society.

How each society deals with its respective storms will shape not only its own destiny, but that of the rest of the world. This is because these two nations are behemoths, the first and the fourth (soon to become the third) largest economies of the world, and because one in every five humans on the globe is either an Indian or an American. China is on the path to the impending RORE storm, but because it is not a democracy, it may have some more time. Ultimately China, and every other nation, will have to face one of these two revolutions and either win or lose in the revolutionary raffle. A revolution is impending and it will be entirely up to us, the people, to decide as to whether it will lead us to deliverance or disaster.

The two societies and their respective revolutions urgently need new kinds of leaders. Not just new leaders; those we get quite frequently. We need new kinds of leaders to weather the storms of these two revolutions, at the two ends of the world, literally and figuratively, in India and in the US. Each will be a role model if they succeed in fulfilling the vision of democracy. While the US can show the way to other developed nations, India can be the prototype for the rest of the developing world. But this will only come to be if they summon the right kind of leadership in every sector of their respective societies. Each revolution can derail these societies and every other society on earth if the right kinds of leaders do not emerge to create new types of structures, processes and institutions and rejuvenate or eliminate the old ones.

Hence, the challenge our leaders face is:

a) In the case of SORE (especially but not exclusively in the developed countries), how to resurrect hope and how to sustain it; and

b) In the case of RORE (especially but not exclusively in the developing countries), how to fulfil the hopes of these discontented billions.

## Basic Propositions in this Chapter

Leadership is the most critical and urgent need of our age because of the 'mother of all revolutions'—the promise and belief in equality (PROBE)—and its two offspring, the revolution of rising expectations (RORE) and spiral of reduced expectations (SORE). These are effects of the information revolution, industrialization, globalization and capitalism, and have emerged like Aladdin's genie out of a lamp.

RORE—Revolution of Rising Expectations (with the demographic-dividend or disaster looming large):

Too many youth thunder with hunger for 'more, more, more' like a billion Oliver Twists all at once. Is it going to be a symphony of energy and synergy, or a cacophony of class wars and mutually assured destruction (MAD)?

SORE—Spiralling of Reduced Opportunities and Sagging Expectations (with the further impact of the 'Shock of Grey'—advanced societies greying away into death un-replaced by new births):

The growing divide between the rich and poor restricts the access to opportunity for the poor, leaving them frustrated and without hope.

Which result in five consequences—VUCAI

- Volatility
- Uncertainty
- Complexity
- Ambiguity
- Interdependence

To deal with which we recommend four prescriptions in the other chapters of the book:

- Development of self: the ideal and the practical
- Development of leadership that transcends: the ideal and the practical
- Management of transformational change: leader as the change agent
- Creation of leadership institutions

That is it, in a nutshell. Now let us grow these 'seeds' into 'trees' in the rest of the book.

# 2

# DEVELOPING A TRANSCENDENT LEADER

I was once in a golf cart with Dr A.P.J. Abdul Kalam, now an ex-president of India but at that time 6 months from the presidential post, and N.R. Narayana Murthy, co-founder and chairman of Infosys at that time. Introduced by N.R. Narayana Murthy to Dr Kalam as the leadership expert, I was asked by the future president, 'Do you really think leaders can be made? Don't you think they are born? Either you have it or you don't, isn't it?' Given that these were two self-made men who had achieved iconic status by dint of their own mettle, by the sweat of their souls so to say, the question was clearly rhetorical...and the right answer is, or ought to have been in their company, 'Of course sir, they are for sure born and not made.' Mercifully, our journey ended in 50 seconds at a hall where the imminent president was going to speak and I was spared the task of expounding my wisdom on this thorny issue of 'nature vs. nurture' or 'heredity vs. environment', as applied to this phenomenon of leadership.

## LEADERS SPEAK

**Do you think leaders are born? Is leadership in one's genes? How much, if any, is 'made'?**

**N.R. Narayana Murthy**
'Often people ask me whether leaders are born or made, and I have always said that each one of us has leadership attributes latent in us, sometimes it is quite alive in a different context.'

## Vivek Mansingh

'I have worked with five phenomenal leaders from the IT industry: Dave Packard, Bill Hewlett, Michael Dell, John Chambers and Steve Jobs. They are all extremely different people. What I have seen is that they have one key strength and then they develop other skills. For Steve Jobs, for instance, creativity was his hallmark...he is an out-of-the-box thinker. He can develop other capabilities like communication skills and an ability to inspire—*that* he can develop. So my take is that if we can find people who have at least one or two strong skills that are required, the rest you can groom or make it happen. In a nutshell, my answer is that we can create leaders. 90 per cent of people can be trained into becoming better leaders. If these people are exposed to structured information, monitoring and coaching, and if they are taught to approach problems with a certain attitude, they will become better leaders.'

## Rajiv Kuchhal

'Some are born to be leaders; some make themselves leaders. I think it's true, all of them are true. I do believe that there have to be innate leadership skills; there is clearly something inherent. I have sometimes been thrown into a position—it's what you have to do to step up to and do it—but again the question is, what is leadership? So, if leadership is the ability to influence people so that you achieve your objectives, then you can actually do it by learning. I have seen people stepping up to the occasion after they have been cajoled, pushed and thrown into the deep end of the water. I think there is some of it in all of us, it's just that some are more fearless about it, and some are fearful about it. So, one of the best things I've heard about [whether] leadership is born or built is that it is like a sport. Everybody can run, but not everybody can be an Olympic champion. The people who are Olympic champions have to be natural runners, but if you run every day you can be a good runner, and I think that leadership is about the same. Some people have natural leadership abilities, but some others continue to practise and be aware that they can suddenly perform a leadership role.'

## Ashok Kamath

'MBA stands for Master of Business Administration. It doesn't say Master of Business Leadership, so it is training you to have a mastery over processes and functions. Leadership is, to my mind, this combination—some of it inherent + some acquired + some little bit thrust upon oneself. Plus, experience and wisdom over the years. You really build the skills. I am a better listener today than I was 20 years ago. This helps me address my role better today, given the nature of the organization that I am in now. I can't possibly use the techniques I used in (a famous firm) in this environment. So, how did I acquire it? I had to listen; I had to appear as the dumb guy for the first 2–3 years. Then, when you are able to grasp it, articulate and push for it, make it happen—then, the acceptance happens. So, I think it's the born + thrust upon perspective + experience and wisdom gained over time. Can it be taught? I don't know if it can be taught, if you didn't have, let's say 7–10 years of experience. You should be able to relate your life to the education that is offered: "This is similar to this, therefore I made a mistake there or did well there." That builds on you, I think that's where the leadership development is—being able to apply what you are "taught" to your life experience, and hence come to your own internalizing.'

**Experience or Training?**

If you are from the school of hard knocks, you may say, 'Experience is not just the best teacher; it is the only teacher.' To think, let alone accept, that what you have learned over the period of a lifetime can be canned or bottled and taught to greenhorns, wet behind the ears, and lo and behold, they'll emerge from the phone booth with a cape on, ready to leap from tall buildings—many from my generation would shudder at this sacrilegious assumption. They would mutter, 'What is the world coming to?' As the curmudgeonly swimming teacher said, 'Oh yes, my methods are very sophisticated. I drop the kid on the first day into the deep end. No other way. You may lose some, but that is the price you pay for learning how to swim on your own.' This is the faction of the group that believes, 'If you can't stand the heat, get out of the kitchen,' as Truman said. (When was the air conditioner invented?!). To all this we have to respond, 'No, this programme is not a substitute for experience. It intends to prepare an aspiring great leader to know what to experience and then how best to learn from it.' To paraphrase Ramakrishna Paramahamsa (one of my favourite parable men), a bullock which goes round and round a milling stone works for an eternity without gaining any expertise on what is being produced as a result of its mind-numbing labour. The same arguments have been advanced every time professional education has been proposed in any discipline—medicine, law, business, arts, literature and so on. The only major field of human affairs in which this philosophy of 'experience comes before learning' still prevails is politics—and look where it has got us. (Sorry, that was a cheap shot. I take it back. There are very good politician leaders out there. I've met some of them, but alas, they may not be with us for long.)

All through history, there has been a tradition of educating kings with knowledge specific to matters of the state, even if the royal students were often indifferent or indolent and the *rajaguru*—Sanskrit for the royal teacher—may have despaired at the prospect of that particular ignorant lout holding the destiny of the kingdom in his hands. (We are not the first ones to feel that way, I'm certain.) The most famous leadership development programmes in history were taught by these legendary teachers: Confucius (551–479 BC) taught the Shu, Ji and Meng families; Kautilya (350–283 BC) taught Chandragupta Maurya (340–298 BC); and Aristotle (384–322 BC) taught Alexander (356–323 BC). Many 'gurus' theorized and prescribed guidelines for the conduct of the ideal leader. The most famous among them were Plato (427–347 BC) with his concept of a 'philosopher king' in *The Republic*, Machiavelli (1459–1527 AD) who authored *The Prince*, and Kautilya who wrote *Arthashastra*. Roman emperors and senators were often, but not always, scholars. Marcus Aurelius (121–180 AD) was a philosopher and an emperor. Greek scholars were the 'gurus' for many a Roman emperor, often as honoured, well-paid slaves. ('Nothing much has changed,' mutters my leadership development consultant friend, after a sneak preview of this sentence.)

This ancient and hallowed tradition of future leaders who inherited their mantle in a dynastic way, preparing themselves formally for the role they would play (more 'followed in the breach than in observance'), fell into disuse under tyrants, of whom there were many. Some tyrants like Genghis Khan were probably autodidacts. And the Kings of England were most often unlettered. All the development of leadership took place on the battlefields, and they were respected for their roles as warrior-leaders. However, with the advent of democracy, leaders were chosen on the basis of popularity and were no longer required to be formally trained for their role. The death of leadership development in a formal manner, and any expectation that leaders should be developed and not just thrust upon people with no preparation, dates from the birth of democracy, of PROBE. (Alas, what price to pay for freedom and equality! Democracy comes with a heavy price tag—there is no special knowledge demanded and no other qualification needed to be declared a leader, except a victory by one vote at the polling booth.)

**A Good Leader**

But before we can train good leaders, we must know what a good leader is.

Imagine you are on the board of directors of a corporation, a sports team or a hospital. Please write down the top five attributes of a good leader for this entity. Don't evade the question by asking for the context. Just ask yourself the following question and write down your answer after thinking for a few seconds: what do you think are the five 'generic' qualities you would want in your leader if you had a magic wand and could create such a person?

When I asked this question to a group of faculty and consultants in a leading leadership development institute, here are just some of the 63 attributes listed by just 10 of them, and then I ran out of flip-chart paper:

**As seen by ten experts:**

Simplicity / trustworthiness / faith in the people and the team / sensitivity towards the needs of the team / sacrifice / listening / speaking / honesty / dedication / integrity / principles and values / clarity of vision / passion / leadership by example / knowledge / open to new ideas / unselfish / unconditional / team builder / team player / task achiever / planner / implementer / decision maker / owing up to failures / ability to bounce back / learning / empathy / courage / self-awareness / confidence / think out of the box—innovator / optimistic / humble / versatility / positivity / ability to motivate and inspire / nurtures people to help them grow and develop / delegates and trusts people / multi-tasking, prioritizing and focusing on the right set of issues / thinking big, taking risks and pioneering/large-hearted and broadminded, not reactive/respectful/transparent, straightforward, honest and cool-headed even in a crisis/extraordinary determination/discipline/punctual/follower of truth/creativity/networking with the right people/a leader is one who creates leaders/fairness/a sense of humour…

Please! Who do you know who can walk on water? What can we do with such an extensive list? And can we really expect one person to have all these qualities? A recruiter will give up and resign if you, as the directors, gave him or her this list of requirements. And this was only part of the list suggested by the 10 of the 20 people in the room, and they were all experienced consultants and former executives.

In order to find an answer to this question, I have collected the responses of the chairman of a multi-billion dollar corporation, the founder-directors of several non-profits, the senior leader of a political party and professors of management. I have also catalogued the lists of such attributes from the vast literature on leadership. I gave up making the list after it crossed 100 attributes.

In scientific theory, the optimal model used to explain a phenomenon is expected to follow the 'Law of Parsimony', also known as Occam's razor. The principle states that 'one should not make more assumptions than the minimum needed… It admonishes us to choose the simplest model from a set of otherwise equivalent models of a given phenomenon. In any given model, Occam's razor helps us to "shave off" those concepts, variables or constructs that are not really needed to explain the phenomenon.'[1] In Albert Einstein's words, 'Make everything as simple as possible, but not simpler.'

Let us be parsimonious and decide which few of these hundreds of attributes are the ones that would get us the best leaders. Which of them are absolutely essential, which are desirable and which ones are for special contexts only.

I will attempt, in the coming pages, to distil the generic qualities and the identity of a leader, in his being and in his becoming.

## Failure to Transcend the Past

I propose that the holistic and integrated model for a great leader is transcendent leadership. Let us start with some real-life examples to see why firms succeed and fail.

Instances abound of leaders who succeeded eminently in one milieu at one time, and lost out when they became the slaves of the success that they had achieved. What was the key to success yesterday is the recipe for failure today, and leaders must learn to steer the organization from the glorious but extinct past environment to the uncertain but promising future. Please read each of the 10 cases below—they are instances of leaders not being able to transcend. No other factor can account for why they would fall off the log.

As you read the cases as recounted by various sources, please note—the organization cannot be separated from its leadership. When an organization's life is described as though those successes and failures had just happened without any human agency—'Sony did not...', 'Apple had the foresight...', 'P&G created...'—we absolve any accountability on the part of the leadership. In fact, those firms whose lunches got stolen and those who stole their competitor's lunches are both the victims and beneficiaries of their respective leaders and their ability to see beyond self-imposed blinkers or, as I term it in this book, transcend the contours of the present to the scenarios of the future. It is the leader, stupid, as Mr Clinton may say.

> Quick quiz: Name a leading company today that was just as dominant 25 years ago. There are a few, but many of the world's top companies in 1985 have floundered, shrunk, grown obsolete, or been acquired by rivals that grew stronger. Vijay Govindarajan, a professor at Dartmouth's Tuck School of Business and co-author of *The Other Side of Innovation* says successful companies tend to fall into three traps that make the glory days fleeting. First is **the physical trap**, in which big investments in old systems or equipment prevent the pursuit of fresher, more relevant investments. There's a **psychological trap**, in which company leaders fixate on what made them successful and fail to notice when something new is displacing it. Then there's the **strategic trap**, when a company focuses purely on the marketplace of today and fails to anticipate the future. Some unlucky companies manage a trifecta and fall into all three traps.[2]

Here are 10 companies and their 'Greek tragedies', as listed by Rick Newman, based on Govindarajan's work. Note the words and phrases which at first describe the rise and then the fall of these industry leaders. Observe that all the three traps identified by the author play in the minds of the leaders; no external obstacle causes these traps. It is the myopia of the leaders—the failure to transcend.

**Blockbuster**: This video-rental chain survived the transition from VHS to DVD just fine—but then it failed to adapt to the next big change. Netflix, phone companies and Redbox made video stores hopelessly outdated by making access to and delivery of the product very easy. The firm is closing hundreds of stores... And it's now chasing its industry instead of leading it.

**Dell**: Dell cut out the middleman and sold directly to the consumer. With this act of transcending the tradition of the industry, Dell came to dominate hallowed names like IBM and HP. But a decade later, Dell faltered as mobile devices began to displace personal computers (PCs), cheap Asian machines cut into profitability and big customers began to demand end-to-end service, not just hardware.

**Eastman Kodak**: For almost all of the twentieth century, camera was synonymous with Kodak. But Kodak's storied run began to end with the advent of digital photography and the rapid spread of printers, software, file-sharing capabilities and third-party apps. Since the late 1980s, Kodak has tried to expand into pharmaceuticals, memory chips, health-care imaging, document management and many other fields, but the magic has never returned. Its stock price is now about 96 per cent below the peak it had hit in 1997.

**Microsoft**: Even the mighty Microsoft is no exception to the rule—transcend or decline. It has fumbled or passed up many great ideas that others capitalized on, like Web TV, e-books, smartphones and the tablet PC. Sticking to one business line can be risky, especially in an industry as fast-changing as technology. And sure enough, the market is shifting away from the PCs that Microsoft's software is designed for. Bill Gates, like his friend and rival, Steve Jobs, was a prophet who transcended the straitjacketed ways of thinking and saw the PC as the future. He took from IBM the same way Jobs took from Xerox the golden gift which was unrecognized by the original holders of the miracles. But prophets of yesterday ought to know that the price of transcendence, like that of freedom, is eternal vigilance. What you did to yesterday's prophets you can be done unto by tomorrow's seers.

**Motorola**: Motorola built the world's first mobile phone. It dominated that business till as recently as 2003, when it introduced the trendy Razr, the highest-selling mobile phone at the time. But Motorola failed to focus on smartphones that can handle e-mail, Internet browsing and other features, and it rapidly lost share to newcomers like Research in Motion, Apple, LG and Samsung. Motorola was vanquished so swiftly that its cell phone division became a perennial money-loser and the firm announced plans this year to spin it off into a separate company.

**Sun Microsystems**: Its Java programming language made Sun an industry giant by the late 1990s. As PCs became more powerful, fewer big customers needed Sun's costly servers, and Sun spent most of the last decade downsizing and retrenching. With Sun's market value at just a fraction of what it had once been, Oracle bought the company in 1999.

**Sears:** The iconic American firm has all but disappeared from the news. A Norman Rockwell image of the American retail company is popular enough to be considered folklore, 'Sears put catalogues on the map, sold suburban Americans many of their household belongings, and introduced sturdy, affordable brands like Craftsman and Kenmore.' But then fleet-footed Walmart, Target and Amazon chewed up its turf. Sears tried to find its way, yet it's still looking for a winning strategy.

**Sony:** Walkman from Sony was, for a time, one of the most ubiquitous products in the consumer electronics market. What tripped up Sony and some of its competitors was the move from hardware to software, which put the emphasis on the brains of the device rather than the circuitry. As a result, faster-moving competitors like LG, Samsung, Vizio, Apple and the various makers of cell phones—which of course come with cameras these days—have outpaced this old-school innovator.

**Toys 'R' Us:** This retailer thrived in the 1980s and 1990s, riding on a surge in American consumption. As it went national, Toys 'R' Us drove many competitors out of business and gobbled up others. Then the tables turned, and the once-mighty toy giant was suddenly bested by discounters like Walmart and Target, online sites like Amazon and smaller merchants with better quality and service.

**Yahoo**: A pioneer in Web search and aggregation, 'Yahoo tried to charge for services like e-mail and file sharing, while upstart Google offered everything for free. Customers flocked to Google, which surged to a commanding lead in search that it still holds,'[3] according to Rick Newman.

It is important to emphasize that none of the strategies that the competitors of these once-mighty firms deployed were impossible for the firm itself to use. In fact, in many cases like Xerox and Polaroid, the original leaders of the industry invented those strategies, but failed to exploit them fully, and their competitors 'stole their lunch' by milking those very strategies. 'BF Goodrich invents, Firestone markets, and Goodyear makes money on the same product.' If all the other factors are almost the same or, in fact, if the odds are stacked (money, R&D, market position and credibility) in favour of the original firm, then what makes the difference? It is the thinking and acting ability, or inability, of the top leaders to transcend the existing system and hunt in the broader world. As the English poet John Milton wrote in *Paradise Lost* (most of these firms did lose their slice of paradise): 'The mind is its own place, and in itself can make a heaven of hell or a hell of heaven.' It is in the minds of the leaders that the seeds of hope or despair are born, and it is those minds that either transcend the present towards the ascent into glory, or sink into descent and even extinction.

Jim Collins identifies the five stages of decline.[4] His theory is relevant to us because, like all great chroniclers and storytellers about the world of organizations, Collins describes events which we then have to diagnose and ask 'Why did this happen?' I contend that in each case, as in the firms presented earlier by Govindarajan and Newman, it is the ability or inability of the leaders of the system to be eternally vigilant and systemic (everything depends on everything else), transcend in their minds the boundaries of the past (time, space, people), and with calm objectivity reinvent their futures.

In *How the Mighty Fall*, Jim Collins confronts these questions and offers leaders hope that they can learn how to stave off decline, and if they find themselves falling, reverse their course. Collins' research project—more than four years in duration—uncovered five stages of decline.

By understanding these stages of decline, leaders can substantially reduce their chances of falling all the way to the bottom. Great companies can stumble badly and recover.

Every institution, no matter how great, is vulnerable to decline. There is no law of nature that states that the most powerful will inevitably remain at the top. Anyone can fall and most eventually do. But as Collins' research emphasizes, some companies do indeed recover—in some cases, come back even stronger—even after having crashed during Stage 4. Decline, it turns out, is largely self-inflicted, and the path to recovery lies largely within our own hands. Sounds like a clarion call to transcendent leadership (also see Chapter 3 for the 'Rise and Fall of an Open System').

The five stages are as follows:

**Stage 1: Hubris born of success:** 'Great enterprises can become insulated by success,' says Collins. This should be read as 'leaders' instead of 'great enterprises', for no one ever met and shook hands with a 'great enterprise'. We better call a spade a spade. Whether the company is a success or failure, the enterprise is a reflection of its leaders and their ability to be honest with themselves and ask, 'How much of our success is fortuitous, and has the world changed enough for us to change?'

**Stage 2: Undisciplined pursuit of more:** Companies in Stage 2 stray from the disciplined creativity that had led them to greatness in the first place, and make undisciplined leaps into areas where they cannot be great, or they attempt to grow at a rate where they cannot maintain excellence—or both. When an organization grows beyond its ability to fill its key seats with the right people, it has set itself up for a fall. As seen later, the TCL juggles five balls at the same time, all the time—from self → interpersonal → team → 'our world' → 'the world'. This multi-tasking enables it to 'fill its key seats with the right people' or conversely, 'not to rush in where angels fear to tread'.

**Stage 3: Denial of risk and peril:** 'In Stage 3, leaders discount negative data, amplify positive data, and put a positive spin on ambiguous data,' explains Collins. Here is a parable from Ramakrishna to explain 'selective listening':

The spiritual teacher told his student, 'God is everywhere.' The student, having heard this, walked out onto the street where he heard a big commotion. An elephant was rushing down the street, wild and angry, and the mahout, the driver on top, was shouting, 'Get out of the way, get out!' The young man stood in the middle of the street while everyone else scattered pell-mell to the sides. The elephant rushed down, picked up this fellow, and threw him to the side before rushing on. Bruised and shaken, the disciple went to his master and complained, 'Sir, you said God is everywhere, so I thought the same God was in me and in the elephant, so why should I fear?' The teacher looked at him and replied, 'But what of the God who was sitting on top of the Elephant God and was shouting for you to get out of the way?'

To transcend the stereotypes and formulae in one's mind, and to look and learn from new data and make judgements with knowledge of the whole of it, that is the leader's responsibility.

Collins quotes the 'waterline' principle by Bill Gore, founder of W.L. Gore & Associates. This waterline, known as 'the Plimsoll line', is based on the buoyancy principle. The ship's equilibrium depends on keeping the Plimsoll line just above the water. When this line is just above the water level, it means that the ship is carrying its maximum load without risk of going under. The leader determines when she has just the right quantity of data to make a decision.

**Stage 4: Grasping for salvation:** 'The cumulative peril and/or the risks of Stage 3 gone bad assert themselves, throwing the enterprise into a sharp decline visible to all. The critical question is, how does the leadership respond? Leaders atop companies in the late stages of decline need to have a calm, clear-headed and focused approach. If you want to reverse decline, be rigorous about what not to do,' explains Collins.

**Stage 5: Capitulation to irrelevance or death:** 'In Stage 5, the accumulated setbacks and expensive false starts erode financial strength and individual spirit to such an extent that leaders abandon all hope of building a great future,' according to Collins.[5]

The following paragraph by Collins is revealing in terms of our central theme—the imperative on the part of leaders to grow the qualities described in this chapter as 'transcendent leadership'.

> The point of the struggle is not just to survive, but to build an enterprise that makes such a distinctive impact on the world it touches (and does so with such superior performance) that it would leave a gaping hole—a hole that cannot be easily filled by any other institution—if it ceased to exist. To accomplish this requires leaders who retain faith that they can find a way to prevail in pursuit of a cause larger than mere survival (and larger than themselves) while also maintaining the stoic will needed to take whatever actions must be taken, however excruciating, for the sake of that cause. [...] Failure is not so much a physical state as a state of mind; success is falling down—and getting up one more time—without end.[6]

## LEADERS SPEAK

### Rohini Nilekani

'I think sometimes leaders are more to manage expectations; sometimes people's expectations from them exceed their ability to deliver. Secondly, I would say they fail in not doing enough self-reflection in terms of how far they can deliver. You make a public statement or action and you are not able to follow through. Of course, many of us don't live up to our high ideas of ourselves; it could be a failure of integrity sometimes. Perhaps they underestimate the extent of what one has to do to achieve what one has talked about, and perhaps people's expectations from you are much further ahead of your ability to deliver.'

We will define and describe TCL by comparing and contrasting it with the concept of 'transformational leadership' (TFL), first formulated by James Macgregor Burns in 1968. TFL has been considered the highest form of leadership and is offered as a concept and a model worth emulating in organizations that aspire to high achievements.

This chapter argues that the concept of TFL is too limited to serve as a comprehensive model for what a truly great leader does in his or her leadership career. The good-to-great leaders, including those whom humanity acknowledges as the greatest leaders in different sectors of life, are to be understood by a far larger and more rigorous conceptual framework of which the TFL concept is a necessary but not sufficient component. TFL is inadequate to explain the power and influence of great leaders unless we go beyond transformation.

At the same time, we must highlight the fact that it is not just a handful of 'immortals' like Gandhi who exemplify transcendent leadership. While famous examples are most commonly used because the biographical details about their lives are easily available, there are many TCLs out there, as observed and experienced by us directly. They are working away in relative anonymity or with only a local identity, taking their organizations to greatness.[7]

I submit that TCL does not always reside in one leader, but may be shared among a team of leaders, even if in a hierarchy, who complement one another and hence make the whole leadership 'mutually exclusive and collectively exhaustive'. In these cases, substitute 'we, the leader' for 'I, the leader.'

**Transformational Leader as Defined in the Literature**

Transformational leadership is a process in which 'leaders and followers help each other to advance to a higher level of morale and motivation.' It is a mutually influencing transforming group. There is a conspicuous absence of any other activity by the leader or the followers. I do not mean to imply that the TFL theorists left no space for other activities within TFL. However, they accord to one facet of the leader, namely intense bonding with followers, the most seminal influence and central role. This, in my view, makes the model a limited one.

In consonance and in contrast, a transcendent leader 'transforms' in the sense of this definition, but also transcends the boundaries of the 'leader-follower' relationship and understands the 'soul' of their common world (India as a whole for Gandhi, America as a whole for Martin Luther King, South Africa for Mandela, the American North and South for Lincoln, and all of humanity for Buddha, the *Upanishads*, Jesus and Mohammed).

Transcending even that specific world, she senses the vision of the universe that surrounds her world and communicates with that larger universe and whoever cares to listen. In fact, she talks to herself as much or more than she does to the universe of followers that surround her. Dialogues with oneself is one of the hallmark features of the personality of a TCL. She is ultimately her own best teacher and best pupil.

A TCL has her own conception of her world around her and the larger universe that surrounds her world. She studies these and evolves her vision, values and strategies, often but not always, in dialogue (or 'multilogue') with close-knit followers who are 'solar systems' unto themselves—with simultaneous citizenship of multiple worlds and roles therein. This is not a secondary act as it may be inferred in TFL; it is a primary seminal act without which the TFL virtue of 'connecting at a deeper level with followers' will be a non-starter.

The TCL's multiple worlds connect to the multiple worlds of followers (the attempt at transformation) and the negotiations, intellectual and emotional, that ensue determine the fate of the enterprise. Regardless of what a group of followers say, a TCL relentlessly pursues proselytization of her vision and values, not just to individuals, but also to organizations and institutions. The TCL does all of her thinking, linking and acting before, during and after the transformational process has set in. Eternal vigilance is the price for transcendence.

TFL is a subset and a by-product of the 'open system' that is TCL.

'Enough,' says my editor, my son who is finishing his PhD in political philosophy at Berkeley and is reading this for me. 'Enough, Dad. Can we bring down these abstractions with some concrete examples? Preferably any that do not involve world-transforming figures like Gandhi? How should the ordinary business leader understand these differences?' He does not mince his words. He is right. I am not, absolutely not, proposing that a TCL is someone who is born once in a millennium and has statues erected for her on which pigeons sit. Instead, just like there are fantastic mothers and fathers, great husbands and wives, there are transcendent leaders in settings that may be little known outside a small world. (The last line of the poem at the end, 'A sunflower seed is a whole system too'?)

There are instances, some that I know and have been in awe of, and others which I've heard about from reliable sources. Let me recount one case.

## The Case of the Little Jack who Suddenly Grew Up

In Midwestern United States, the 65 employees of a small firm shivered in the bitter winter, but not because of the cold. They had grown up with the cold, but they had not grown up with poverty, and poverty faced them imminently. It was a family-owned firm run by the founder who had grown into a benevolent patriarch and an autocrat; it had seen better times. It had been one of the main sources of employment for generations in that small town, and the firm and its owner were revered by the people, but the town was abuzz with discontent and anxiety about the future of the firm and their jobs. The old man had lost his business acumen but not his grip on decision-making, and the firm's revenues and profits had been gradually sinking. The product, blades for outboard motors, was still in demand, but the firm had lost its competitive edge and its prices had risen so much that most their long-time customers were quietly moving to lower-cost, better quality competitors. And then suddenly, the leader died. His son who inherited the firm had been assisting his dad for many years, but he was an executive assistant, not an executive in his own right. His father had not allowed him to share power.

On the day after the funeral, the son gathered all the employees who had known him and each other all their lives. The gloom in the room could be cut with a knife. 'What can poor Jack do? He doesn't know anything,' whispers of despair had been going around the town. People were packing up, putting up their homes for sale and were preparing to try their luck in the big city. Jack stood up in front of them and said, 'I know I don't know how to run this business. I certainly don't know how to get a lot of contracts and make a lot of money for all of us and keep all the jobs for you and your children. But I know someone, in fact many, who know how to do all that. The only question is, will they agree to help?' He paused and the senior-most worker said, 'Heck, Jack. Whatever it takes, let us pay him and bring him on. It is our jobs, families and life as we have known it at stake, kid.' There were loud amens and 'Yeah, do it, Jack, we will back you.' Someone said, 'Who is it?' Jack then said, 'You. All of you. You know how to run this business. I do not. Come run the plant with me. But why should you? What is in it for you? Well, here is my idea: either I sell the firm, or you help me run the plant. In return, I propose a bonus plan which is called the Scanlan plan. We work for the bonus profit. You decide how much each one gets.' Someone from the back asked, 'Does that include your share?' 'Yes,' Jack replied, 'without you, my share will be zero. I'm sure you will give me more than that.' The workers put up bumper stickers all around town, 'We have no bosses here; bonus plan is our boss.' In two years, the firm had gained 65 per cent market share.

Jack, the son, during a weekly meeting with the employees three years later, spoke to a consultant. 'I was not being good-hearted to our employees even though I was fond of the people in the town. I was being strategic because I did not have the capital needed for the survival of the plant. I knew our industry, the big and small competitors, and the banks—the banks especially. I needed capital badly to upgrade our old equipment and compete with the big boys. The banks wouldn't touch me with a 10-foot bargepole because they too knew that I didn't know anything about outboard motor blades and how to make them good and cheap. But they knew our people, and that was my ace-in-the-hole. And it worked. Once these guys and gals said they would run the place, the banks lined up because their depositors were sitting in front of them.'

As Jack finished, a voice spoke up, 'Don't you believe that baloney, Mr Fancy Consultant! Jack here is a good kid who does not want us to feel like we owe him anything. Heck, we owe him everything. He could have sold the firm for whatever he could get and could have gone to the lights of the big city—we couldn't have done nothing whatever. He stayed, came up with an idea that, yeah, got the banks to put us up, got the vendors to wait for their money and continue supplies and the customers to place orders with us—but he was doing it for us.'

The young consultant, as he left for the airport, wondered who had it right.

Of course, all of them were right. Jack, the ordinary Midwestern youth, did 'leap tall buildings' in his mind. Jack analysed what faced him and took into account the objective facts—he lacked the credibility to run the plant alone and the prospect of selling for a low price and leaving the only life that he and his family had known did not appeal to him. The thought that shutting down the firm would leave half the town's families, who had been his friends all his life, under the shadow of bankruptcy, and would mean the destruction of a way of life that they all cherished, motivated him to keep the firm alive.

He put it all together, called it a holistic vision and came up with an integrated plan which would get him the most experienced labour at the lowest cost, and the most motivated, even inspired, workforce which would feel a sense of ownership, and no one needed to leave, including his family. Call it thinking outside the box or connecting the nine dots... or perhaps transcendence, anyone?[8]

What Leonardo Da Vinci was to any famous painter in history (a Renaissance man who was a great painter but also a lot many other things), so is TCL compared to TFL. A leader can be transformational without rising to the summit of being transcendent. But a transcendent leader is necessarily transformational and more.

Leo Tolstoy, when speaking of Abraham Lincoln, compared him to other great leaders of history, '[...] why was Lincoln so great that he overshadows all other national heroes? He really was not a great general like Napoleon or Washington; he was not as skilful a statesman as Gladstone or Frederick the Great; but his supremacy expresses altogether in his peculiar moral power and in the greatness of his character.'[9]

A transcendent leader is not God, but is an attempt on the part of a human to be god-like. It is not the pursuit of fame and glory that motivates her so much as the challenge of being the best and doing the best.

When someone sees an elephant for the first time, they may describe it as four big pillars because they noticed only the four great legs. But on seeing the elephant as a whole, they realize that the legs, big as they are, are not the only, or even the most important, part of the elephant's body. The mammoth body, the flexible trunk, the broom-like tail, the fan-like ears, the small eyes and the brains inside—all of these put together make up this gentle giant. If we have only a limited picture, we stunt our understanding of leadership, and we miss the prime qualities that have gone into the self-making (no one else can make a TCL) of the greatest of leaders. By using a definition that captures only one aspect of this fascinating product of genius of the human race, we lose the ability to understand, appreciate and possibly emulate the greatness of transcendent leaders.

In a short while, I will present the qualities of a TCL in the form of a *mantap* (sacred bandstand). However, before that, here are some smaller case studies of transcendence in organizations.

## The Case of the Sinner-turned-Saint

Du-Pont Chemicals, when faced with stringent new environmental regulations in the United States in the early 1970s, launched an environmental consulting division which exploited the extensive and deep knowledge which Du-Pont had of chemicals and the impact they had on the environment. Yesterday's polluter became today's saviour. On the one hand, Du-Pont responded to the regulatory mandate and gained enormous goodwill as an environmentally conscious corporation, and on the other hand, it created a new business opportunity for itself by selling 'environmental compliance consulting' to its peers and fellow-industry firms.

## The Case of the Red Meat Turned into White Milk

Seminal Inc. (a pseudonym), an artificial insemination firm, faced bankruptcy in the early 1970s. The beef market had ceased to be bullish (pardon the bad pun!). The small, but very profitable, boutique firm was reeling under the threat of the vegetarian movement. The baby boomers were coming of age and there was a strong move towards encouraging a healthy lifestyle (red meat came to be viewed as unhealthy and vegetables as 'good for you'). This made the future bleak for the firm. The leadership deliberated for over a month and emerged with a solution—artificial insemination, their area of expertise, could be sold not just to aid beef production, but could also be used for milk production, milk being one of the staple foods for vegetarians. Milk was touted to have untold virtues and the underground culture on both coasts of the US with 'back to nature' beliefs swigged milk as though there were no tomorrow. So the former beef experts reinvented themselves into the milk movement while waiting for the American public to tire of namby-pamby milk and revert to their old habits of consuming large quantities of the all-American meat.

## The Transcendent Leader

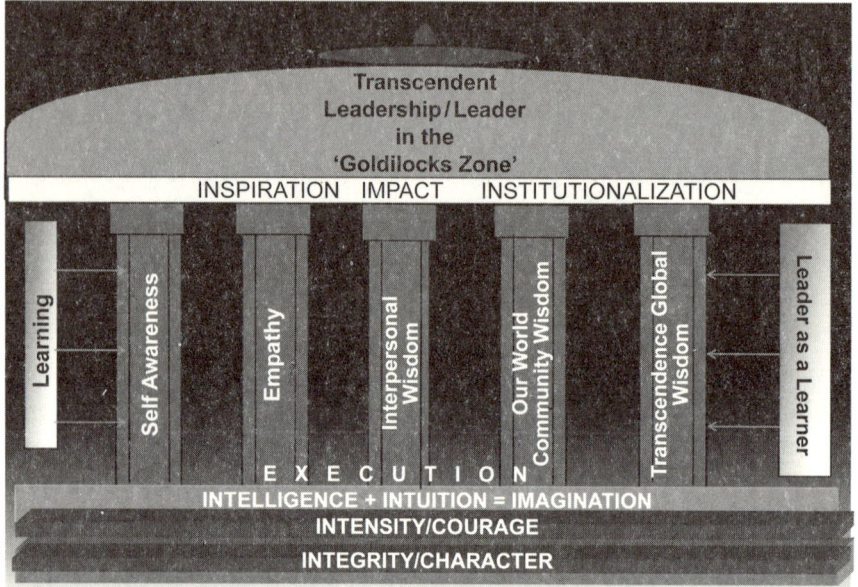

*Figure 2.1: '3+5 Transcendent Leadership' model*

In interviews with leaders, I introduced the model of transcendent leadership as seen in Figure 2.1 with the following rationale:

Imagine a young, aspiring leader asking me to provide the recipe for great leadership. She asks, 'What should I be and do to become a great leader?' My answer is the '3+5 Transcendent Leadership' model you see in the *mantap*. It has three layers of foundation: integrity/character, intensity/courage intelligence+intuition = imagination, in that order. This citadel of leadership is held up by five pillars moving from left to right. The identity of the great leader is in optimizing this system of qualities. The model is multi-dimensional—to be seen as projected in time and space, so that there is continuous learning on each quality. It is not immaculate conception. One is not born with all these qualities—one may have a little more of something or none of the other—but these are the 'eight commandments' I would prescribe to understand, absorb, practise and perfect throughout one's life.

As you can imagine, the reactions from the leaders were an emphatic 'yes' on some ('integrity'), and a slow and thoughtful 'yes, I can see that' on others ('Our world? Come to think of it, that is the description of my role—to know and act upon my knowledge of our world'). But on the whole, they were immensely encouraging of this proposal. Some suggested alternative words that they thought would better describe the quality I was trying to present ('Imagination rather than intelligence?'); some debated whether one quality was not the natural result of others ('Wouldn't you have interpersonal wisdom if you had the first two, self-awareness and empathy?'); but none demurred on the overall comprehensive model. Perhaps they were being polite, but they did seem convinced. In any case, I will leave the question of its value to my readers. You be the judge. And since you are only virtually in front of me, you need not be burdened with the task of taking my feelings into consideration. So go ahead, tear it apart if you like. But then you must promise to develop your own unique recipe for great leadership. If you create your own model, then I would have succeeded in my mission—to assist you in your leadership journey by helping to create a model of what to look for and nurture in yourself and in your people.

Let us now enter this *mantap* and explore each layer and pillar.

## The Foundation—The Three Is

The three layers of the foundation of this edifice are 'integrity/character', 'intensity/passion' and 'intelligence + intuition = imagination' in that order.

Any true leader needs this foundation. Great leaders develop these three qualities in the core of their being. The sequential order is important; integrity is the most fundamental. It is the prerequisite for all others to succeed. Without integrity, the rest may be used for good or evil. They are neutral instruments. What Richard Feynman said about science in 1988 applies equally to the 'great forces' in a leader without integrity now:

> It was once thought that the possibilities people had were not developed because most of the people were ignorant. With universal education, could all men be Voltaire? Bad can be taught at least as efficiently as good. [...] Education is a strong force, but for either good or evil, as are such great forces as peace, sobriety, material power,

communication, honesty and the ideals of many dreamers. Why can't we conquer ourselves? Because we find that even great forces and abilities do not seem to carry with them clear instructions on how to use them. As an example, the great accumulation of understanding as to how the physical world behaves only convinces one that this behaviour seems to have a kind of meaninglessness. The sciences do not directly teach good and bad.[10]

**Integrity/Character:**

Listen to the Sage of Buffalo, Warren Buffett, 'Somebody once said that in looking for people to hire, you look for three qualities: integrity, intelligence and energy. And if you don't have the first, the other two will kill you. You think about it; it's true. If you hire somebody without [integrity], you really want them to be dumb and lazy.'

What is integrity? According to Stephen Carter from Harvard:

[…] Integrity requires three steps: (1) Discerning what is right and what is wrong; (2) Acting on what you have discerned even at a personal cost; (3) Saying openly that you're acting in your understanding of right from wrong.

[…] The first criterion captures the idea of integrity as requiring a degree of moral reflectiveness. The second brings in the ideal of an integral person as steadfast which includes the chance of keeping commitments. The third reminds us that a person of integrity is unashamed of doing the right.

The word integrity comes from the same Latin root as integer and historically has been understood to carry much the same sense, the sense of wholeness. A person of integrity like a whole number is a whole person, a person somehow undivided. The word conveys not so much a single-mindedness as a completeness, not the frenzy of a fanatic who wants to remake all the world in a single mould, but the serenity of a person who is confident in the knowledge that he or she is living rightly. A person of integrity lurks somewhere inside each of us; a person we feel we can trust to do right today, to play by the rules, to keep commitments. Perhaps it is because we all sense the capacity for integrity within ourselves that we are able to notice and admire it even in people with whom, on many issues, we sharply disagree.[11]

Now reread Carter's three steps and compare it with what Mahatma Gandhi had said: 'Happiness is when what you think, what you say, and what you do are in harmony.' So Carter's integrity is Gandhiji's happiness, right? The scholar and the saint arrive at the same place.

*The American Heritage Dictionary of the English Language* (fourth edition) defines integrity as:

1. Steadfast adherence to a strict moral or ethical code.
2. The state of being unimpaired; soundness.
3. The quality or condition of being whole or undivided; completeness.

Why is integrity (or the lack thereof) suddenly the stuff of headlines?

Cynicism about governments is not new. As far back as 300 BC, Kautilya in the *Arthashastra* said, 'Just as it is impossible to know when a swimming fish is drinking water (or urinating in it), so it is impossible to find out when a government servant is stealing money.'

So, this degeneration is not a recent phenomenon. What if I told you that the following was found in the ruins of a castle in northern India, probably part of a long treatise on politics and probably by Kautilya around 349 BC?

## 'How to Get Power and How to Retain It': A Primer for a Politician

*The rules stated below are to be followed implicitly for success.*

*Do not trust anyone at the start, for they all need something from you and you may not want to give them what they want, or you may get nothing in return. Do not worry; they will come to you at any price as a bee does to a flower. Power is an asexual aphrodisiac. No one is immune fully to its seduction; once tasted it is addictive and holds its victims in its sway beyond all reason. One would sell one's mother to keep feeding at the trough of power.*

*Do not trust anyone fully* (underscored in the original), *anytime, no matter how long you know him or her. It keeps them on their toes if they feel uncertain about your trust and will spur them on to do more and better to gain your trust which you dole out unpredictably, but repeat, never fully.*

*Beware of principled people, for they are the most dangerous. They have no permanent friends, only permanent interests. The purer their principles are, the more undependable they are to you in your quest for power. They owe their loyalty and allegiance not to a man but to an abstract idea such as honesty, goodness or justice. You need such people, to use them where your interests align with theirs, but be prepared to discard them when your interests are no longer served by them (like a small cloth you use when you have a cold).*

*Unprincipled unscrupulous followers are to be cultivated, for they seek the same goals as you do—power and more power. But if you achieve better results, they will follow you loyally as the moon does the sun, reflecting the glory. They will do this as long as they see that you have power and patronage to dispense, which you should do in a measured manner to keep them hungry.*

*Keep the principled and the unprincipled at each other's throats and appear to favour one at one time and another at another and none at all at times. This way, they will fight each other, control each other, and will not focus their rivalry on you. As for virtues, proclaim them on every possible occasion. The ordinary subject may or may not believe, yet needs to believe you may be virtuous. For what choice does he have, poor gullible fool?*

*Vices you indulge in, but never publicly. A man needs his vices as a dog needs to sniff new smells. But to let someone see you indulge gives them power over you and you will be vulnerable to blackmail. Feed your followers many vices so that you can get a hold on them and manipulate their behaviour as and when you need to.*

*Truth is precious, economize it. Tell the truth sparingly and use it as a strategy to get something, but never be addicted to it. Learn to lie unselfconsciously, without embarrassment or guilt or shame. Learn to enjoy lying. Truth lacks variety and is uncreative, dull and boring. Lying has infinite variety—a veritable art form to be practised at every opportunity and enjoyed for its own sake. Practise lying early and often so that you gain expertise in the nuances of lying. Have just enough verifiable truth to allay suspicious minds, and then the rest will be accepted as genuine, as milk mixed with water is accepted because it is white. Put people off-balance by not maintaining any patterns in your lying (or in any of your behaviour) so that they can't predict your words or actions. Confuse them constantly as they argue within themselves, 'Oh this can't be a lie, because I caught him telling the truth last time,' or 'He will never lie to me; he depends on me, but let him lie to others.'*

*Insist your followers tell the truth. To keep them honest or to rattle them, catch them in a lie and make a big fuss about it.*[12] *Lying is a privilege only the powerful deserve, because they are above such paltry bourgeoisie values and common morality. The truly powerless and the truly powerful are similar in this respect, neither has anything to gain by telling the truth or to lose by telling a lie.*

*Of all the vices, women are the most dangerous and you should be ever vigilant. The intoxication of wine is temporary, but a woman can impair you permanently. If you have to have a woman, choose a woman who loves power as much as you do and helps you get it. You need not fear a woman as a potential rival, for she will never hold power in a man's world in a true sense.*

*Never give away any information. Be vague in your responses [...]*
(the tablet inscription is lost from here on).

Honestly? Beg your pardon for putting you up to a little mischief, but no such inscription exists as far as I know, because I just wrote this based on my observations over a few years. These guidelines are not fiction or cynical reflections, though; I have met and heard those who hold these 'truths to be self-evident and that all men are not created equal' and they intend to keep it so.

This fictitious inscription indicates that it is possible that instances of questionable ethical behaviour in both business and public life have been happening all the time, but it's only now that such instances are coming to light, thanks to enhanced public scrutiny. Regardless, never before in independent India's history has there been such angst and such widespread anguish and anger at the depth and breadth of corruption at the highest levels of governments and corporations. Consider this debate held at the Indian Institute of Management, Bangalore, on 21 December 2011:

## The Unethical Indian? A Debate

One of India's iconic business leaders, also the first Indian to be the CEO of a major global consulting firm, is charged with insider trading in a US court. Not so long ago, one of India's top five software services firms imploded when it was revealed that funds had been diverted to another business. Several national and state ministers have been in jail, charged with corruption and misuse of their office. Another iconic former police officer, the first woman to enter the Indian police service, and herself a crusader against corruption, is accused of repeatedly claiming more money than she spent on her travel. Viewing this unfolding crisis, a top ethics watchdog of the government has commented that 'India's moral fabric is tearing apart.'

Is it possible that this release of people's 'animal instincts' is an inevitable outcome of pursuing a capitalist model of development? Or could it be that we, as a society, don't have a strong enough moral compass, and are instead ambivalent about right and wrong in many contexts? Or perhaps the problem lies not within us, but in the structures, processes and systems that we have created that encourage self-serving behaviour? Do we have a role to play in changing this situation? Or will the creation of a strong Lok Pal be the panacea that we are looking for?

At the minimum, the consequence of this mammoth rise in corruption has been the erosion of the public's trust and respect in leaders, especially political and business leaders.

There are two kinds of integrity—integrity of vision or purpose and integrity of values. It is not always easy to differentiate between the two. Vision is about direction and values are about setting boundaries for the actions taken towards that direction. An example of a vision statement would be, 'I wish to generate wealth for my shareholders and employees, but by using ethical means.' A large Indian firm used to call this latter phrase 'not managing the environment'. I admired it because it meant not bribing officials to gain licenses or government contracts!

Sticking to your vision steadfastly even in the face of failure may seem stupid, even suicidal. Yet, what use is a vision if you change it every time the wind blows the wrong way? The important part here is to know the core of your vision that you want to stick to at all costs, and the peripheral parts which you can let go. If you are a Hewlett Packard (HP) who is committed to a vision of carrying your people with you all along and a big contract is offered to you, which you need badly but which would entail hiring and later firing a bulk of the new hires at the end of the contract, you reject the contract, as HP did. If you are Shell Oil in the UK, sworn to making socially useful products, and your R&D department comes up with a 'new' product which you know and they know is merely cosmetic and caters to the ignorance or vanity of consumers and provides no lasting value at all, you reject it, even though it is easy money for the pickings. But it is not easy to know always what is core and what is peripheral when you have temptations leading you astray. For Infosys,[13] a small struggling Indian firm in the 1980s, 40 per cent of its business came from a certain multinational. The giant Goliath had the fledgling Indian David information industry 'over a barrel' and proposed drastic reductions in its rates with a 'take it or leave it' ultimatum. Infosys decided to leave it, to walk out rather than accept a demand which went contrary to its vision of being respected globally. It decided to keep the integrity of its vision at a cost, a heavy cost at that juncture—a significant proportion of its business. What if it had turned out to be disastrous? Integrity extracts a price, and the higher the stakes, the higher the challenge to keep integrity intact. And why does one stick to one's integrity even at such a high cost? Because the benefits are equally high. The most important benefit is the trust you generate and maintain in your stakeholders, because they know what your vision is and what your values are, and that you will stick to them come what may and hence they can trust you with their money, their careers and sometimes their very lives. This buys you trust and customer and employee loyalty (even from those who themselves may compromise their values all the time and have no vision except expediency of the situation).

What if the prevailing norm in the community or society is against such 'goody-goody' values like integrity?

Edward Luce, in his book *In Spite of the Gods: The Rise of Modern India*, says,

> In Kerala, some people even admired corrupt officials. They say if you're not making money, you must be really stupid. Keralites have a word for honest officials—*pavangal,* which means a highly moral person with good intentions, but it can also be defined as naïve and gullible. Likewise, those who know how to give bribes are described as *buddhi,* which means cunning and implies the 'power of discrimination which distinguishes adults from children'. It is a revealing vocabulary.

To be fair to Kerala, a lovely state which advertises itself as 'God's own country'—and God, I am told reliably, has approved of this advertisement—it is not by a long chalk alone in having citizens who make this candid distinction about the naïve simpletons, the suckers, the losers; and the street-savvy citizen who knows how to get along by going along.

Integrity may have been the 'hot button' issue in politics from the time human beings invented governance. So what if we gave a seminar to young politicians on 'transcendent leadership'? Here is a brief report from one such seminar on political leadership:

## On the Education of Young Politicians

Preamble: We have recently concluded the first workshop for young politicians. To evaluate it we use the two definitions by Peter Drucker.

a) Effectiveness—Doing the right things
b) Efficiency—Doing things right

On (b) we scored 8 of 10, both in our view and in the participants' evaluations. So far so good.

But on (a) I rated the workshop a 0 on 10. We discussed 'how' to be an efficient/productive/knowledgeable/popular/election-winning MLA. We learnt our place in the structure and processes of legislatures and how to understand budgets, statistics and behaviours—all knowledge and skills which are 'value-neutral'. The knowledge we shared could be used by the worst of crooks and the best of saints with equal results. We responded to what they wanted, but we did not deal at all with 'what to want'. We dealt with the mechanics of leadership, but not the morality of it. We did not dwell on 'why be in public service' and what were the 'right' goals for that and 'why'. We were good 'consigliores' (trusted advisors) for the Godfathers of politics. 'Ours is not to question why, ours is but to do and die' is the soldier's motto; we fulfil it.

Who is the 'we' I referred to in the earlier paragraph? It is all of us, citizens and scholars alike, who are accomplices after the fact. These are not 'politically wrong' questions; the real rebirth of the nation lies in asking these very questions, especially by those in the next generation who will inherit the legacy (and thereby the contamination), and by those who are poised to be bequeathed the podium (and the odium). Hence the accountability—the 0 out of 10—resides in all of us. We cannot afford to agree with Oscar Wilde's 'What has posterity done unto us that we should anything for posterity?' We, the old folk who have enjoyed the fruits of freedom, must hold ourselves accountable.

Hence, I propose a series of workshops which ask the following questions instead:

What is the image of a politician in the mind of the aam admi, the common man? Do we agree with the image? If we do, what are its implications for our ideals when we develop the 'new age' of leaders? What should we ask of them, teach them, reward them for and sanction to them?

What are the realistic constraints to professing and practising professed values which may be different (not in formal statement but in practice)? Do the constraints compel us to abandon the 'born again' ideals totally or partially? Are we finally for training the elected office bearers for fighting, winning and retaining power at all costs, and all else be damned (based on the hypothesis that 'We are the (relatively) good people. They are the bad people. Hence, if we earn and keep power then it is to be assumed that our people will do good by the Indian people. Q.E.D.'). In a court of law can the defence be, 'Yes I murdered, but they did it, so they have no moral right to condemn us.' But why did you let (name any of the crooked ministers) have a free go? Because we needed to keep power and... (Repeat: We are the good people. They are the bad people. Hence if we earn and keep power then...) Imagine a play and on the stage the two political parties come to say the same words, 'Yes, what happened in (that year) in that place was a heinous pogrom. But so were those that happened in (that other year) and (in that other place). How come you can hound (so-and-so) for the first one but no person of stature has been brought to book for the second (or third or fourth or the nth).' Because we are good people; they are the bad people... (You know it by heart by now).

Can we design the following modules for young politicians:

- How to serve the people of your constituency?
- How to resist the temptation of corruption?
- How to measure your performance serving your citizens in your constituency?
- Using the Millennium Development Goals—how have you improved education, healthcare and other sectors for your ordinary citizen? ('people index vs. party index')?

- Under what circumstances would you resign rather than accept certain conditions?
- What is the legacy you want to leave for your constituency if you're an only one-time MLA?
- What if an astrologer you trust implicitly told you that you will never be a minister and you will be a one-time MLA only? What would you want to know and do?
- If you had six months to live what would you want to do as a as a minister, a MLA, or as a MP?

Can we ask these questions and demand answers? Rhetoric apart, this is the point of epiphany—I don't know if we have the 'testicular fortitude' for this.

'These are all good questions, but we need answers,' says my editor. My answer: questions of integrity are the exclusive right and responsibility of each individual, like physical exercise, and hence the answers to these questions are only of value when a human being says them and acts on them according to Stephen Carter's three criteria, 'Integrity requires three steps: (1) Discerning what is right and what is wrong, (2) Acting on what you have discerned even at a personal cost, and (3) Saying openly that you're acting in your understanding of right from wrong.'

Here are some quotes heard in the marketplace (focus group sessions at various forums) about integrity (the speakers preferred to remain anonymous):

**Speaker #1:** 'Integrity is like mother and apple pie, as the Americans would say. It is politically correct to agree that integrity is fundamental to a leader. But real life is not that simple or straightforward. It is not black or white. If it were, that would be easy. There are shades of grey. For example, I don't want to pay bribes, so my company has strict rules about this. But I know we do employ agents or (laughs) when they have fancy college degrees they are called 'consultants' or 'lobbyists'. They charge us 'fees' which you know is partly towards paying bribes to move our files or even to just simply sell our products. We have to live with it.'

**Speaker #2:** 'That quote of yours from Lincoln—"Any man can bear adversity; give him power and it will test his character". I don't think he is right about bearing adversity being easy. In fact, that too tests character. You compromise a lot in bad times, just in order to survive or keep up appearances. You ask vendors to bill a month later so that you can show a better bottom line for the quarter; you exaggerate your product's qualities in order to get an order knowing full well it is not that good; the white or "brown lies" you say to keep vendors from guessing that your cash flow is in trouble—it is not easy to keep integrity (that is what character is for me) in adversity.'

**Speaker #3**: 'My principle is: Trust everyone a little and trust no one fully. I know that sounds cynical (sounds like something Kautilya or Machiavelli said, right?), but I don't mean it that way. In fact, I include myself in it. I mean that real life is hard and every one, or at least most people I know, makes compromises. You know the saying, "Every man has his price." If I have to lose Rs 3,00,000 I may refuse to pay a bribe; if it is 3 million at stake I may pay up under the table and get on with it. I think if the stakes are high enough, then one may give up some "purity" to gain some necessity, if you know what I mean? And this is not for merely selfish reasons. You have "stakeholders", is that what you call them? Shareholders who are pensioners and are dependent on your dividends to live and employees whose jobs are at stake and would not have jobs if you did not win that contract (however big you are as a firm, you are still at the mercy of the forces outside your organization).'

**Speaker #4:** 'Integrity in public life, by and large, whether it is politicians, whether it's the bureaucracy, whether it's our business leaders, for all of them (it's seeping into our education system now as well) integrity in public life is completely gone. You need to pay 2–3 lakhs for a primary teacher's position in a government school, so how does a 25–26 year old young lady start her life in the field of education? She starts with the thought, "I have to recover my 2–3 lakhs." What is the ethics you have to transmit to your work? Businesses have done the same thing. We spoke about inequality earlier—it is widening substantially. Earlier it was not so pronounced, but today you have somebody building a 2.5 billion dollar edifice to himself in the middle of Bombay, the view from which is slums in all 360 degrees and you're okay with it. Now you can turn around as a leader and say, "What I make is mine, what you make is mine too." We have started to lose our life ethics dramatically. To me, this combination—the lack of a life ethic, the lack of principles and the degradation in law and order—has created the loss of integrity. Maybe a lack trust is a symptom of it all, but the large hitters are these factors… Trust is the consequence of the positive versions of these, and you're saying neither an internal monitor nor an external monitor exists anymore—the ethics which are internal and the law and order force which is external. I am honest because I want to be honest or I am honest because you are going to punish me if I am not honest. Neither one exists now. Neither internal integrity nor external enforcement exists, and therefore, in that sense, we are screwed.'

**Speaker #6**: 'Our society is deteriorating and the social fabric will explode at this rate in the next 10–20 years in some form. And the reason I'm petrified about that is because our population's average age is going to be around 30 years for the next 20–25 years, and when you've lost law and order, life ethics and integrity, you end up preparing youngsters to become entitlement cases. They think, "This prosperity is mine by right and I have to get my slice of the pie. Doesn't matter if I can't read or write and have no skills… But I still need to go to malls and, have my whatever…." They expect that to happen, and they are not equipped to make that happen. As a result, you either break the social fabric or you go into large-scale crime. Either way, crime is the consequence of breaking the social fabric right? But that's the most dangerous thing that could happen, you are talking about significant numbers; you are talking about 2-3-4 hundred million youngsters over the next 20 years. Most economists say that we will add one million people to the workforce every month or so for the next 20 years, so that is 240 million discontent youth. Now where is your demographic dividend, if those children are not equipped with the basics of organized society, which is trust, law and order, ethics and integrity? If you're a small country, you could say—if you're a Singapore, a city-state—someone can take over, relatively simple. But this is 1.2 billion people—what do you do? (At one point of time, Indira Gandhi made an effort to take over for her own reasons, and she had to move back because it just couldn't be done). So, the question becomes, "What are the alternatives?" and that's really what I think needs some thinking.

That's an area of opportunity for people like you and me, to be able to impart to well-meaning next generation leaders some of these issues. This building will not have people who are appreciative of this conversation, because they are not aware of it. You got to be able to integrate. If you want to call upon the rich and poor, India and Bharat, you got to integrate both of them...'

**Speaker #7**: So, three things are needed—awareness, caring, then acting upon the awareness and caring. If the awareness itself doesn't exist, then the other two don't count. But awareness does exist among the well-educated middle-class, but they may not care and therefore nothing happens. Maybe those who wring their hands may care but they do not act; the caring does not automatically imply action, converting the caring into action. And those—at least the best in the development sector that I have seen, the best in each sector—a few actually have all these three, but the critical mass that is needed by society is missing. Therefore, people like us meet once in a year or so, maybe lament on the state of affairs, and then we go back to our individual sand boxes, and do things that may not finally have synergy to act upon that situation, the overall body politic...'

## Integrity and Power

At a workshop two years ago, I asked, 'Two people have identical knives. One is a great surgeon and the other is a great thug. What is the difference between their uses of the knife?' A woman answered: 'एक जान देते है; दूसरा जान लेते है' (one gives life; the other takes away life). When it rains, it brings life to earth; when it floods, it brings destruction; when the rain becomes a tsunami, it brings death. Fire goes from the beauty of life-giving to the horror of death as the *lakshman rekha*[14] is crossed. A cancer cell is nothing but a healthy cell gone greedy.

So what is this *lakshman rekha*, this rubicon, which separates life from death, constructive from destructive, embrace from smother, caress from throttle? The same instrument of power (a knife) has different purposes, one imbued with morality ('care for others') and another imbued with narrow gains. The same intervention (rain) brings at one stage life and at another stage death, because Indra, the Rain God, comes sometimes as a friend of humans and sometimes as a tyrant raining down terror and destruction.

The instrument is the same; the difference is one of purpose, of morality, of concern for others. So, when we see the knife, how do we know whether to lie down or to fight back? This was the question I faced when I first heard of the Anna Hazare movement, a recent attempt at acquiring power to reform Indian society by creating an 'anti-corruption' movement. A leader rose up overnight and for a few months held sway over the airwaves and peoples' minds in India. Tens of thousands gathered in person and more watched on television as the new messiah challenged the establishment to appoint a judge-jury-prosecutor called 'Lok Yakut'.

In the beginning, I was for it. I saw Anna as the welcome rain, bringing the freshness of idealism to the parched cynical earth which is India for many; voicing the near-universal cry of every honest human being in India for a life that was just ordinarily decent and leaders who were boringly honest. Someone had to stand up and say, 'I have had enough; I can't take any more of this.' I believed this despite my recognition that many good things have transpired in the last two decades and that the glass is half-full. But then I changed my mind and felt that the so-called 'movement' was throwing the baby out with the bathwater.

In fact, precisely because we have progressed, we know not only what we have, but also what we don't have. We have climbed a mountain and can now see the next peak. An optimal mixture of frustration and hope is the recipe for a revolution in all social transformations. Neither one by itself is enough. India now has both, at least for the middle class (not for the poor yet, but it is coming; to the rich it will come as a threat to their vested interests). When this potent mixture explodes it creates a 'movement', a temporary system lacking structure but compensating for it with aspiration and passion. It is highly unstable, but while it lasts it is exhilarating, and like a forest fire, it consumes the lives that it touches. With a clean sweep of creative destruction at its best, it transforms the system. If it succeeds, if its values and purpose resonate with enough followers, it becomes a precursor of more permanent structures and could lead to the formation of an organization and to a long-term vision of an institution. While a movement is a necessary but not sufficient cause in certain contexts where profound issues are at stake for society (or some significant chunk of it—the Bhakti movement in Hinduism or the evangelists in the US vs. the civil rights movement or the independence movement which were holistic and relatively all-embracing), it has to convert itself into an institution at the right time to be of any use to the long-term transformation of the system (see Thomas S. Kuhn 1962, *The Structure of Scientific Revolutions*).

I thought that Anna was creating such a movement, which would be within the *lakshman rekha*.

But then Anna and his core committee demanded not just that their version of the Lok Pal bill, the 'Jan Lok Pal Bill', be the only bill to be presented in parliament, but also that it must be passed! Till then they were exercising their right to free speech, but were not denying that right to anyone else. He flagrantly violated the right of elected parliamentarians to consider alternatives for achieving the same goal—the eradication of corruption—and dictated terms to the constitutional body that it should, in fact must, vote only one way and no other, or else Mr Hazare would fast unto death. This was blackmail of parliament, of civil society proponents of other versions of the Lok Pal Bill, and of ordinary citizens of India. It was 'my way or the highway'. Gandhiji, the greater of my two heroes, undertook fasts, but only against the illegitimate authority of the British Empire. There, the *lakshman rekha* allowed any moral means to oppose the usurpers. Even there, Gandhiji insisted on the primacy of the means over the end, of non-violence over violence. He never used a fast unto death as a means of coercion, even against the hated enemy regime. A martyr is the nightmare of a dictator and is morally right to be one; but it is criminal to be a martyr against democracy. That is where Anna lost the moral power he had gained by drawing the attention of the nation to the issue of corruption in a peaceful, non-violent way.

In short, 'The operation succeeded but the patient died.' One sure way to 'cure' the cancer is by killing the patient.

Looking back, I should have known what would happen with the Anna Hazare 'movement'; it is obvious from the history of movements (including revolutions of all kinds). At the beginning, at the birth of a movement, the 'mover' creates the movement. As time passes, as support gathers for the cause, as the temptation increases for the abuse of power (if the mover lacks the wisdom to put the genie back into the bottle), then the roles reverse. The movement begins to carry the mover who is the now the 'effect' rather than the 'cause', a cork floating in a giant wave imagining that it is causing the wave (Robespierre in the French Revolution; Nehru and Jinnah at partition; Jayaprakash Narayan in 1977). It is only a matter of time before the cork disappears and the sharks appear, because they love and thrive on chaos. Of course, the cork can itself transform into a shark as has happened numerous times in history ('One has to compromise for the cause, so let me kill those who oppose me.') The mover starts humble, a servant of the masses who leads them towards the light, but he comes to believe that he himself is the light and hence the master, not the servant or just the mover. This has happened to most of our post-independence leaders (but, thank God, not all).

Movements are not a like a scalpel; they are at best more like a hammer in the hands of a smith and at worst like a bludgeon in the hands of a marauder. They are not for precision bombing; they are for carpet bombing. If you get in its way, innocent bystander or guilty perpetrator alike, you will be the indiscriminate target. Movements cannot afford the luxury of nuances and subtleties. There are no shades of grey, just black and white. This is why it is difficult to predict the outcomes of movements. Either you overestimate (three cabinet ministers wait to receive a yoga guru at the train station) or you underestimate (you arrest and jail a far more powerful adversary). So, I ask you, 'What is the "just right" reaction and how do we judge it?'

In this recent instance in Indian history, an episode which promised for a time to become historic but then faded to nothingness, both parties failed to use power wisely. The 'mover', Anna Hazare, the protagonist, wanted to shake the system, but was himself shaken. He could not transcend his limited vision ('I want Lok Ayukta, the panacea for all ills of my society') to proclaim a broader vision (adapting the immortal words of Gandhiji, 'I want each one of us to be the change you want to see. I want each of you to stop paying any bribe whatsoever and then protest every bribe-giver.') The government, the antagonist, was equally clumsy in the use of formal power vested in it by the people. It succeeded in neutralizing the protagonist, but it did not transcend the immediate crisis and respond to the deeper cry of the people. The messenger was defeated in the end and the message was ignored, adding to the cynicism of the general public who think nothing will ever change.

This deep cynicism is not unique to India.

## 'Leaders without Followers'[15]

> The annual 'Trust Barometer' survey published by Edelman, a public-relations firm, reports widespread scepticism about the ethics practised by political and business leaders. The lowest scores were when those surveyed were asked if they trust leaders to 'tell the truth, regardless of how complex or unpopular it is.' Only 18 per cent trusted business leaders, whilst government leaders scored a yet more miserable 13 per cent.

Why are we seeing this rising tide of distrust in our leaders? It has to do with the misuse of power. In a leader, integrity without power leads to impotence; power without integrity leads to tyranny.

## LEADERS SPEAK

**'Nearly any man can bear adversity, but if you want to test a man's character, give him power.' Do you agree with Lincoln? What does power mean to you? How important is power for a leader? Kissinger said, 'Power is an aphrodisiac,' while Lord Acton held, 'Power tends to corrupt, and absolute power corrupts absolutely.' Comment.**

### N.R. Narayana Murthy

'Look, I have seen one thing, I have rarely come across an incompetent fellow who has a big ego, rarely, there could be some, but it's rare, so as long as this person who is showing ego is very competent, and as long as he doesn't go beyond (limits) it's okay with me because there are more occasions where I can use his competence than suffer from his ego.'

### Ashok Kamath

'I think both are tough, it's hard to share adversity as much as it is hard to share power. When you share adversity you are actually showing real outstanding qualities as a leader. I think sharing power is harder, but I think the adversity one is very difficult. In the circles that I have moved in and known, I haven't seen power as corrupting. But then the circle that I move in, we are people from middle-class backgrounds, we worked our way up, that's what I have seen and those are my friends today also.'

## Ashok Mishra

'You should never let the power get to your head, because at the end of the day power has to be shared with the team, so that everybody is empowered. They have power to do what they would do... to work for you means to derive power from you... I derive mine from my chairman and the board.'

## Manish Sabharwal

'Any man can bear adversity... give the man power and it will test his character.' Ashok and I are the checks and bounds; power has the ability to gets things done; it has the ability to act more than anything else. The best way to run a country is by dictatorship. You end up as Lee Kuan Yew, which I think is the best thing for India given the chaos and politics, or you probably end up in Mugambe.

[...] The difference between India and Pakistan born on the same night is three million people... democracy is the only way to run a country in the long run... and absolute power is a great way to get things done in a country or company, but if you pick the wrong thing, you've had it. So, there are checks and balances between Ashok and me and now there's also the supervision that we brought in, like our CFO, who is quite capable. I think they have put checks and balances on me which has absolutely helped me make better decisions. Sometimes they absolutely drive me crazy, our CFO asks for more MIS in one day than I used to ask for in three months, but I think he has been great for the company because he now keeps the trains running on time which is a different skill set from getting the train out of the station. As the company stabilizes, once the products get defined, as customers get defined, then you need to blunt the authority and exercise of power because at that point you have more to lose and less to gain.'

## Mali Mahalingam

'I think to me power is not a bad word, and I have seen leaders use power, and I have seen my chairman and other executives use power for their self-interest, and things of that sort. I think power is an absolute necessity in my opinion, but I am also of the view that power is not mandatory, and I have always believed that one can lead from any chair, you can influence people without having authority, or by just letting people know you have it. I have also seen people at very senior levels acting as though they did not have authority and power. So to me, the concept of power is that you have it everywhere and have always had—some people grab it and use it for larger benefits, and some people don't create the necessary impact that they need to create in the organization. So I have seen both sides—people seeing power, grabbing it and abusing it, and people seeing power, grabbing it and using it for the benefit of the organization, and people not seeing it and not being able to impact or create any impact for the organization. I belonged to a category where power need not be given to you. You keep pushing the boundaries, till you are being told that you are exceeding your power limits, that's what I have done.

'Most recently, a decision really upset me and expedited my desire to be on my own and not to work for any company. We let some people go to Sweden; there I thought even legally we were obliged to pay a variable incentive. Even if they had left on their own, they've earned it and here is a situation that we are letting them go, how can we deny them, and he took a call. He said if it gets legal then he would handle that, but he will not pay them the variable pay... This is blatantly unethical and a breach of trust in my opinion. I wanted it to be escalated to the chairman of the board. Then my boss said what goes to the chairman is his call and it stops with me period. I told him to please find a good HR manager, all these eight years that I had been heading HR, I always paid out bonuses and variable pay to anyone who had served the company till the date of reckoning, and I think half a dozen other companies do it too. I've seen great leaders who have always had these schools of thought which I tend to completely disagree with. By not agreeing to this I ran the risk of losing my own job, but I couldn't care. That is where I have used power very effectively. I'm the head of HR, and I gave them five reasons why this gentleman must be terminated from the company, and I was given the go ahead to terminate. I am documenting the reasons for anybody to see it. This is where I have used power to challenge the decision, or the decision of someone to veto my decision, when I believe that I have a valid reason for harassment cases or lack of integrity. Those managers who were opposed to integrity; you cannot give them a chance at the higher levels but can probably pardon them at a lower level in the hierarchy for some silly things, but violations of integrity at higher levels cannot be put up with. I have stood by those decisions, and by the way, I have terminated against their bosses and have also called the senior guys and told them what they should've have done. Mali has done this and I am very proud of him and this is where he used his powers to protect me, I would say my authority.'

## Sudip Banerjee
'Very important issue for people and for powerful men in society. "Power if used well can have a huge positive influence on society, on businesses, on the public, etc… power if used badly can cause enormous damage".'

## Rishikesha Krishnan
'I think what tends to happens is that people in India tend to exercise positional power which seems to come naturally, but building up the kind of power which comes from other sources like from your influence, seems to be somewhat scarce. For example, exceptions like Gandhiji and all, so yes, I think power is definitely an important aspect.

'I've always tended to believe that there is actually quite a lot you can do without having formal power, even those who don't have formal power usually have some other form of influence. In fact, many a times when I have got involved in so-called leadership things, I have often seen people on the periphery to start with, but it is possible to influence quite a lot of things like delegation, motivating people and giving them space, supporting them implicitly, all these can get people to create trust actually, the link with trust is that you can't build trust unless you show trust first. People start believing you and I started seeing this on several occasions, in many of situations I have been in.'

## Vijay Mahajan
'I was looking for a successor and I went and hired a 42-year-old guy from Citibank in London, and you know, he was at one level a good man, but later on there is a question of how anybody can deal with adversity; give a man

power and see his character and so his character really came out and within a year he had taken the company in a totally different direction and I had this severe dilemma as to having ceded a position—should I be interfering? I think in some ways it's almost karma or whatever. The peak of that was in the last week of September, we had a big event in Hyderabad and by 15 October, the AP government had gone after the whole sector and within 3–4 months after that this guy left.

'In terms of a well-known leader, although I didn't know him personally, take Nehruji, they say that his best really came out from 1950 onwards when neither Gandhiji nor Sardar Patel nor Ambedkar were there, you know, 1950–51. In a sense, he became the single most important leader at that stage, and that reverse thing did not happen. "Absolute power corrupts absolutely," that didn't happen to Nehruji, and instead the greatest in him came out, as evidenced by the phenomenal amount of institution building and nation building and so on.

'But I think there was a certain amount of naivety in all of his beliefs, whether it was state socialism, whether it was in non-alignment, or whether it was in Indo-Chinese relationships or even his beliefs in parliamentary democracy in India.'

### Madan Padaki
'The way I look at it, as the power to make peoples' lives good or bad around you grows, when you wield that power around you, that's what makes it heady... I have been on a few of these government committees. If you make a policy decision that will impact millions of lives, that, to my mind, is the definition of that power. Power is to make an impact for the good or for the worse.'

### Anjan Lahiri
'What is power? Power is: you say something and it gets done. You say it nicely and nobody will listen to you.'

### Daljit Mirchandani
'I am a firm believer in this word "power". People get it by virtue of positions, [but] if the humility goes away, I will question the capability to lead. I've seen examples of people getting into positions of power and operating from there,

and invariably, you find them acting as a banyan tree—without people being able to grow under them. Power and authority—maybe it's required around a turnaround period—sales crashing, power is required during leadership getting turned around, you have no time for consensus. [But] turnaround situations are not perpetual. You do get those troubled instances when you have to take total charge, but then it doesn't mean that you have that behaviour in stable and growth phases.'

### Kiran Mazumdar-Shaw

'I find women can handle power a lot better than men, because I think women have less of an ego. I find that men have a much higher sense of ego. Socially they have been empowered a lot more than women have, so I think women are far more balanced in handling power because they realize that if they over use that power, society will not be accepting of them. There is a check and balance sort of thing more for women. It is a good thing and a bad thing in a way. I think that's why a lot of women are very scared to assume leadership roles. I find that a little worrying; I find that a lot of good, capable women are very shy to assume strong leadership roles because somehow they feel that... they feel a bit diffident about handling that power... I engage a lot with women who are very strong leaders who have not been given an opportunity to lead because they are women.'

### K.V. Kamath

'The way I look at it, humility is something very critical to make sure that you do not get carried away by power. My assessment is that, ultimately, if you're going to fail, the number one reason you're going to fail is because of power going to your head, which then causes irrational decisions in a variety of ways in an organizational context and outside. And that, ultimately, leads to your downfall. All that needs is some small shift in the environment and then you are going to be hurting the organization that you're in and yourself. So, I would think that humility becomes a big counter and you try to imbibe that, in a way, to stay away from the challenges that power brings.'

### K. Dinesh

'Character needs to be built brick-by-brick, day-by-day in each transaction or action. But it can get demolished in one single moment. It is the character which sums up the leader, rather than the sum total of the rest of the deeds like brand, bottom line, top line, loyalty, excellence, productivity, etc. It is business which drives the agenda, but it is character which shapes the fine-tuned agenda to make it meaningful, joyful and enduring in both good times and trying times.'

**S.K. Raman**
'Power corrupts... that is where a real character of the person comes—by the value system that he has moulded into himself during his younger age. So, when he comes to a position of power, he will not flaunt it. He says, "This is the value".'

**Rajiv Kuchhal**
Power and leadership are linked, but a true leader is one who achieves power through leadership, whereas you have people in power who are not leaders, who are there because of the power they have. It becomes very tempting when you are the leader and you know it's available to you to take advantage of the situation. I think until and unless you have self-discipline at an extraordinary level, because the thing is that leadership is also when a person who is a great leader, also believes "I'm different right and I'm better than others." So when this whole conflict comes in, if the guy doesn't have that strong self-belief, then the guy is not a leader. If the guy has strong self-belief that I am better than others, then he may think that he should get a better (share) than others. What is that line? "To those whom much is given, much is expected." From the Bible, right?[16]

So the strength of a character absolutely comes with a power which you get, how you are able to use the power. Not using power... if you don't use the power then you're not a leader, but if you use the power and don't use it appropriately, you can misuse it. It's a very thin line at times, a very, very thin line and it's not easy to do that, and that is one of the biggest challenges with leadership and many people go along with the rise and then they forget that side of it...

**Anonymous**
A political leader who prefers to remain anonymous (and I prefer to respect that

request) said, 'There is the reverse side of power. It is not only the question of the one who holds power and how does his or her behaviour change. It is equally about the one who is subject to that power and how will they behave in the presence of that powerful person.... People touch your feet, somehow kowtow to you, and they might not even know who you are. The touch, they feel, causes the great leader to appreciate you. And the leader does not discourage it, sometimes actually demands it... Power corrupts not just the power holder, but those who are affected by that power also get corrupted. I found that people who were my close friends before they became famous and powerful...their behaviour changed, money and power changes them, in subtle to gross ways. And my own behaviour, unless I watch out, really changes, even to the form of subservience. Obsequiousness, sycophancy, are the results. As they say, kiss the a** above and kick the head below.'

**Ashok Kamath**
'My big boss at the start of my career once told me that when he goes to the office, he walks in the hallway and there are many who are doing their work in their cubicles and say good morning or whatever. And once in a while he would stop by and say good morning to someone, "Oh, Jayaram, what are you working on these days?" So, the chairman of the company is asking him what he's working on. So, instead of giving the answer, "Nothing or whatever," Jayaram makes a big deal out of it, and the boss will listen patiently and he listens well. Then, out of courtesy, he will tell Jayaram, "When you are done, I will be interested to know the result." It's just courtesy, he's really not... Now what does Jayaram do, instead of doing what he is supposed to be doing, he will work on what he told the boss at that moment. His manager will be tearing his hair, "What do I do now, I can't go to the chairman and ask him why did he say that?" So my boss says, "I noticed several times that asking silly things like that just for courtesy produced such behaviour. I stopped. You know, management by moving around has several hazards like that".'

## Are Leaders Generally 'Good' People?

This was one of the questions in my questionnaire to the leaders; it gave pause to many. One could see the memory wheels rapidly spinning to the leaders that they had known, including themselves. Because Steve Jobs' biography (Walter Issacson 2012) had just come out, there were debates around the world about the multiple facets of this mercurial man called Jobs: a creative genius who single-handedly gave birth to four industries, a child of the California culture of the 1970s, a cult figure who became synonymous with innovation and whose products were awaited by the loyal customers of Apple products with breathless eagerness, matched only by teenage fans waiting for the next hit single. Yet, he was also criticized for his lack of sensitivity towards his fellow workers, for his abandonment of a pregnant girlfriend and other such omissions and commissions. The Internet was full of debates over whether he was worth emulating as a hero and a leader, or to be studied as a cautionary tale.

Similar controversies have swirled around another legend from the corporate world, Jack Welch. Although a phenomenal success in growing General Electric (though since his retirement there have been murmurs of exaggerated numbers), he is unpopular for his people policies, such as laying off the bottom 10 per cent of performers every year. His personal life received some criticism as well, when he divorced his wife of 25 years to marry his secretary, 25 years his junior. Do we compartmentalize it and say, 'The leader's personal life is no one else's business. If the leader delivers business success that is the litmus test', or do we feel disappointment and even disillusionment? Leaving out the personal, what about the layoffs and 'ruthless' personnel policies? Should an aspiring leader conclude that it is okay to sacrifice the careers of your employees to maximize shareholders' returns, or should you accord equal weight, maybe even superior weight, to the interests of the people who work for you?

**Intensity**

The second layer of the foundation of great leadership is intensity. In Einstein's words, 'Only one who devotes himself to a cause with his whole strength and soul can be a true master. For this reason, mastery demands all of a person.'

What is intensity? Passion with, and towards, a purpose. No achievement in history has been possible without a certain set of individuals, the leader(s) and the followers, whipping up an internal storm of intensity. 'Fire in the belly' is too mild a metaphor, it is at its height an all-consuming emotion, a tsunami of energy, and a good leader helps sustain it as long as necessary. It was there when Gandhiji marched off towards Dandi (Do you recall the pace of the old man's stride?!) to make salt and thumb our million collective noses at the empire where the sun never set (now, because of the passionate Indian masses led by this most intense of human beings, they can't dare to sleep even when the sun sets). It was there in Archimedes when he jumped out naked from his bathtub shouting 'Eureka!' (I found it!) and ran through the streets because his intense concentration had just yielded a secret of nature called buoyancy. It is there every time a 'new setting' is created—the liberation of Eastern Europe from communist dictators; seven youngsters creating an Infosys with the leader not seeing his firstborn for the first six months of the baby's life; every entrepreneur in the early months, even years.

Intensity is a love affair with a cause, be it a start-up, a revolution, an affair with a loved one, composing a song, writing a book, a sport, theatre and stagecraft of any kind…the list could encompass every facet of human life. Intensity is in the blood and sinews of the one who commits to a cause. She feels the adrenalin; it does not discriminate among and betwixt causes. Everyone who has ever been in such an affair knows what intensity means—their spouses, families and friends know it too, because they would have seen this person, their dear one, in the throes of an obsession, working day and night, eating, dreaming and sleeping 'the cause'; others may see nothing special in it, but for her it is the centre of the universe.

Steve Jobs, who stepped down as CEO of Apple on 24 August 2011, after having been on medical leave, reflected on his life, career and mortality in a well-known commencement address at Stanford University in 2005. Listen to a leader who seemed to embody intensity of purpose in every pore of his being:

> Don't lose faith. I'm convinced that the only thing that kept me going was that I loved what I did. You've got to find what you love. And that is as true for your work as it is for your lovers. Your work is going to fill a large part of your life, and the only way to be truly satisfied is to do what you believe is great work. And the only way to do great work is to love what you do. If you haven't found it yet, keep looking. Don't settle. As with all matters of the heart, you'll know when you

find it. And, like any great relationship, it just gets better and better as the years roll on. So keep looking until you find it. Don't settle.

Your time is limited, so don't waste it living someone else's life. Don't be trapped by dogma—which is living with the results of other people's thinking. Don't let the noise of others' opinions drown out your own inner voice. And most importantly—have the courage to follow your heart and intuition. They somehow already know what you truly want to become. Everything else is secondary.

One leader on the world stage who was not only full of intensity for his causes (Great Britain and its survival, the British Empire), but created a crescendo of intensity in the people of Britain, was Winston Churchill. He had the passion of a performer and was the quintessential example of a 'Leader as Performer'. With his eloquent rhetoric reflecting his firm resolve, he transmitted his passionate will to win at any cost. He spoke throbbing, pulsating words and memorable phrases in soaring cadences to a population, in fact to a civilization on the brink of utter destruction, and they drank them in, the intensity of his indomitable spirit in the face of overwhelming odds, and rose with him to face the deadly enemy intent on bombing them out of existence. As a member of another nation and race, he could never understand India and hence had disdain for it. I forgive him for his arrogance because he was so capable of grand folly. When he was wrong he was memorably wrong, and when he was right he was triumphantly right.

One cannot do justice to his intensity of purpose in defence of his values and vision by attempting to summarize it. It is worth reading and relishing. Rarely has anyone matched his stirring words, except perhaps Lincoln in his immortal Gettysburg address. I am writing this as one who was born an Indian and feel this man was as wrong as anyone can be about my great civilization.[17] But he is relevant here because he is the role model of passion in a great leader.

At this point many of you may ask, 'That man who thought independent India would not last six months... How can you praise him?' As his pet peeve/favourite whipping boy/arch enemy, Gandhiji ('That half-naked fakir', the over-clothed English aristocrat called him, among many other names) said, 'I hate the British rule, but I love the British.' I would have the same sentiments towards Churchill, transcendent in his masterly leadership during World War II, lacking any such transcendence in his leadership of the British Empire, trapped in the glory of a past which was disappearing like the morning mist in front of the dawning sun. He is still the paragon of 'good' intensity, intensity with integrity, compared to that other thunderbolt of intensity, Adolf Hitler, the poster boy for 'bad' intensity (Reminds you of good cholesterol and bad cholesterol, right?).

Isaiah Berlin, the wise observer of leaders among other things, said of Winston Churchill in 1940:

> There are those who, inhibited by the furniture of the ordinary world, come to life only when they feel themselves actors upon a stage, and thus emancipated, speak out for the first time, and are then found to have much to say. There are those who can function freely only in uniform or armour or court dress, see only through certain kinds of spectacles, act fearlessly only in situations which are in some way formalized for them; see life as a kind of play in which they and others are assigned certain lines which they must speak.[18]

Unlike Churchill who needed certain 'situations' for his intensity to be aroused (like Superman who needs his cape and the telephone booth to transform from man to superman), his gentle but superior adversary, Gandhiji, generated his intensity from within himself. His famous 'inner voice' gave him the inspiration, admonition and ammunition to feel passionate about myriad interests, spanning a wide range from the profound to the mundane, from affecting all humanity to influencing an esoteric dietary group.

A cautionary note: intensity without integrity, without a sense of the whole and a basic sense of right and wrong, can become a distortion, a devouring obsession which, at its worst, destroys the leader and all that he touches.

Its benign manifestation is in our stereotype of the absent-minded professor who is so engrossed in the mathematical problem he is trying to solve that he walks out of his home in his underwear. Archimedes jumping out of his bathtub and running naked down the street shouting 'Eureka!' because he had discovered the principle of buoyancy is an endearing example, apocryphal though it may be, of the intense absorption in one's goal. But it turns lethal when the intensity makes the leader so self-centred that everything else is sacrificed for the 'cause'.

In Tolstoy's *War and Peace,* there is a description of Napoleon on the battlefield. Napoleon is so focused on reaching Moscow, so busy with his map and field glass, that he barely notices a group of his soldiers, Polish Uhlans, who are trying to impress him by attempting to cross a frigid river. Forty of them drown or freeze to death to show him their valour. 'The little man in the grey overcoat,' writes Tolstoy, 'began pacing up and down the bank...occasionally glancing disapprovingly at the drowning Uhlans, who distracted his attention.' Tolstoy ends the chapter with a Latin quote that applies to the soldiers and their leader both, *Quos vultperderedementat* (those whom God wishes to destroy, he drives mad).

Benjamin Nugent, in an article in the *New York Times,* said, 'Monomania is what it sounds like—a pathologically intense focus on one thing. It's the opposite of the problem you have if your gaze is ever flitting from your Tumblr to your spreadsheet to your baby to rush-hour traffic.'[19]

One more example of obsessive focus on one objective and being oblivious to everything else can be found in that delightful movie adaptation (of Bernard Shaw's *Pygmalion*) *My Fair Lady,* where Eliza Doolittle, trying to pronounce syllables as per Professor Higgins's diktat with her mouth full of marbles, Demosthenes-like, accidentally swallows one. There is consternation on her face as she blurts out to the great linguist, 'I swallowed one.' He replies dismissively as he sweeps out of the room, 'There is more where it came from; now keep practising—Aaaa, Eeee, Aye, Oooo, Uuuu.'

## Intelligence + Intuition = Imagination

The third layer of the foundation for the leader is imagination, which I submit, is born out of the interplay of intelligence and intuition.

Reality is limited by what we know as facts. A leader, at any point of time, whatever her resources, cannot hope to access more than a fraction of the data needed to create a future.

In the early 1980s, I used to live in Monterey, California, and often drove at 4 a.m. through the mountains to San José airport. The fog rising from Monterey Bay reduced the visibility in front of my car to hardly a few feet. There were no fancy fog lights then; at least my car didn't have any. Hence, I had to drive imagining the road ahead beyond the brief visible stretch, any creature like a deer or an object like another car may be right there just beyond the pale of my vision, so I used, as I'm sure others did, my mind's eye to conceive of what lay ahead.

A TCL does just that—she imagines a future, creates a dream, and works towards its happening. Intelligence, that which IQ tests measure, the left brain's reasoning ability, can help part of the way but will then plead ignorance, and it is then that imagination takes over. Reason walks, sometimes runs, but imagination flies. Of course, a good-to-great leader has her feet on earth while her head is in the clouds. Of course she cross-checks her imaginative ideas with the available data to see if it tallies, but she has to fly with her intuition on top of the information her intelligence has gathered. That is the role of imagination in a transcendent leader—going beyond the boundaries of the known into the unknown, cautiously no doubt, but nevertheless daring to go. Imagination separates the adult from the child, while using a child's fancy to evoke creativity. Yes, the feet are firmly on earth, but the eyes are to the horizon and the head is exploring the heights, and yes, every once in a while risks are taken to lift oneself up and levitate.

Imagination has had as one of its biggest proponents Albert Einstein, a highly credible witness on issues of intellectual work and a supreme conceptual leader who is arguably the greatest scientific genius ever born (Okay okay, Newton and Da Vinci, you can join him too on the podium; Feinman, please, behave yourself in front of your elders).

His most famous and oft-repeated quotes read thus:

'The true sign of intelligence is not knowledge but imagination.'

'Imagination is everything. It is the preview of life's coming attractions.'

'I am enough of an artist to draw freely upon my imagination. Imagination is more important than knowledge. Knowledge is limited. Imagination encircles the world.'

'Logic will get you from A to Z; imagination will get you everywhere.'

**Others on Imagination:**

'Reason is intelligence taking exercise. Imagination is intelligence with an erection,' said Victor Hugo.

'An idea is salvation by imagination,' said Frank Lloyd Wright.

'Vision is the art of seeing things invisible,' said Jonathan Swift.

'All successful people, men and women, are big dreamers. They imagine what their future could be, ideal in every respect, and then they work every day toward their distant vision, that goal or purpose,' said Brian Tracy.

'All men who have achieved great things have been great dreamers,' said Orison Swett Marden.

The two components of imagination, intelligence and intuition, products of the left and the right brains respectively, are like the visible and invisible parts of one iceberg. Intelligence is seen above, one-fifth of the total ability of a great leader, which is visible to everyone, and intuition is the other four-fifths that operates invisible and serves as the rest of the total resource available to her.

Most of our leader interviewees paused and hesitated when presented with 'intelligence' as a basic quality by itself saying, 'I'm not sure it is that important,' but when combined with intuition, there was resounding consensus that that was the right combination.

What is this 'intelligence + intuition = imagination' iceberg, this $I^3$, in the context of a transcendent leader?

There are five special kinds of 'intelligence' I have found in good-to-great leaders:

1. Pattern recognition and integration
2. 'Vital balance'/'Goldilocks ability'
3. 'Amphibian' ability
4. Judgement of character
5. Postponed gratification/control of emotions/ego suppression

Before we share what these five mean, we have to ask, 'Intelligence for what, to do what?' These qualities ought to be viewed for their value in the context of what a transcendent leader has to do in order to lead. Hence we present, as the pillars in Figure 2.2, the 'Five Acts of Appreciation'. We present the explanation of the five intelligences and the five acts of appreciation starting with Figure 2.2.

| 5 personal Competences/ 5 Acts of Appreciation | Pattern Recognition & Integration | 'Vital Balance' | 'Amphibian' ability | Judgement of character | Control of emotions/ Postpones gratification/ Ego suppression |
|---|---|---|---|---|---|
| **SELF** (self awareness) | | | | | |
| **YOU** (Empathy) | | | | | |
| **WE** (Interpersonal wisdom) | | | | | |
| **OUR WORLD** (Strategy) | | | | | |
| **THE WORLD** (Vision-Values) | | | | | |

*Figure 2.2: Intelligences for Transcendent Leadership*

First for the rows—the 'Five Acts of Appreciation'—an explanation.
1. Self-awareness:                                    I & I
—who/what, where, how and why am I?
2. Empathy:                                             'I—You' vs I & You
—who/what, where/how and why are you?
3. Interpersonal wisdom:                   I—You & Us
—who/what, where, how and why are we?
4. Mastery of the present: strategy & execution    Our World
—who/what, where, how and why are they?
5. Transcendence: Vision—Values            The World
—who/what, how and why are the 'worlds'?

Or

1. I get to know myself and learn to make myself better continuously
2. I get to know you, my 'significant other', and help you learn to make yourself better continuously
3. You (all my 'significant others') and I get to know our relationship and learn to make us better continuously
4. I get to know 'my world'—its people, its organized entities, the structures, systems, processes, values and beliefs (the 'anatomy and the physiology' of my stakeholders), and learn to make my world better continuously
5. I get to know the world of which my world is just a part, and learn to make 'the world' better continuously

The five 'actors' involved in my life's drama (see Figure 2.2) are the two at the centre—me and you (all those I relate to) (1) and (2); the relationship between us (3); the relevant environment—'our world' (4); and the universal environment—'the world'—the context which holds our world with many other worlds and ultimately sustains or destroys us (5).

There are five kinds of relationships which together make up my, and your, entire life. Let us talk about these five relationships.

The first 'people' I meet constantly is myself. I am many people. 'One must be true to one's selves,' said Smith reportedly. Literature is full of examples of a single person being a host colony for multiple selves. Psychological research and clinical practice strongly support this. Religions recognize this and base their prescriptions to their faithful ones on ways to manage this 'federation'. (Many of us silently say to the world often, 'No, I am not a schizophrenic, nor do I suffer from a multiple personality disorder. I just am a multiple self').

The other day I met me and was thoroughly elated. As Oscar Wilde said, 'Self-love is the everlasting love.' You do agree, don't you?

The very next day I met another 'me' and was utterly disgusted.

But whether I like me or hate me, I am the only one I got, and all the time too, 24×7, so I better learn how to get along with me. Understand, accept, improve and change—I am my own laboratory where I am the scientist, the experiment, the apparatus and the result. The unique triple paradox of human behaviour is that, as said elsewhere in this chat with you, we are human minds studying human minds using human minds.

The second relationship is between I and 'You'. The two 'actors' can be assumed to be any two people—like spouses in a nuclear family or two organizations or two nations, etc.

The third actor is the relationship between the self-realizing I and You. Many readers have at this point asked, 'Why do we need the relationship to be the third actor? Isn't it enough to have I and You?'

It is not enough.

The relationship between the two, the third 'actor', is as distinct and different as each individual that constitutes the relationship. The character of the relationship is most often different from that of the individual elements which produced it. It is analogous to chemical relations in which, for instance, hydrogen reacts with oxygen to produce water ($H_2 + O_2 = 2H_2O$), the latter product being entirely different in its properties and characteristics from its constituent elements. It is a fact of experience that each one of us, as individuals, has subtle to substantial differences in our behaviours depending on who or what we are with.

The fourth actor is 'our world', the relevant environment, or the realm of immediate relevance. This refers to those domains of the immediate environment (in terms of space and time) which impact the three actors—namely the two of us (1) and (2) and our relationship (3).

The fifth actor is 'the world'—the realm of universal relevance. Imagine a pebble thrown into a pond. There is an immediate disturbance in the water—a sound, a plop, and then concentric circles of waves begin to recede from the centre of action. The circles visible to the naked eye seem to cease after a short distance. But we are told by scientists that the ripples go on for an enormously longer distance (theoretically forever, exactly like the Big Bang, which created the present universe) and it is the limitation of our eyes and ears that prevent us from being able to observe the continuance of the phenomenon. Similarly, the limitations of systemic capacities (human minds) makes it difficult, at first, to take into account those regions of the environment beyond the immediate and the obvious. These are, for instance, the higher parts of the space-time graph in Figure 2.2. If this fifth actor is not taken into account in terms of its impact on our system, we would end up with a 'closed system diagnosis', an unreal picture of what the reality is.

Have I told you the one about the drunk who was looking for a key under the street lamp? A passer-by asked, 'Poor chap. Did you lose your key here?' The drunk answered, 'Oh no! I lost the key over there, but here is where the light is.' In Einstein's words, 'We cannot solve our problems with the same thinking we used when we created them.'

1. Self
2. You
3. We
4. Our world
5. The world

I propose five qualifications, or as I label them, 'acts of appreciation'—one for each of the 'actors' identified earlier—as those acquired and continuously honed by a transcendent leader. These are firmly based, as stated before, on the three layers of the foundation—integrity and character, intensity and courage, and intelligence and intuition. These five acts of 'appreciation' are essential for a healthy and life-affirming relationship between and among the 'actors'. The term 'appreciation' is used here in the sense as ascribed by Geoffrey Vickers (1968).[20] The word 'appreciation' is used for those combined judgements of fact and value which we constantly make. We notice and we value. These are like the warp and woof of a net.

As Einstein said:

> A human being is a part of a whole that we call the universe—a part limited in time and space. He experiences himself, his thoughts and feelings as something separate from the rest...a kind of optical delusion of his consciousness. This delusion is a kind of prison for us, restricting us to our personal desires and to affection for a few persons nearest to us. Our task must be to free ourselves from this prison by widening our circle of compassion to embrace all living creatures and the whole of nature in its beauty.

The models I discuss in this book are based on the intention, as Einstein prescribes, 'To free ourselves from this prison of "interpersonal few" (my paraphrase), and expand by widening our circle of compassion to embrace all living creatures and the whole of nature in its beauty.'

## A Summary of Each Act of Appreciation or 'the Five Pillars of the *Mantap*'

In this section, I present a succinct summary of the meaning of each term. Then I elaborate on each act of appreciation through mini-essays of unequal lengths. (Integrity runs away with the prize for the longest discussion; most of the leaders interviewed spoke about it at length.)

First, the underlying pattern of these 'acts of appreciation'.

A great leader learns as a human baby learns—the five areas of knowledge and wisdom that I present here for a great leader are very similar to the progressive steps by which a baby learns about itself and the world around it. Harvard psychologist Robert Kegan, in his brilliant 1982 book, *The Evolving Self*, and later in the introduction to his follow-up 1994 book, *In Over Our Heads: The Mental Demands of Modern Life*, presented a model of how a human being develops knowledge within him or herself. I present a brief summary. Based on Jean Piaget's description of the pattern by which knowledge grows and develops in a human mind over time, there are successive layers of appreciation. Each successive layer of knowledge uses the previous layer as a foundation. Knowledge is cumulative. More advanced and abstract understandings are not possible without first having less advanced, more concrete experiences.

Kegan suggests that as babies grow into adults, they develop progressively more objective and accurate appreciations of the social world they inhabit. They do this by progressing through five or more states or periods of development which he labelled as:

- Incorporative
- Impulsive
- Imperial
- Interpersonal
- Institutional

Thereafter, conscience is born and the potential for guilt and shame arises, as well as the potential for empathy.

As a child's sense of self continues to develop, it can be said to have values or commitments to ideas and beliefs and principles, which are larger and more permanent than passing whims and fears. Kegan refers to this new realization of and commitment to values as the institutional period, noting that in this period, the child's idea of self becomes something which can be, for the first time, described in terms of institutionalized values such as being honest. 'I'm an honest person. I try to be fair. I strive to be brave,' are the sorts of things an institutional mind might say. Values, such as the Golden Rule (Do unto others as you would have them do unto you), start to guide the child's appreciation of how to be a member of the family and of society. The moral, ethical and legal foundations of society follow from this basic achievement of an institutional self. Further, children (or adults) who achieve this level of social maturity understand the need for laws and for ethical codes that work to govern everyone's behaviour. Less socially mature individuals won't grasp why these things are important and cannot and should not simply be disregarded when they are inconvenient.

A leader traces exactly the same pattern of behaviour.

## Self-Awareness

The first act of appreciation is self-awareness.

'Honesty is telling truth to other people, integrity is telling truth to oneself,' said Spencer Johnson.

The first duty and 'strategy' is self-awareness, the understanding of the many people one is. The first step is just understanding, not managing, growing, etc. This is the converse of empathy. Each system tries to deeply engage in an act of self-empathy. The question is, 'Who, what, where, how and why am I?' Self-awareness has been held up as one of the highest philosophic ideals by many Asian philosophies. At its most profound level, it has been considered the highest goal of a human being. According to Hindu philosophy (and personality theories) there are, apparently, two selves—the individual self and the universal self. Hindu philosophers consider this separation of selves illusory. The curtain of illusion, called '*Maya*', shrouds the individual and alienates him from his true identity— which is that of one indivisible self. The true goal then, of the path of life, is to unveil the curtain of *Maya* and to become aware of one's true identity. Such is the non-dualistic philosophy.

### LEADERS SPEAK

**Values: What are they to you? Why?**

### R. Sriram

'Purpose is the heart of leadership. Our purpose defines who we are and what we do with our life. Thinkers over the years have proposed various motives for human purpose. Freud believed in the "will to pleasure" while Adler believed in the "will to power" as the force that drives human actions. But Viktor Fankl believed that the "will to meaning" provides the central purpose to human life; this resonates powerfully with me. Finding and providing meaning is the central task of leadership. And this starts with voyaging within, for only when the leader finds meaning in her life can she connect with others and their meaning.

'As Tao Te Ching states:

*Knowing others is wisdom;*
*Knowing the self is enlightenment.*
*Mastering others requires force;*
*Mastering the self needs strength.'*

### Ramesh Ramanathan
'The real danger is getting trapped in any one bucket—being too cerebral or being too tactical and operational. And these two are not the only two dimensions. You have to be tough, you have to be friendly, you have to know when to be serious, and when to be jovial. That is the real pleasure of leadership, when a combination of all this results in people and the team getting motivated, getting excited, getting energized and seals in the purpose to the larger vision.

'The leadership journey begins with your own personal development because nobody has reached a certain destination. As long as each of us individually keep growing every day, then you are taking an active amount of one's own time to invest in your own growth. Then you automatically become tuned into the fact that others in your organization are in a similar journey and therefore need be nurtured and space needs to be made available in a systematic and fair way.'

### Jacob Kurian
'It's better at times to be humble about it, to recognize that you can't know everything. You need to be humble enough to say that there are always things to learn and I constantly keep telling my guys that when you say that you are the manager and keep telling them what to do, maybe it's acceptable in a more hierarchical set-up in a factory, or in a remote set-up too it is still acceptable, but not in their minds; in their minds they are saying, you don't deserve to be one.

'So leadership needs to be earned over and over again; you don't have any preordained right. Position gives you an opportunity, but it doesn't give you a right to be a leader, you have to earn it and if you lose it then you have lost everything as a leader to be credible and consistent.'

### Binny Bansal
'Meritocracy, for instance, is a major value for us. There is equal opportunity

for all; we will not have favouritism. We will have fairness and justice and equity so that if the criteria for performance are met, the guy gets the preference over somebody who might be liked or is related.'

## Ashok Kamath

'To me the most important values are: humility as a leader. Humility allows you to listen, to respect and to make your call, because as a leader the buck stops with you, and you have to make that difficult call, that's why they pay you the bucks, and you want to make sure that it is a fair deal. In a large enterprise there is no bailing out. Obsessiveness to me is passion; if you don't have it, then you can't pump energy into your organization, and if you can't do that, then there is no vision, then you become a manager and not a leader... Compassion vs. humility—I think there is a relationship, I think it may be very hard to be very humble and not be compassionate, I can't think of an example of that...'

## N.R. Narayana Murthy

'Values, like visions, are time- geography- and context-invariant guiding principles. We may be able to cope with the lack of a vision, but not with the lack of values. I would not call them the three most important values, but the three most frequently implemented values in my own personal and professional journey are:

- Lifelong learning—This is our only insurance against becoming obsolete. There is no end to learning and there is something to learn from everyone—be it your subordinates, peers or superiors. Even from my office assistant, whose job it is to get me a glass of water when needed and ensure that I attend my meetings on time, I have learned the importance of having an unwavering focus on outcomes.
- Leadership by example—One should not ask anyone to do what they are not prepared to do themselves.
- Fairness, honesty, integrity and transparency in everything that we do— There is no other path to success.

'From my own experience, I am convinced that the only path to achieving sustainable quality and meaningful growth or success is by fulfilling our responsibilities to all our stakeholders. No stakeholder is expendable, no stakeholder is more important than the other and no leader or individual is greater than the organization.

'Finally, someone rightly said that if you love what you are doing, then there is no place for a discussion about a work-life balance.'

## Subroto Bagchi

'Integrity—those who have an affinity to fairness have integrity, fair is whole, fair is integrity. The state of nature is inherently a state of fairness. In the whole animal kingdom rape does not happen; it is only when there is consensus that they mate.

'I have collated my own components which, I tell my leaders, are my four principles:

- Principle no. 1: If there is a rule, I'll follow the rule. If you are part of a social contract, you cannot say that you don't like it. When individual citizens are selective about what law they will follow and not follow, collectively the system breaks. I will follow the rule if the rule is acceptable. If the rule is inconvenient to me I will protest, but pending resolution, I will still follow the rule.
- Principle no. 2: For everything in life there cannot be a rule. Where rules don't exist, I will follow fair judgement; it's the man-made law all the time. There will be times when I will be confused about the rule and also about fair judgement; when confusion happens I will seek counsel. I will not first shoot and then ask whether it is right or wrong.
- Principle no. 3: When in doubt, call somebody who has no vested interest, ideally somebody whom you love and respect, but do call before you act.
- Principle no. 4: The fourth thing is that my private act should stand public scrutiny without causing me embarrassment, because only human beings have shame actually, nobody needs that...shame is an override... and our sense of shame makes us different from all other life forms, you lose that and then everything goes.'

## Anil Jain

'I think this is what it leads to...there can't be a disconnect within the various parts of your being, the man and the manager; the person at home and the father and the husband or wife, whatever the case may be, and the person who is there in the office, cannot be at war with each other.'

**Deependra Moitra**
'I think moral values are certainly important; I mean they are basic hygiene... they are necessary even for an individual's own well-being. If I do not have integrity I know that inside me a lot of energy is going to be lost in simply resolving all these conflicts between right and wrong. Hence it is necessary for my own well-being; it is a necessary condition for me to assume leadership. So I definitely attach a lot of importance to these so-called hygiene factors.'

**Devapriyo Ghose**
'The problem with most characteristics that one associates with leadership, particularly extrinsic qualities, is that you can always find a counter example of a leader who didn't have that quality. I'm sure you will find some person acknowledged as a leader in the corporate world who is not a visionary or a great communicator or a persuasive influencer or inspiring and motivational or great with people. Possibly the only defining characteristic for leaders who are sustainably successful that I can think of is authenticity born of reflective self-insight—being secure enough to see oneself clearly, strengths, weaknesses, blind spots and all, and therefore being able to be true to oneself and the larger purpose that one serves. Of course this assumes that the leader has the required capabilities, motivation, self-belief, etc. All of those are required and necessary, but to my mind, not sufficient for a leader to be successful over time. To do that, the differentiating quality that the leader needs is to be able to continuously reassess himself in terms of what the context requires from him in terms of leadership and is open enough and agile enough mentally and emotionally to move himself to his next orbit using his moral compass as a guide.'

Self-awareness is the ability of an individual to know and experience deeply one's strengths and limitations as a whole human being at any point of time, and over a lifetime. As such it is the platform to launch all the other seven qualities in a leader. It is the instrument with which one accomplishes everything one has as a vision and values. Self-awareness is a prerequisite for integrity. How can you be whole and loyal to your values and principles if you don't know what those are?

## Self-awareness

Be forewarned! As the cliché goes, fools rush in where angels fear to tread. We are now, you and I, entering into the realm of philosophers, psychologists and holy people. Who am I? Who are you? Who are we? What is 'our world'? What is the world beyond our personal worlds? These are questions that have haunted human consciousness ever since humans gained the mixed blessing of being conscious. They deal with my life and yours from the most superficial and mundane to the most profound and spiritual levels. They are as concrete as our limbs. When our bodies need exercise, we train them. When they get sick, we go to expert physicians. Yet, we do not examine the health of our individual and collective minds, neither exercise them nor heal them of their sicknesses. There is no wellness programme for minds. Yes, there are myriad prophets, seers and wise people who promise to take this 'burden' off our hands and give us peace in its stead. And many of them do mean well.

Every religion promises solace in return for the surrender of the self. Yet, it is important to note that even as religions promise salvation in return for self-surrender, they too emphasize and exhort the faithful to make themselves better human beings. Paradoxical as it may seem, religions ask for discipline and hard work to aid the evolution to a higher state. A TCL never asks for self-surrender from herself or her people, she asks for self-realization. Humility does not mean negation of one's self; it means proud acceptance and enhancement of all that one is and can be, and yet feeling genuinely one with others and with the world to which all of them belong. A mother does not feel superior to her child, nor does a teacher to her pupil. The relationship is not one of competition, nor is it a contest. Instead, the relationship of transcendence is one of synergy towards a common cause. Together the leader and the followers empower, enhance and enable the environment and all that is in it, human and non-human, to be their best.

Many of us outsource this psychological-spiritual need to agencies outside ourselves and obey the commands of that external healer/therapist/guru. Oscar Wilde once said, 'Physical exercise is very important; I hire someone to do it for me.' There are some needs in life—hunger, thirst, sex and salvation—that can only be satisfied by one's direct participation. I have to be accountable for my destiny no matter how wise you are and how much you want to help me. At the apogee of such self-reliant conviction is Nelson Mandela's favourite poem that he recited every day while he was imprisoned in a 6 × 8 cell at Robbins Island: 'Out of the Night That Covers Me (Invictus)' by William Ernest Henley.

> Out of the night that covers me,
> Black as the pit from pole to pole,
> I thank whatever gods may be
> For my unconquerable soul.
>
> It matters not how strait the gate,
> How charged with punishments the scroll,
> I am the master of my fate:
> I am the captain of my soul.

I contend that we must take care of our minds and nurture them because we are the instrument of change, we together. No single individual, however great a leader he or she may be, will do it for us. All abstractions called organizations, institutions, societies, nations and governments—all these structures and processes are merely the offspring of our collective minds. They cease to be useful the moment we cannot control them with our collective psyche. We have lost control of them, if we ever had control. We need to regain the mastery of our creations. Then we become true leaders. We are riding wild rogue elephants, helplessly cowering as the wild beast rushes forward hither and thither. We need to tame them and make them again what they were intended to be in the first place, our servants, 'friends', tools for transformation of life on earth. They are extensions of our minds, no more and no less. They are a part of us and we should know deeply how to use them, which needs us to understand how to use us.

This chapter is about using ourselves to transform our world.

## Empathy

The second act of appreciation is empathy. It could be simply stated by the question, 'Who or what, where, how and why are you?' It is a question that each system asks about the other. Each involves itself in the other. In common practice in behavioural sciences, empathy is encouraged through role-playing. At its most profound, empathy is almost an attempt at the transmigration of souls—to be able to move into the mind, body and spirit of the other system, to be able to feel the feelings and think the thoughts as the other system does, to be able to understand the moods, passions and the value systems of the other system—referring to the space-time continuum, to be able to empathize with as broad and deep a life-space and as long a time horizon as possible. Self-realization is not enough; 'other realization' is needed—the realization of the whole, which is a mixture of the internal and external environment, now and in the future.

Let us dwell on this a little so that we can compare and contrast TCL and TFL—the system-centric vs. anthropocentric models. Sorry for the jargon. I promise more examples soon to illustrate these terms.

Philosophies that exclusively stress self-realization to the subordination or even exclusion of the world surrounding the self are artificial, isolationist and ultimately self-defeating. The self is an inseparable part of the universe. In fact, in the lives of the greatest leaders, even of those who profess self-realization as their ultimate goal, it is very evident that they expand their mission to the larger world and keep the development and/or the realization of the self as a solitary luxury to be indulged in occasionally.

A great leader transcends the contemporaneous situation—the internal and external environments existing now—to imagine possible future environments and hence is able to prepare the organization for such a future. Longevity at high levels of success depends on this ability more than any other quality. 175-year-old Procter & Gamble, 132-year-old General Electric and the 144-year-old Tata conglomerates are all living and are dynamic demonstrations of transcendent leadership. Younger organizations are attempting to become role models of TCL. Such firms boast not only of transcendent creators, but also of a self-consciously evolving culture that encourages transcendence in the top echelons of leadership. In the public domain, the democratic 'four estates' (legislature, judiciary, executive and free press) owe their very birth and continued existence to the TCL that such societies have had at their cusps. The absence of such leadership in later years has led to the degeneration of certain democracies. Religious institutions—the instruments of propagation of faith by the great and small religions of the world—are important manifestations of TCL. Again, the presence or absence of TCL has made the difference in the character and success of such institutions. All these entities have had periodically transcendent leaders who continuously conceived of the possible and probable futures and then 'invented' the appropriate transformations of the internal and sometimes external environments to create the optimal future for their organizations and institutions.

A transformational leader may not be a transcendent leader, but every transcendent leader needs to be transformational in order to take her vision into the long-term future, influence the course of history in her field, or, as in the case of the greatest of transcendent leaders, in the life of the species.

In this profound sense, TCL is like the concept of 'revolutionary science', introduced by Thomas Kuhn in his 1962 book, *The Structure of Scientific Revolutions*. TFL is the intermediate stage to TCL. Gandhiji was transcendent in his invention of *satyagraha* and transformational in his freedom movement. He was less than a TFL in the social realm such when it came to the Harijan movement, village reforms and in building institutions for his ideas. Lincoln was TCL in the emancipation proclamation, less so in the execution of that proclamation.

What the concept of TFL lacks is the vision of an open system in continuous interaction with its environment and in negotiation with its long-term future. In this sense, TFL is non-systemic. It focuses on the individual leader and her followers but neglects the milieu, 'the worlds' in which they are embedded. TFL deals with an internal world called the followers; TCL deals with all the internal and the external worlds.

Most leadership models propounded in the literature and by scholars and leaders alike are non-systemic in their essence. They focus too much on the individual or individuals and neglect the context, the internal and external environments in both time and space. In this sense, they are Newtonian rather than Einsteinian. They are static models which stress the 'here and now', while the fate of the organizations is in the 'there and then' as much as or more than in the 'here and now'. I do not mean to suggest that the present orientation of leadership models is wrong or even misplaced; it is that that the perspective is limited and inadequate to create a long-term future. Yes, as Lord Keynes once famously said (probably in exasperation at hearing the term 'long-term' prefacing every hopeful or hopeless prediction), 'In the long term we are all dead.' But a leader must ensure that the system survives and prospers in its long-term vision. A good organization manages its present by great execution, but managing the future requires great leadership to conceive of that future and understand what it ought to be and how it should be created.

A river flows past and one can say, 'We can quench our thirst from it; bathe and clean our bodies; look at and feel the beauty of it,' but where does the river come from? How does the river acquire these qualities? Can we enhance its thirst-quenching, navigation and power-generating capacities? Can we learn how to recognize other rivers by studying its sources? And how do we 'create other rivers' by exploring the sources of this river? (hint hint—river is the TCL in this analogy).

The TCL does exploit the present, but unique to her role is the creation of alternative future scenarios and pursuing both present and future scenarios in parallel until the optimal one reveals itself.

TFL does not address the 'why' of great leadership qualities; it merely states the impact of those qualities on followers.

The *mantap* presented and described in the rest of this chapter attempts to answer the question, 'What qualities go into making what we call a transcendent leader?'

(Please add in your mind the third and fourth dimensions to Figure 2.1—time and territory; the process of acquiring the '3+5' is an eternal quest, and neither the leader nor the system is static).

The TCL does not just connect deeply with her people, but she also connects with the broader and deeper areas of the environment. She does not just connect to deeper values but 'creates' them in her people. She does not just deal with values but transforms the vision of her people to a more universal, holistic and integrated one with the larger environment.

From *The Tell-Tale Brain* by the famed neuro-scientist, V.S. Ramachandran (2010):

> A patient named Smith is undergoing neurosurgery at the University of Toronto. He is fully awake and conscious. His scalp has been perfused with a local anaesthetic and his skull has been opened. The surgeon places an electrode in Smith's anterior cingulated, a region near the front of the brain where many of the neurons respond

to pain. And sure enough, the doctor is able to find a neuron that becomes active whenever Smith's hand is poked with a needle. But the surgeon is astonished by what he sees next. The same neuron fires just as vigorously when Smith merely watches another patient being poked. It is as if the neuron (or the functional circuit of which it is a part) is empathizing with another person. A stranger's pain becomes Smith's pain, almost literally. Indian and Buddhist mystics assert that there is no essential difference between self and other, and that true enlightenment comes from the compassion that dissolves this barrier. I used to think this was just well-intentioned mumbo-jumbo, but here is a neuron that doesn't know the difference between the self and the other. Are our brains uniquely hardwired for empathy and compassion?

## LEADERS SPEAK

**Vijay Mahajan**
'I think people's trust in interpersonal relationships and their trust in institutional functioning are quite eroded right now. But really leaders, literally all the way from our President of our welfare association, or indeed from the head of a family in a house all the way to institutional leaders... I think it's a very important point to restore trust at all levels...as to why I think it's so fundamental, it is because without that you engage...you tend to engage in aberrant behaviour... You know what happens immediately after a major event, whether it's a football match or a gang rape...you know when the people come out on the street and then the rioters come in and very soon there is a breakdown of law and order...it's because the aberrant behaviour takes over (once there is no trust)...

'But what I am saying is that in different places you have to do different things to build trust... In every case there will be something which will be convincing to a large number of people and then you kind of talk on it.... build on it....

'I have also got exposed to systems fairly early in life...actually, the second year of my electrical engineering...but then repeatedly...I was fascinated by it and I did some reading... So either because of that or because I was oriented towards it... I have always had a systemic view of thinking... So I think the first decision that I took...the meta decision....which I am really thankful for is that I decided to work systemically but to improve a whole system...

'The point here I want to make for the future is whether it is justifiable to say in every good to great leader who accomplishes something, naivety plays a role; unless you're a bit naïve... Like the Bernard Shaw quote, "The reasonable man adapts himself to the world: the unreasonable one persists in trying to adapt the world to himself. Therefore all progress depends on the unreasonable man." So is the role of naïvety...'

### Binny Bansal

'You might have self-awareness, you might have empathy, I understand myself, I understand you. But over and beyond one's own understanding of self in successful relationships... Understanding is not enough; acceptance is necessary and beyond that, if you want to create something together, the leader has to create enthusiastic acceptance...and a leader often has many relationships... [There may be] one leader and there may be hundred, thousand million people following and that one has to be so interpersonal in a sense for each one of those people that are the followers [with whom] he has a relationship...'

**Comment on the following qualities in a leader's context: compassion vs. ruthlessness; 'laid-back' vs. obsessive; humility vs. narcissism.**

### Devapriyo Ghose

'I think leadership qualities, other than perhaps a strong moral compass, are hardly ever so binary, so black and white. It's the balance of qualities that helps a leader do the 'right' things, and like in every other sphere, too much of anything is probably not a good thing. Words like compassion vs. ruthlessness tend to be so laden with meaning and tend to be thought of as unequivocally positive or totally pejoratively that they can cloud one's judgement. A leader can hardly ever be ambitious for others if she is not, also in some measure, ambitious for herself—it's the balance and the moral compass that determines how that ambition is directed. Without being obsessive in some measure, would a leader be persistent, resilient and focused? Take Steve Jobs. Eventually it's about intention and impact. Compassion and humility, while admirable qualities, in and of themselves, if applied for the wrong reasons may not be unquestionably "good". With all the good intentions, if too much humility prevents a person from pushing himself forward and doing the very best he can, the impact of that humility to my mind becomes sub-optimal—surely for others, if not for oneself.'

**Interpersonal Wisdom**

The third act of appreciation is interpersonal wisdom.

The world revolves around the health of interpersonal relationships. The vital functions of such health—its blood pressure, temperature and pulse—are mutual trust and mutual respect. (Note: liking each other is not essential, and under certain circumstances, may even be counter-productive as a distraction from making responsible decisions ['How can I hurt his feelings?'] on issues of gravity). It is not trust or respect; it is both. There are those who we trust implicitly, but we may not respect their abilities in terms of our shared task. My brother may trust me totally, but he will not choose me for the swimming team because I cannot swim. Then there are those whom we respect for their abilities but will not trust as far as I can throw an elephant. When we expect and get from one another these two precious gifts, a fully-functioning relationship blooms. In marriage (love is beautiful, but...), in parenting ('dad, you promised'), corporations, governments (oh yes), politics (no, don't say politics with trust and respect is an oxymoron in the case of recent events in India; 'for betraying public trust and being unworthy of public or private respect we sentence you to...') and international relations (Israel-Arab, Indo-Pak).

Social communities (Dalit and the rest in India, races, genders) and every type of human pairing or organized entity is based on the fundamental need to establish trust and respect, enough to facilitate the common purpose that they are supposed to share among their members internally and all the stakeholders externally.

From a discussion on trash collection, to issues of global strategic imperatives, to carving out areas of influence among superpowers, it is noticed that the results of negotiations will, to a significant extent, bloom or wither based on interpersonal amity or discord.

The relationship that forms when two open systems meet and interact has a unique identity of its own. When a relationship is at its best ('ideal'), the whole is greater than the sum of its parts. Also, synergy, defined by R. Buckminster Fuller as, 'The unique behaviour of whole systems, unpredicted by the behaviour of their respective subsystems' events,'[21] is a result of this interaction, and it justifies considering the relationship as a distinct actor. The question is, 'When/what, where, how and why are we?' 'We' constitutes the whole system of which the two sub-systems are now elements. The act of appreciation here involved mutual cogitation and diagnosis. The instances of these are facts of universal human experience. 'I am so different when I am with you'; You two together hit off so well'; 'Hay would catch fire between them'—such statements are heard many times daily by all of us. We are all multiple personalities, like Eve or Sybil, for we respond to different relationships differently. Over a period of time, a sustained relationship takes on a distinct character. Complementarity of couples in many marriages is an instance of synergy in action. In a more complex way, larger systems like organizations exhibit the same characteristics. Inter-organizational relationships cannot be deduced from the study of each in isolation and away from the other. Can one doubt that a federal agency would react differently to a large corporate vis-a-vis a local community agency?

As we begin to move from the realm of intra-personal and interpersonal relationships in the first three pillars of transcendence to the fourth and fifth pillars—'our world' and 'the world'—the worlds of strategy and execution, of vision and values—we pause to identify a crucial factor which separates a transcendent leader from lesser leaders. For this, a bit of theory would be needed. (As my mother used to say about every bitter medicine, 'Drink it up, it is good for you.' But if you wish to skip it and go ahead to the five qualities, I won't tell).

The fundamental paradigm is one of an open system in mutual interaction with its environment. This model underlies, in one way or another, all the models in Chapter 3. Looking at this simple model, we can state that a transcendent leader needs to create and manage these three elements: the environment, the setting itself (the open system) and a viable relationship between the two. (The relevant environment for an open system consists of those domains which have 'nontrivial' interaction and impact with the setting).

To expand on the basic concept stated here, let us look at the following model, first introduced by Emery and Trist in their 1965 book, *Casual Texture of Environment*.

Consider the following paradigm:

**Domains of Environment**

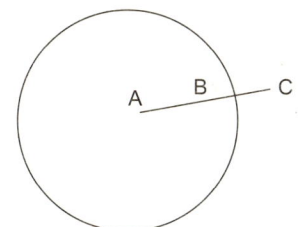

A–Internal Environment
B–Transactional Environment
C–External Environment

To facilitate expansion of the basic notion stated above, let us both look at the following model:

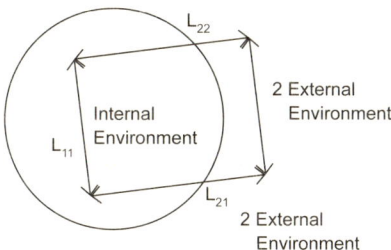

Legend:
L—relationship
1—Subscript for a systemic element—a subsystem;
2—Subscript for an environmental domain;

This model depicts three classifications of the environment that could influence a setting;
$L_{11}$—the relationship between (and the events thereof) two or more elements within the setting (called 'the internal environment');
$L_{11}$ and $L_{21}$—the first subscript stands for the 'source' or the initiator, and the second for the 'sink';

$L_{22}$— the relationship between two environmental domains in the external environment, which has a significant impact on the setting in part or as a whole.

I apply this model now to one of the ultimate responsibilities of a transcendent leader. The central task consists of the evolution of a 'vital balance' in the transactional environment (3) by maintaining two balances—the balance of the internal milieu ('the internal balance') (1), and the balance of the external milieu or contextual environment ('the external balance') (2).

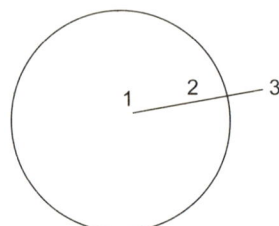

1–Internal Environment
2–Transactional Environment
3–External Environment

## LEADERS SPEAK

**According to Fukuyama, '[...] a nation's well-being, as well as its ability to compete, is conditioned by a single, pervasive cultural characteristic: the level of trust inherent in the society.' Do you agree? Do you think our leaders have failed society in this crucial task of creating and maintaining the trust levels needed to nourish the social fabric?**

### Terry Moodley

'That applies to one's professional work and professional journey as well. You find that you choose to surround yourself with people whom you can trust. Connecting to people becomes a lot easier when you have such high levels of trust, but I think the same applies to one's self as well. You got to stay true to certain principles and certain values so that you create a personal brand that is recognized as a trustworthy brand. A lot of people think about ways to connect better with stakeholders, either up the ladder in the corporate world or with key customers.'

## Rohini Nilekani
'I think good leaders are non-judgemental because they understand the frailty of human nature. They can rise above being judgemental...especially today's leaders have to do that. I also think that good leaders are very tolerant of imperfection. Leaders who stand the test of time are good and tolerant [of others' frailties].'

## Sudeep Banerjee
'Without question trust is a very important element... I think it is important to the extent that the absence of it almost guarantees failures and chaos in societies, including nations, companies and businesses... The presence of it strengthens not just the social fabric, but it also strengthens the bonds between people, between co-workers, and the bonds between management and workers. If it is a factory context, it strengthens the bonds between leaders and their followers, and in a political context, it strengthens the bonds between politicians and their people, etc.'

## S.K. Raman
'I would like to use a broader definition of trust. One of the most crucial things, whether it is the society or a business or a family, is the value system. When I say value system, trust becomes one of the elements of the value system. By the value system, I mean one's commitment towards society, one's commitment towards family members, one's commitment towards the country and one's commitment to the whole global society.'

## Kris Gopalakrishnan
'I feel a sustainable leadership model is one where you have a team; you have a set of people you can depend on, and you have more than one person who is thinking about the company, is passionate about it, and is willing to sacrifice for it. This is probably a more stable model. Whenever you depend on a hero to salvage the company when it is not doing well, it typically fizzles out and then the company doesn't do well after that. In today's environment when you look at what is required of a leader in our 24x7 world, the pressures and demands on leaders are very high and so we need to make sure that there is a team around them. I feel that is a better model for leadership.'

### Anu Rao

Leaders surround themselves with handlers, and there are times when some handlers don't give the leader important information. At organization X, a bunch of senior men and women close to the CEO/President prevented the relevant information to reach him. They never allowed other employees to talk to him even though he was easily accessible; they actually censored what information got through to him [sic]. I think that's very unfortunate because the leaders of such organizations don't have the best information to guide their strategies. Loyalties were directed towards individuals rather than the organization. At that time, I really had to look within myself to find the courage to cope with all this politics in the organization.

## Strategy—Our World

The fourth pillar or act of appreciation is mastery of the present. This mandates a continuous monitoring of the environment by the leader. The question is, 'Who/what, where, how and why are they?' Those parts of the world around them which directly affect them are usually known (consciously or otherwise) to the concerned systems. The transcendent leader is the ultimate strategizer for her system. In the next chapter, 'Management of Transformational Change', strategy is discussed at length.

This pillar is particularly relevant to women leaders who compete with men for positions of power and influence and often make it to the top of the leadership ladder. A mastery—or 'mistressy'—of the world in transition where gender roles are ever so rapidly changing and yet not changing wholly is a unique quality that women leaders develop. They have to maintain a 'Goldilocks balance' between fighting for one's place in what was, and still is, a man's world, and yet allow enough acceptance of the old world ways in order to move ahead, get things done, and not feel constantly at war. This is the unique ability of women leaders who have made it to the helm of organizations.

### Chanda Kocchar

'Actually, I have learnt from a whole lot of people along the way. When it comes to learning, I have always believed that the entire outside world is open to you and it's really up to you to determine much you learn.

'I was born into a family which was gender neutral and joined a gender-neutral organization again, so my experience ever since I joined ICICI has been that of a pure meritocracy organization. Decisions are taken on the basis of merit; people are given responsibilities based on their capabilities; a person is rewarded based on their performance and it doesn't matter if the person is male or female, and I think that is the most important requirement for any organization to ensure that women flourish. When the system runs on merit, women are capable of flourishing...but what is important is that it must be ensured that merit is recognized on a gender-neutral basis.

'I think it is probably related to two big trends in society, the first is the pure economic requirement as India grows. I think companies are realizing that 50 per cent of the talent in India is women, and if the economy has to grow, it cannot grow by ignoring 50 per cent of the talent base. This is a talent base that is intelligent, hard-working, passionate about work, and is made of people who aspire. Second, one should credit the societal trend of giving higher and higher recognition to gender neutrality in our world, whether it's the family or spouses becoming more accepting of the fact that a woman can work...the entire society has started to accept it.

'Men and women differ in certain characteristics and certain attributes, but that doesn't necessarily mean that the attributes that men have make them better or worse leaders and similarly with women. I think leadership is a combination of many attributes that you have and that combination differs from person to person.'

### Kiran Mazumdar-Shaw

'You can do things very differently in this country and lead in a very different way; it is even possible to be a one-woman show.

'I find women can handle power a lot better than men; this is my personal opinion. I think women have less of an ego, I find that men tend to have much bigger egos... Socially, men have been empowered a lot more than women have, so I think women are far more balanced in their handling of power because they realize that if they overuse that power, society will not be accepting of them. There are more checks and balances when it comes to women and power.

'I think women can bring about big societal changes in this country, it is happening but too slowly, and we are not given the voice or appropriate platforms.

'If you look at gender discrimination, I really think it has to do more with society at large rather than individual organizations. If you look at the media today, the way they report women business leaders and others is very discriminatory. I went to the US to sign a big deal recently, and it's interesting that the CEO of that company is a woman. She is a very tough woman, strong and very driven. So we were having a chat about women's role in business leadership, and I was telling her about how tough it is in India today for women business leaders to be taken seriously. Few of us get noticed and we keep feeling that there are very few women in business when there are many more but they don't get noticed. Women are not recognized because it's the men who dominate all the time, even if they are doing useless stuff and useless business they get more attention than women, so there is a problem.'

### K.V. Kamath
'A lot has been said about the way ICICI has gone gender neutral, and the basics of this is very simple. We need to have a very open mind in terms of meritocracy from recruitment onwards till the time the employee starts working, and you need to believe that a job can be done by women. Treating the evaluation and promotion process as just quotas might not work. You need openness to say every job can be done by women, and though you may run into objections and challenges within the organization, you have to overcome it. Once you do that, then recruitment comes in and over a period of time leadership will develop.'

### Vinita Bali
'I have never thought of gender as a criterion to judge anybody. I'm one of those who firmly believe that the gender discussion needs to give way to a competency discussion. I can show you two men who have nothing in common, and I can show you a man and a woman who have more in common than these other two men. We tend to overemphasize gender in most organizations, at least now, and the ratio is skewed more towards men than towards women. But I think men are struggling in these new environments as well, where they are not just dealing with their own kind, but are dealing with diversity—diversity

that comes not from just gender differences, but also from differences in experience levels, diversity in ethnicity, diversity in socioeconomic backgrounds, diversity in one's upbringing, and diversity in beliefs and value systems. I think gender is just one of those criteria by which a workforce can be divided, but since it's the most convenient criteria to talk about, everybody talks a lot about it and I really do believe that the debate or discussion around gender needs to give way to a discussion around competency.'

## Transcendence: Vision/Values or 'The World'

The fifth pillar or act of appreciation is transcendence—vision/values or 'the world'.

The origins of the word 'transcendence' are located in mysticism and theology, and as such a lot of fog surrounds it. In fact, it is a simple concept to comprehend, but it is supremely difficult to practise in reality. I have described at length the concept of transcendent leadership in the earlier section, and I will repeat it briefly here for the sake of 'optimal redundancy', as they say in information theory. The hallmark of a truly great leader is to acquire and use this unique ability to transcend temporal and spatial limitations and plan for the long-term future of the 'system'.

A transcendent leader identifies ultimately with the larger world as a 'citizen of the universe' belonging to a race called the human race, and as such he is a statesman rather than an organizational politician, even though he does don that hat too when he is in 'our world'. Gandhiji said, 'People think I am a saint trying to become a politician; I am actually a politician trying to be a saint.' A transcendent leader is one with her head in the clouds and her feet on earth. The fourth pillar—strategy and execution—explains how the leader's 'feet are very firmly on earth', whereas the fifth pillar—vision and values—shows her having her 'head in the clouds'.

After Tagore read Jawaharlal Nehru's autobiography in 1936, he commented, 'Through all its details, there runs a current of humanity which overpasses the tangles of facts and leads us to the person who is greater than his deeds and truer than his surroundings.'

## On Vision

Three sequential questions—why? What? How? —have to be asked before any intervention. I find this gives the leader and the team great clarity of mind, and great action follows from this clarity. You will find on the next page two images for a model of VISTAR (vision, strategy/structure, action and plans/review). A leader who achieves and then shares this global vision with her 'warriors' is somewhat like Krishna who shows Arjuna the *Vishwa Roopa Darshana* to give Arjuna the systemic context in which his challenges, dilemmas and opportunities are to be played out. The big picture permits a crystal-clear understanding of the smaller picture and the interrelationships between various elements.

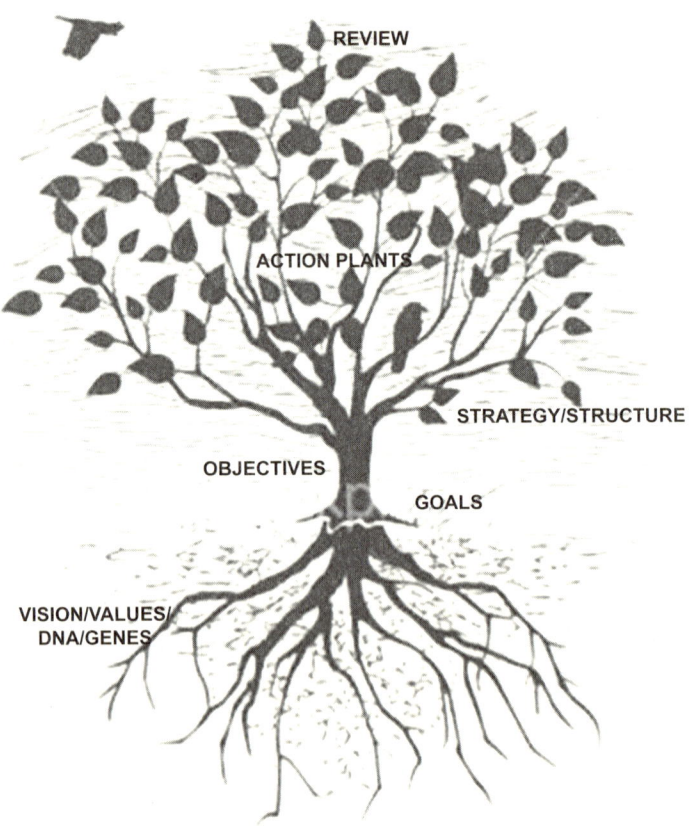

*Figure 2.3: The VISTAR Tree*

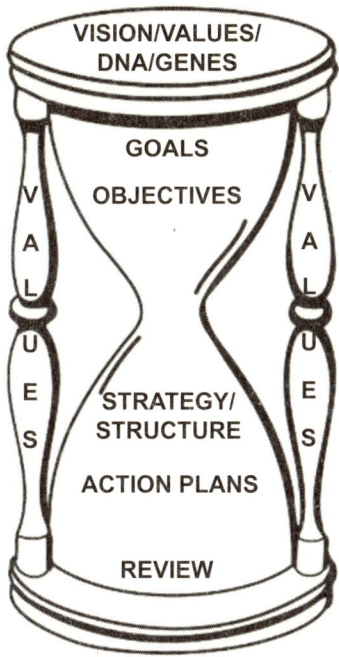

*Figure 2.4: The VISTAR Hourglass*

- A friend of the about-to-become president (Sr.) Bush had urged him to spend several days at Camp David thinking through his plans for his prospective presidency, to which Bush is said to have responded in exasperation, 'Oh, the vision thing.'
- When Lou Gerstner was recruited in the early 1990s to rescue IBM, he declared, 'The last thing IBM needs now is a vision. It needs lower costs and better market focus in every division.' On another occasion, he is noted to have said, '[Changing a culture] is not something you do by writing memos. You've got to appeal to people's emotions. They've got to buy in with their hearts and their beliefs, not just the minds.' And so he toured the country and told his employees a new identity story, 'I'm one of us now.'
- Bill Gates is reported to have said, 'Being a visionary is trivial. Being a CEO is hard.'

## LEADERS SPEAK

**Comment on the necessity, or the lack thereof, of having a vision**

### Trilochan Sastry
'The good ones stayed focussed and ask the questions, "Why am I here? What am I doing, making a new organization? Where are you going?" So whether it was a Verghese Kurien or a Mahatma Gandhi, I think their real contribution was the vision... It is a word that is misunderstood and misused even today... it's a very important concept [...] It is the courage to stand up for what you believe in and if you lose that faith, then quit...but I don't do enough of that...'

### Ashok Kamath
'We were talking about vision—does it really matter? I think it's critical for a very simple reason: how else do you measure yourself in a crisis? The vision becomes a guiding beacon. You have to ask the ultimate primordial question, "Is this going to make it and be successful or not?" Our vision actually builds on to universalization and the quality of education and equity. These link back to our ethics and our integrity, because from vision you go to values.

### Ashok Mishra
'Vision definitely and absolutely matters. I believe that every organization needs to have a vision. Sometimes people tend to write long vision statements, but it has to be a shared vision and can't be the vision of the leader alone. For example, in a great service provider company, that vision has to percolate down in different ways, because everybody is contributing to it, even the people at the lowest rung. As you said, in smart jargon, one needs to "build to excel" [...] In fact, when you talk of leaders, one of the ways to describe a great leader is to describe him as a "visionary" leader [...] It should be absolutely clear in your mind that the vision should be followed by the mission statement; vision alone is not good enough...what you need to achieve that vision becomes the mission...'

### Sachin Bansal
'So, when you're small, the vision statement, although not stated, is very clear to everyone. In big, high-performance organizations, if a vision statement

did not guide people every day, it's hard to imagine how they would make decisions. Consistent values, vision and a mission become a necessity in big organizations... It also becomes the reason why people want to join you; it also influences all your decisions on what kind of people you want in your organization. For those on the outside, it helps them decide whether they want to join the company or if they relate to it values. You don't want people who don't relate to it, and you obviously only want to hire people who relate to those values.'

### Jacqueline Novogratz

'I agree 100 per cent that being a CEO is hard. It's much harder than I ever thought it would be, and it's as humbling as anything I have ever done. I think you get the privilege of learning in the most acute way what your limitations are as well as what you're good at. I think there is enormous power in vision, without romanticizing it. For Gandhi to help India, he had to see it as an independent nation first...it required a vision that allowed an entire billion people on the planet to realize how much they were worth... I don't think things like this happen without a vision. Our mission is very audacious; we want to change the way the world tackles poverty. We will not be able to do that without that sense of audacity and vision. It's possible, and at the same time, we have the humility to understand what the world is and what we believe it can be. I think it's both the audacity that comes with the vision and the humility that comes with what it takes to actually execute it... Preparing those values becomes so critical [...] A vision without execution is a bunch of words; execution without vision is tactical drudgery. It's that combination of vision plus execution that leads to change...'

### Manish Sabharwal

'If you don't set point A or B as a destination, then it's like Alice in Wonderland. By which I mean, if you don't know where you're going, then any road will get you there. So, I think in our firm, whether you call it vision or not, we were working towards the idea of "fun, profitability and good for India"; it was our lighthouse. Our motto is putting India to work right. And we wanted it to be big. We didn't want it to be a dwarf, we wanted it to be a baby that would grow into something huge, and we were very conscious of that. To my mind, vision gets a bad rap when it goes into airy-fairy stuff. But having said that, your vision has to be unrealistic, your reach must exceed your grasp or what's a heaven for, as Robert Browning used to say. So to me, visions are about expectations more than anything else, having high expectations of oneself is very important. [...] I think the greatest companies and entrepreneurs are those who make you realize the strengths that you don't have. And in my mind, my vision is about expectations and how events evolve to fulfil expectations and people rise to expectations.'

## Mali Mahalingam

'In my previous organization, I think that a lot of our employees, all the way from our engineers up to our VP of engineering, joined us simply because we had a vision and the Chairman articulated it every time. Every time the Chairman visited India, which was about once a year, he was able to articulate this dream, this vision, which we used as an employee value proposition across the company. [...] The vision has come alive in the company, I've seen the Chairman articulate it, and it rubbed off on all of us with whom he had initially built the company. He seeded the company with 40–50 of us who shared the vision with him, and we have never even once had to disbelieve his vision, nor have the engineers that we hired out of campus. So I have had a very different, positive experience about how vision can mobilize people and bring in the very best of talent to be part of what you set out to do. I think, here, the vision translated into sharing a big picture, a dream that everybody wanted to be a part of—that was the vision here. Put simply, we wanted to be the preferred company to get engineering done anywhere outside, and we wanted to do it better than Oracle, SAP and Microsoft—we wanted to be faster than them, and hopefully, cheaper. This is a vision a lot of us shared and for good reason we became, and I would say this with all humility, the market leader in outsourced product engineering.

'The other thing is that over the last 12 months we've started diluting and are becoming [something] other than a services company in the product domain, so that's a deviation and I think it's not without consequences. People are becoming very disillusioned with our departure from the vision that we initially set out with. So, I have a firm belief in a vision which is articulated well, consistently, and is a vision that people can relate to. It does not work well when its 500,000 feet and full of vague English in which people don't see any meaning. That's when it really suffers, I think. Otherwise, I have a reason to believe that it's a very powerful mobilizing force and it's valuable.'

## Sudip Banerjee
'I think the choice of words is important, and sometimes, I think that creates room for doubt, misleading people into thinking that it is just PR or a pep talk. I think, without using that word "vision", I can still say that we have to think big, we have to think about the future, and we have to think about where we are going. All of that is crystallized into one word—vision. If we don't have a sense of direction or know where we are headed, we will be lost. First, we need to know where we want to go, then, where we are headed. And then we need the roadmap to get from here to there, otherwise we can't go anywhere tend to lose our way. So, therefore I would say, vision is real. It is something that is important in this context.

'I think Premji had some ideas, and the good thing about him was that he used to say, "Let's sit together and get somebody to facilitate." Premji built the vision along the way, and all of us participated in building it. Premji always had targets that were 10 times larger than what we currently achieved. Premji said, "Look, I think the only thing we did right was that we always think BIG and say that we will do something, not knowing where exactly or how we will do it, but we did it." I think the purpose of this exercise was to set us thinking, it gave us a sense of direction, it gave us something concrete to pursue. I think that was important otherwise you don't have anything driving you, there's no purpose or sense of direction. So from that point of view, I think it's very necessary.'

## Rishikesha Krishnan
'There is a lot of confusion about these words since a tremendous amount of word play also happens here. Setting a stretch goal for example—anybody could set that stretch goal. But to actually envision something that doesn't necessarily exist [...] that can actually be quite invigorating. For example, if you say that Infosys is going to be a $20 billion company by 2015, or something like that, I don't consider that a vision. Infosys will be just a company valued at some rate at that point of time, maybe $20 billion, maybe $15 billion. I don't think that is what vision is about. I think, for example, John F. Kennedy made a fairly big leap. A lot of this technology didn't exist at that point. They knew some things were possible, but they were doubtful about a lot of other

things [...] He created that image when he said, "We going to conquer space; we are going to go out there," I think that was a tremendous leap and shot in the arm for NASA and the whole space programme. I would be reluctant to dismiss all vision. I think a lot of vision, or rather what's called vision, is just a stretch goal or just some number. Those don't need any great visionary skills, but I think one has to be careful in trying to distinguish between what is genuine vision, what can possibly happen, and what is just extrapolation.

'One company that I have been reading about quite a lot and I also ended up talking to recently, is Bharat Forge. 25 years ago, Bharat Forge was a very small forging company. It's interesting if you go back and look at some of the early decisions which they took which were very critical to the transformation of Bharat Forge. I don't see any trace of a vision that Baba Kalyani was going to create the largest forging company in India. I don't think that is what he was trying to do. He studied at MIT, and he came back to India in 1972. From the day he came back, he started working at his father's forging company. After 15 years of working there, he wanted to start exporting forging outside India. He wanted to basically export to developed markets, but they weren't able to do it because of various reasons like quality issues, product issues, etc. It just wasn't possible. And then, in the late 1980s, he called a Japanese consultant. He told the consultant that this was his dream but he was not able to realize it. This gentleman told him that his employees were all the time trying to find the time to eat. So, he said some vague things and basically what he understood from this meeting was that we are not able to do things consistently. And then he thought about it and he realized that they had always hired unskilled and semi-skilled people, assuming that it would keep the cost low. When they had calculated the quality of the product they could make, they had come to the conclusion that it's most probably going to be difficult to do that with manual labour. So, he decided that he needed to automate the process. He decided—a very courageous decision—that he would completely upgrade the whole process, and move from a manual process to an automated process. He ended up doing it—he took a whole lot of decisions. He also decided to completely change his manpower. He gave VRS to all the unskilled guys, except a few potential ones, and hired a completely new workforce of people who were engineers and graduates and who could run the organization. My point is, I don't think even then he had any illusion or vision that he is going to be the number one forging company.

He wanted to make good forgings and also export good forgings. And this is the problem he tried to solve and he put this infrastructure in place. And this became the seeds for the take-off for the company.'

**Rohini Nilekani**
'I am very disappointed with today's corporate leadership—they cannot combine those hats and tackle the real question of externalized profits and socialized profits and privatized profits. I think that is a huge failure of corporate leadership, considering their knowledge about the social and environmental effects of doing their business, they should surely be able to create a platform where such trade-offs are analysed and they could say that they would not do this because of the externalities.'

## The Five Kinds of Intelligence

Great leaders are great pattern readers, and even more importantly and uniquely, they are pattern choosers. Of course they are also planners, controllers, executers and so on, but for all of those roles they can hire others to fill in their shoes. But [in] the ultimate gamble, because it is always a gamble when they have to make the final call—otherwise someone lower down would have made the decision if it had lower risk—it is time to look at the forest for the trees. All the available data would have been gathered, analysed, sifted, prioritized and alternatives—options and scenarios—drawn up for her consideration. From this differentiated mass, she has now to integrate. Data is always limited in some way or another; if there was a perfect database, a computer would be able to make the decisions. A human being, a leader, is needed to make the decision because there are gaps; pieces of the jigsaw puzzle are missing. The behaviour of some of the significant players in the environment—internal or external—will be a mystery. What will the government do on this pending bill? The competitors? The market?

A leader's life is suffused with this phrase—vital balance (first used by Karl Menninger, a distinguished psychologist, and founder of the Menninger Clinic in Topeka, Kansas). Leaders hope to create and maintain a vital balance—this 'Goldilocks ability' to strike the optimal balance between any number of dichotomous variables.

In cosmology, there is a term, 'the Goldilocks effect', and that is what we have at this pinnacle of the system's functioning. Writing about why the miracle of life appeared and is sustained on earth, Bill Bryson says, 'Gravity is just right—"critical density" is the cosmologists' term for it—and that it will hold the universe together at just the right dimensions to allow things to go on indefinitely. Cosmologists in their lighter moments sometimes call this the Goldilocks effect—that everything is just right.'[22]

Nature had got it just right. Great leaders know that the Goldilocks effect—this vital balance between or among dichotomies, two or more seemingly contradictory ideas or policies or strategies or vested interests—is composed of 49 per cent science and 51 per cent art.

The leader has to balance the short term and the long term; the people and the company; honesty and expediency; shareholder returns, customer service and employee benefits; the environment and development; leases and assets acquisition, meritocracy and loyalty, theory and practice, situational ethics and work life balance for others and for oneself, organic growth and inorganic growth…the list of issues which an organization's top leader has to balance is long.

### Box 2.2
### The Blind Girl and the Two Suitors: a Parable

She was so pretty and gentle but had never ever seen the world. She had been born blind. But she had not one, but two young men who were in passionate love with her and constantly, sometimes in turns, sometimes simultaneously, described to her the world she couldn't see. All well, you say? How sweet and romantic, you murmur with a twinge of envy maybe? Well, there was a catch. The two young men each had a special gift or a curse, depending on how you see it. One was born with telescopic sight affixed permanently to his eyes, whereas the other one had microscopic sight affixed permanently to his eyes. And what is more, neither one knew of his affliction. Each described the world around him according to his vision and proclaimed it as the truth, the whole truth and nothing but the truth, and said that the other guy was pathetically wrong. The telescope man had lyrical descriptions of things far away, but he kept stumbling and let the poor blind girl fall at every step because he could not see what was under his nose. The microscope man, on the other hand, could see with exaggerated clarity every speck of dust, and every pebble appeared like a huge boulder to him. He was paralysed with fear and the poor blind girl never got to move a step. Yet each man swore to protect and cherish her till death do them part. The blind lassie did not know where to look (Sorry, bad pun. No sensitivity at all. Go to the back of the classroom and stand upon the bench).

Then lo and behold, the miracle happened. An eye surgeon with laser beams came to town and she was cured. Her vision was completely restored and the first thing she saw was a world which was unlike anything her lovers had described. She felt bad for them but she got married to the surgeon.

Moral of the story: You have to have balance—the vital balance—between the distant future and the immediate present, between the short term and the long term, between the family and the universe, between the 'blue sky' idealism and the sceptical and cynical pragmatism, between the self (that all-important entity—as Oscar Wilde said, 'Self-love is the only everlasting love') and fellow human beings (even those who are not like me).

Arthur Schopenhauer said, 'Talent hits a target no one else can hit; genius hits a target that no one else can see.' The difference between talent and genius is that talent leaps a 10-foot ditch and lands at 9 feet 11 inches, genius leaps the last inch. I hope that the ideas presented in this book will help leaders develop themselves to leap the 10!

Sexist as it may sound, the quote given below from an article published in the *New Yorker* (27 November 2000, p. 161) about Samuel Johnson illustrates amphibian intelligence, an ability in transcendence:

> [Boswell's Johnson] had both existential gifts: he could take a specific case and instantly raise it to the level of an abstract principle (of the man who married twice he declared that it was "the triumph of hope over experience") and he could break down a general proposition to a pungent particular instance (of chastity he said, "The great principle which every woman is taught is to keep her legs together"). [...] He can see the point and grasp the principle [...] He could count the

trees and see forests. These two gifts for getting down to cases and for seeing the big picture are the whole of intelligence.

According to Vickers, 'All management models, theories and concepts are merely meant for sensitizing the intuition of the decision-makers.'

## Judgement of Character and the Ability to Find and Inspire the 'Right' Talent

A leader need not be the smartest person in the organization and need not necessarily possess a high IQ, though some may. It is, among many other facets, an ability to recognize and 'sell' your cause (company, movement, project or programme) to a high IQ/EQ person so that she voluntarily, and beyond the lure of lucrative incentives, wants to work with you, for you, and under your flag. Einstein said, 'I don't have to know everything as long as I know where to get the answer when I need it.' A leader may have her one strength, and she may learn a few more essential ones, but she will never be able to be an expert in everything. Great leaders choose wisely, and when they find the right people and the right opportunities, they go all out for them. They grab them and keep them as long as they can.

Every human being is, by necessity, in order to function in the everyday world, a bit of an amateur psychologist. But a leader has a much greater need to read other people—his 'constituency', so to say. A great leader is most often a self-taught psychologist who learns the 'Triple Paradox'—the human mind uses the human mind to investigate and understand the human mind. Intuition, empathy, self-awareness and interpersonal wisdom all depend upon this ability. US Supreme Court Justice Stewart once said, 'I do not know how to define pornography, but I know one when I see one.' Begging pardon of leaders, same can be said of the far frontiers of great leadership. You know a great leader when you see one.

The 'fifth column'—the fifth type of intelligence—mean the control of emotions, or the capacity to postponed gratification, or refers to ego suppression.'

Of course, the term 'fifth column' is notorious in its connotation. Wikipedia defines the fifth column as, 'A group of people who undermine a larger group, such as a nation or a besieged city, from within. The activities of a fifth column can be overt or clandestine.' In our schema of the five intelligences which are the tools, the equipment and the competencies of a transcendent leader, I have deliberately placed this in the 'fifth column' because the absence of this can upset the whole apple cart and undermine all the other 'intelligences' and 'acts of appreciation'. The other nine in the model depend on this 'emotional intelligence' to be allowed to play and influence events. Like the proverbial finger in front of one's eye blocking the whole universe (Go ahead and try it. Extend your forefinger two inches from your eye and slowly bring it closer until your finger finally reaches the eye. It blocks all vision, right?), the absence of emotional control blocks all our other abilities and makes one a slave of non-rational emotion. Once, a grandma advised her granddaughter, 'Count to 10 when you're angry before you speak; on second thoughts, count to 100, or keep counting till you can say what you want to say without anger.' This applies universally. A leader who keeps her feelings under control, who can wait for the results patiently, and one who can suppress his sense of self-importance to the achievement of the greater or longer good—winning the war by losing some battles—such a leader is the ultimate victor.

## LEADERS SPEAK

### Anu Rao

> 'We cannot solve our problems with the same thinking we used when we created them.'
> —Albert Einstein

I found this quote from Albert Einstein valuable in my work as an organizational ombuds person, where my role in the organization was to assist everyone as a neutral officer and help resolve problems and issues within the organization, regardless of whether it was fact or not, or whether it was one's assumption or interpretation, or even when the issue was embedded in the construction of a problem itself.

Can the problem be traced back to the organization's leadership and its culture? What are the leadership concerns? Is it accountability? Loyalty? Results? Ensuring that the organization looks good? Cost control? Serving their customers? Surely these are not mutually exclusive. Conflict resolution entails issues related to organizational resources, issues of perception, motivation and self-esteem concerning individuals and personalities and finally those which affect the values, that are both personal to the individuals and the organization. Further, conflicts are dynamic, they change (usually for the worse) with time, and they are affected by communications or the lack of it.

The five intelligences are the weapons in the armoury, the arrows in the quiver, to arrive at the 'five acts of appreciation.'

## Execution

This word—execution—runs across all five pillars for good reason. Vision, values and goals are all mere words till they are translated into deeds on the ground. The weatherman's promise of rain tomorrow is not rain. It is merely a declaration of an impending event, a forecast, even wishful thinking till tomorrow when the heavens may or may not execute the prediction. Great leaders are great 'doers'. They think, they conceptualize, they design their organizations, their systems, their movements, but above all they execute those designs as though there is no tomorrow. With the 3Is—integrity, intensity and intelligence—they translate ideas into reality with hard work. I have never known any leader worth her salt who was not the hardest worker compared to all around her. I know you are just dying to say, 'How about Ronald Reagan? No one ever accused him of sweating it out, and yet he won landslide victories.' (They were minority presidencies. When Reagan carried 44 states in 1980 and defeated Carter 489–49 in electoral votes, he won only 26.9 per cent of the adults. The winners in the 1996, 2000 and 2004 elections received 24, 24.1 and 28.2 per cent respectively. So 'landslide' is a very relative term).

My response to the Reagan comment, in random order is:

1. Landslides are not synonymous with great leadership. Popularity does not connote greatness. Some of the most cruel tyrants in history (you supply your favourite one) have had overwhelming followings. Who said the *vox populi* was a moral voice or a discriminating one? The masses may not be for long periods of time be any wiser than the courtiers of feudal times.
2. The jury may be out on a President whose two terms saw the greatest deepening of the gulf between the rich and the poor, the greatest

increase in national debt and the largest federal bureaucracy in American history.
3. Picking a good team and delegating wisely can reduce the need for very hard work if you do not want to work.

Charles Knight, Chairman of Emerson Electric, had led a company which had 30 years of uninterrupted profitable quarters when he wrote this article:

> Several assumptions underlie our management process. We believe, for example, that profitability is a state of mind. Experience tells us that if the management concentrates on the fundamentals and constantly follows up, there is no reason why we can't achieve profits year after year—even in manufacturing businesses that many observers consider mature and unglamorous. We also believe that companies fail primarily for non-analytical reasons: the management knows what to do, but for some reason, doesn't do it. That is why Emerson has a strong action orientation; we see to it that our strategies get implemented properly.[23]

A third belief is that the 'long term' consists of a sequence of 'short terms.' Poor performance in the short term makes it more difficult to achieve strong performance in the long term. The basis of management is management from minute to minute, day to day, week to week. Finally, it is crucial to keep it simple. While effective management is simple in theory, it's difficult in practice. As Peter Drucker noted, managers seem naturally inclined to get caught up in complicated ideas and concepts—ideas that look great on paper but just don't work. A corporation has to work hard to have a simple plan, simple communications, simple programmes and simple organizations. It takes real discipline to keep things simple.

'You all know what we know; we just do it,' that's what he says here, right?

## LEADERS SPEAK

**Execution: Who thinks 'strategy' in your organization? Who leads the execution of strategies? 'Ideas are dime a dozen; it is the execution that separates the men from the boys.' Do you agree?**

**S.D. Shibulal**
'I agree. From my experience, I am convinced that an idea without an

execution plan is of little value. I have seen the most brilliant ideas fail because not enough attention was paid to planning its execution. At the same time, rather simple ideas have witnessed great success because they were executed flawlessly. A general saying we follow is that strategy is 10 per cent ideation and 90 per cent execution.'

## About the '3+5 Transcendent Leadership' *Mantap*

### K.V. Kamath

'This is very nicely put. It clearly resonates. I think all of the aspects you have placed in the foundation are clearly necessary. Intuition plays a huge role in leaders. What is intuition? Intuition is the sum total of all that you have learnt, consciously and subconsciously, in whichever form, which becomes a force that can be honed... integrity and character have to be at the base. From our own case, if you look at ICICI from 1955, it has been about defining our character and values and it has grown more enriched as we moved along.'

### Rajiv Kuchhal

'What is leadership? At least in my perspective, the only leadership that matters is the leadership of people... If you can't lead people, it doesn't matter if you're a brilliant sales guy, if you're a brilliant strategy guy, or if you're extremely articulate, or if you're very bright. It doesn't matter... Ultimately, you should be able to lead people, people should be able to look up to you or at least identify with you. If it is a skill gap you can bridge that skill gap, but if you are not a people leader then you can't bridge that gap. That's why most organizations end up using HR to talk to their people, saying it's an HR problem. It's not an HR problem. That's where my run at my recent company ended; I saw people doing various things and they were very successful at them, but what I thought was missing was leadership. While people admired those at top, or at least respected what they had achieved, they were not great leaders of people. They were risk-takers, they were entrepreneurs, but they were not leaders of people. Ultimately, if you can't get people together, you can't do anything. You can't do any change management, you can't grow, and you can't scale. I realized this only in this company, because till then I didn't see the gap and that's when I started seeing the gap and saying, "Oh, this is what leadership is all about, you should be leaders of people".'

## Madan Padaki

'I completely resonate with it. I don't think it could have been demonstrated any better. Whenever anyone asks me, "What do you look for?" when hiring anybody as a leader, I must go back to these 3Is. First of all, he has to be a person who says what he does and does what he says. Our interviews are almost 8–9 hours long. We start by meeting for breakfast and stay on till the evening, because you can put on a façade for an hour in an interview, but unless you're a fantastic actor, you can't hold on to that façade for a long time and there will be a slip up. The second thing I look for is intensity. As a leader, especially in an entrepreneurial world, intensity is what drives outcomes. You can't have a *chalta hai* kind of attitude. You need to be an intelligent person, and you need to develop that intelligence. I think we are not talking about IQ here. That's why, on my side, I believe that intelligence is born out of these three wisdoms. And therefore, if I were to make one change to the *mantap* structure, I would look at intelligence as coming from the world of experience. A lot of it is genetically codified, but that does not mean that if you're genetically not intelligent, you can't be wise. And therefore, these three pillars will infuse the intelligence. It's not a must-have trait, but a nice one to have. But you know that the person has everything else and has the ability to accept the wisdom, intelligence will be built over time. I concur with the sequence at the bottom; that's the most fundamental, absolutely.

'The way I look at it: self-awareness is when you put your own self in others' shoes and understand who you are because that's the lens through which you look at the world. I need to be aware of what lens I am putting on, whether it is good, bad, right or wrong is not the question. I need to know what is the lens through which I view the world. When I'm viewing the world, I also need to figure out what their supposed lenses are. Again, it's not a question of how good or bad that lens is. When both these lenses interact, that's when interpersonal wisdom comes in and that evolves.

'The way I would interpret it: if you look at the triple bottom line, this is where profits happen; this is where the people side of things is; and this is where the planet side of things is. The sustainability, the impact and the profits. In this progression, the profits are only the means to these other two ends.'

## Jacqueline Novogratz

'Intelligence, courage, integrity...I think that is great. I wonder if there is something around resilience and optimism down there...maybe it could be intensity, courage and resilience. I'm not sure if intelligence is clearly a piece of it. I'm not sure that leaders are always intelligent. Intuition is probably right. I'm thinking of great leaders and the first thought or word that comes to mind is not intelligence.

'I think that integrity indeed has a moral dimension, and in fact, I think that what we are seeing across the world today is a craving for an integrity that is connected to a sense of moral purpose or moral priority... We are clearly in an organization that carries its values on its sleeve, but I also see young people all over the world today who are clearly yearning for this idea... It makes it more difficult for young people to understand what the roadmap looks like, and I keep saying to them that there is no roadmap. There is more to accomplish and that includes learning how to do what is right rather than what is easy, because we are living in a world where things are going so quickly—where young people are doing things that are easy rather than doing things that are right... I deliberately use the word moral.

'The idea of a moral imagination... You use the word empathy, but I will say that we have to actually go beyond empathy and prove yourself to be in another person's shoes to understand how they are feeling and build better solutions. That way, you can build it from there, not just from your own perspective... I think we need to have the humility to see the world as it is, and then combine that with the audacity to imagine what it could be—a nexus of humility and audacity. Then, we will be able to lead from a transcendent place. It's so often that we see leaders who refuse to acknowledge what is, and therefore just live in an audacious place; a place where they often can't build anything. Or, there is so much humility that they stay focused on the very small and don't make much change.'

## Sudip Banerjee

'I think the foundation...integrity, that's the real question...if you don't have it, you won't go anywhere... Intensity, I am not so sure of, because I think it means different things to different people. If there were two to three other words, such as, regain passion, drive, or fire in the belly, all of that I would probably say is more fitting. That needs to be paraphrased... You would obviously need to have intelligence. I would say above-average intelligence, but you don't need to be super intelligent. I don't believe that any of these people I talk about—let's say those whom I look upon as leaders in my personal experience, have been super intelligent. I thought, IQ-wise, he was huge, but others, yes, intelligent people but not super intelligent. Self-awareness, yes, that's very important. I am just wondering where humility fits into this? In the context of today's times, I think that's something which should be emphasized because it's important. I don't know whether it's clubbed in with 'world' or empathy. But somewhere I think that should be introduced or maybe it should be added. Humility, self-awareness, empathy, certainly...'

### Ashok Mishra

'Definitely all three are important: integrity, intensity and intelligence. You really don't have to be Einstein to be a great leader. Self-awareness is good, but just listening is not good enough. It's good that you're listening but just empathy is not enough—good negotiation skills are required. A leader should also always be is a learner; if a leader thinks he knows everything then he stops growing.'

### Sanjay Anandaram

'I think all of this is extremely crucial. Intelligence, I take as a prerequisite. Obviously every human has intelligence and intelligence has multiple meanings. I would rate self-awareness and empathy as extremely crucial. Obviously, the three horizontal layers that you have laid out—the '3Is'—are the foundation and I think you have shown that well. If I have self-awareness and empathy, the rest of it follows—interpersonal wisdom, global wisdom and community wisdom—I think they are actually derivatives of the foundational elements and of the first two are pillars, namely self-awareness and empathy...'

### Vinita Bali

'Another aspect that a leader requires would be the ability to see the bigger picture and the ability to holistically see the business. A third related aspect is the ability to look at the business as a microcosm of communities and societies and the role businesses play in shaping communities, societies and the larger world. Leaders also need to know how to inspire others to give their best, how to give people credit for what they have contributed, and also how to create this wonderful alignment.'

### Kris Gopalakrishnan

'The highest goal is to create an institution which survives generations. The thinking and the leadership required encompasses transformation, leadership development and the creation of a value system. A thinking organization should come first and individuals second, creating a set of people who truly believe in those values. A transformational leader is somebody who takes the company through certain challenges—be an external environment, a technology change or poor performance—and you need to turn it around... so that's the transcending nature.

**Tolstoy, in *War and Peace*, said, 'Great men are but the labels that some serve to give a name to an end, and like labels, they have the least possible connection with the event.' The leader is a 'slave of history' according to Tolstoy. What do you think of Tolstoy's view?**

### Devapriyo Ghose

'Insofar as a leader has to be in the right place at the right time, I guess history provides a starting point and a context to every leader in whatever sphere. History is after all the accumulation of a million things that people big and small do. But to my mind, leaders shape history, and in turn, they are shaped by history. The people we remember as leaders in whatever field—Hammurabi, Ashoka, Bach, Picasso, Keynes and Nelson Mandela—to take some names from history pretty much at random—or for that matter the person who invented fire—these leaders, in whatever different spheres they inhabited, were in no way destined to succeed by divine right—they struggled, in some cases with circumstances, in others with their inner worlds, but in every case they persisted and were able to, in their time, change the course of history.'

### K. Dinesh

'Execution excellence: it is always important to translate plans into reality through excellent execution. The hallmark of a great leadership team is relentless execution—day in and day out and learning from it to shape the next course of action. It is like the breath which never stops even as we sleep or like the never-ending athletic relay race where the batons are handed over from one to another till the goal is accomplished!'

# 3

# THREE GENERIC MODELS FOR CHANGE

I believe life should be a process wherein one sets up ideals and, if absolutely compelled, beats a reluctant and minimum retreat from those ideals. Throughout this book I have presented 'ideal models' and their practical compromises to help us think about leadership and organizations.

This mini-chapter presents a prelude—a sort of 'rehearsal'—to the management of transformational change. I wish to prepare the ground with three models, which are like the accompanying instruments in an Indian music concert; they are intended to enhance your appreciation of the main model by complementing the final model. You will hopefully understand the comprehensive model better if you were to have these three in your mind first.

But first: what is a model? A model is simply an ordered set of assumptions about a complex system. It is an attempt to understand some aspect of the infinitely varied world by selecting from perceptions and past experiences a set of general observations applicable to the problem at hand. Every person approaches his problems, wherever they occur on the space-time graph in Figure 3.1, with the help of models. A farmer uses mental models of his land, his assets, market prospects and past weather conditions to decide which crops to plant each year; a surveyor constructs a physical model, a map, to help in planning a road; an economist uses mathematical models to understand and predict the flow of international trade.[1]

We need to be able to understand and diagnose why some settings fail and some succeed. If 60 to 90 per cent of all small business ventures attempted in the United States and in India fail within one year of their initiation, surely we need to understand why, so we can save this monumental effort going waste. To help us in this diagnosis, we first create models of 'ideal' conditions. These are conceptual statements about a system which has reached a level which can be considered 'fully-functioning' or successful. We present phases of the developmental process and a catalogue of essential roles and activities. Such a description should aid us in retracing the phases of the development process to the beginnings of the system.

Let us use an analogy. Suppose we find a fully functioning aeroplane. Then we proceed to take it apart to see what components it consists of, what relationships they had to one another, in which order and with what degrees of centrality. Then we put it back together and fly it to find out how it works while flying. We now have two sets of data—one, the structure of the system, and two, its dynamics of performance—the 'anatomy' and the 'physiology' of the aeroplane. Add to this the following verifiable assumption: whatever state the system is in now, it owes that state substantially to its design (that is, the process and content of its creation). The two sets of data now available to us should enable us to hypothesize basic assumptions about effective design. It still does not tell us what exact processes and components went into creating these products. But we have a set, at least, of products to play with, to retrace to the possible alternative origins.

Models should be used as ladders and props; they are like the scaffolding a fresco painter sets aside (for later periodic use) when it has served its purpose. Models help provide a set of concepts, relatively well-used and tested in various settings, to bite and chew on as it were, to use and retain or discard as the need arises to understand the creation of change. I will now describe each model in turn.

## Model 1: Rise and Fall of an Open System

Look at the curve in Figure 3.1. At the bottom of the 'mountain' there is a level titled **'purpose or teleology'** of the system. Every open system fundamentally needs a minimum definition, at least an explanation of why it wants to exist and what it hopes to achieve by existing. This definition need not be a conscious formulation, but may be subconscious or unconscious; this is the teleology of the system (from the Greek word 'tele' meaning 'distance').

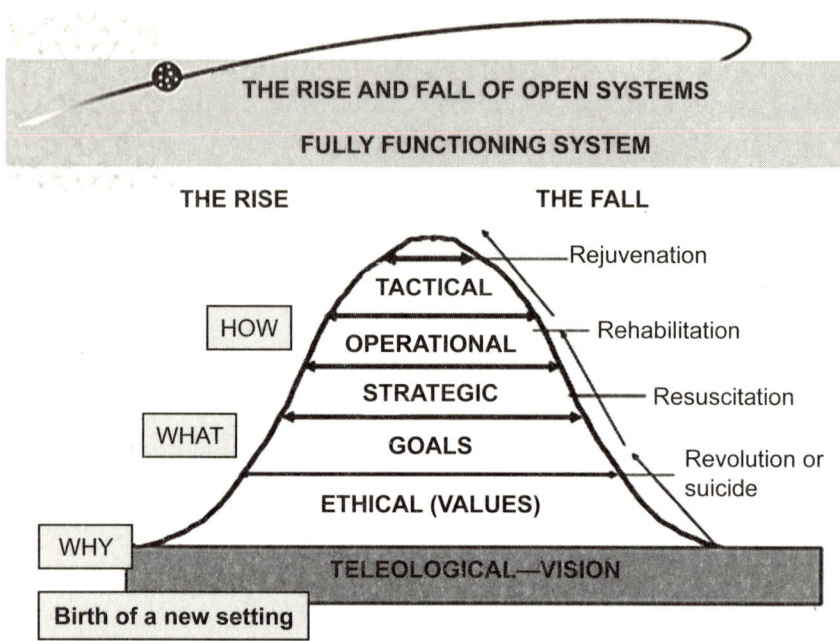

*Figure 3.1: The Rise and Fall of Open Systems*

By 'purpose' I mean here an overall, super-ordinate guiding theme that motivates the system to come into being and sustains it in its lifetime. The next level on the bell curve is the **ethical or value level**. Values define the boundaries of the system. They influence significantly the limitations and the strengths of the system. They differ from the purpose in the sense that they state a set of conditions that define the working of the system, rather than what the system is supposed to achieve. Values, in their ultimate and most fundamental manifestations, define the conditions under which the system decides it is willing to survive. This includes, for instance, definitions of prosperity and despair, happiness and grief, good health and ill health.

### LEADERS SPEAK

**Values: What are they to you? Why?**

**Ashok Kamath**

'In terms of values, the first is integrity, the second is respect for other people—which means you need to listen carefully before you make your calls—and the third is passion and commitment.'

## Binny Bansal

'Personally, my values at work and the values I believe in, that is, my personal values and my professional values, are a little bit different. Not very, but a little bit. [...] We did an exercise a year back on what should be Flipkart's values. What we have learnt is that we want Flipkart's values to reflect our personal values, according to what we now have as values rather than what we should have. You can dream that you should have certain values, but you can't really change your values, that has been another learning. You can't really say that we should have these values...you have some values and those are the ones you can afford to have. [...] The values that we have come up with are service to the customer and there was something between passion and pursuit of excellence.'

## Jacqueline Novogratz

'I have learnt from my parents' generosity, openness and kindness. Everybody was welcome at the table and there was always room at the table. My parents had consent for the poor always; my father in his time had started an orphanage. I would not call it a liberal household, but they were an immigrant household which had both military and catholic backgrounds. I would say they were socially very conservative actually, although they were learners. Generations changed and the world changed, and they changed with it and I would say the values they gave me were less about being liberal and more about being generous and inclusive and having very high expectations. You were expected to do something in the world... You were expected to take care of the family and friends and then the world and you were expected to be independent...'

## Manish Sabharwal

'I struggle with absolute values and relative values. Are there absolute rights and wrongs, or it is relative? Should I not pay a bribe, should Manmohan Singh not have done what he did to get the nuclear bill passed, should Kennedy not have lied during the Cuban missile crisis? I struggle with this when people tell me there are absolute rights and wrongs. To me, the more important values are how you live your life, to me that sort of patience, that sort of long view, is more important. People's capabilities are like their shoe sizes or height, is it worth investing in them? I'll shy away from the bigger absolute values or relative values because I haven't resolved that debate in my mind and obviously there are absolute values. Sometimes, I try to think like that the person in that context...for me the most important way to live your life is to take the long view. [...] I think long-term greed is a very important value where you make calculated decisions on the basis of the long-term good rather than the immediate short term. High discount rates in terms of finance versus low discount rates. Your values should be long term and let's not maximize today at the expense of tomorrow, but tomorrow doesn't need be so small either.'

### Hema Ravichandar
'Finally the values that matter are the values that people live by and demonstrate, and sometimes there are contradictions in those core values or beliefs...to me that is the ultimate truth. I will not go by those framed statements, I will go by what you do, I will not go by what you say.'

### Ashok Mishra
'Values are very important because values actually describe [...] the right way to reach goals without doing wrong [...] They help you not to step on people's toes to get your vision done...'

### Rajiv Kuchhal
'Values, I think, are a lot more important than vision because values tell you what is acceptable and what is unacceptable. It defines what is in your boundary and what your character is, and people relate to that much better. If leadership is about people leadership, then I think values are paramount, way more important than vision because with those values you can move and be something.

'My three most important values: you should be trustworthy because that leads to a very low cost of transaction and leads to openness and really reduces the friction; if something is not there you should be very open about it. Now trust itself has multiple components, but I'll say leading by example is one of them; you cannot be a leader if you can't follow what you want others to do. Second, I very strongly believe that there has to be a system of fairness, you have to be unbiased, it's very important, then only you can build the trust of your people. Third, don't outsource your thinking, don't stop thinking about what you can do differently. Doing or bettering yourself or bettering the things around you every day makes things better. So don't stop thinking, that's the best thing human beings have. I don't know if it's a value, but in my mind it is.'

## Sachin Bansal

'In 2009, because of our success, we didn't really think of the values that were important to us and which we live for. We knew in tiny bits that integrity is important. We hired a person who we thought would fit in handsomely. He brought with him all the data he had used in his previous organization; he had copied everything. He said he would get the job done for us and we really didn't care how he was going to do it. He had worked for a large corporation before, and we thought that he would bring in the best practices. Once we came to know that he was copying data from his previous organization, we told him that he needed to stop doing it. Once we did this he was of no use, he was using their data to make decisions here and that's not what we wanted; we wanted real capable guys. That's when we started thinking integrity is important, and if the company grows these values need to be followed. There were also a couple of other examples where we hired one head of a department, she always said that she would look at what the competitors are doing and then come up with a similar solution. She didn't have any first principles, no originality or creativity. In all probability you might come up with the same solution, but first try it your own way. The next hiring mistake we did was with an IIM-A graduate. Overall, I think it was a matter of capabilities, which we misjudged. We need to look at capabilities, from our own lens, our own criteria, and not that he is from a Stanford, IIM-A etc. That doesn't mean that they are (great)... We need to look at capability ourselves and there are some values that we like in people and we will stick by them.'

## Mali Mahalingam

'From the time I started my management career, all the way till I had the opportunity to lead large corporations like HP and IBM—very few people in this country have had the opportunity to be the head of HR for both HP and IBM and I've had the fortune and privilege to be in those positions—I've found that the companies that I worked for did believe in certain values and this translated into the daily behaviour of employees and was more than just PR slogans on the wall. The rules of the garage that HP believed in, the values that defined the company, was that they respect the individual and they give world-class customer experience. I think that the companies that I have worked with have lived up to their values a great deal, personally for me, those organizational values highly reinforced my own personal values. IBM respects the individual, I think they have done so much to live that value. Every IBMer feels extremely proud of being an IBMer. More and more managers leave IBM, not because they didn't deliver, but because they didn't live up to the value of respecting the individual. You cannot shout at an IBMer and then get away...this is something that I have seen. I don't think we are close to IBM when it comes to being true by a long way. Every year (once in two years), they validate the IBM values through what they call "value jams". The chairman of the company, starting with Lou Gerstner earlier and now Sam Falmisono who took over recently as chairman, all of them believe in conducting value jams. They get online and leverage technology to get people to comment on how values are lived in different parts of the world and how they are reinforced. Employees are asked to narrate examples of how the values were lived or not lived. These values jams are a very powerful exercise that IBM does to revalidate and reaffirm their values year on year. The value jam is a 4-hour long exercise; globally hundreds of thousands of people participate and have their voice heard by the chairman of the company. Then a booklet is made which consists of what people said and what they expressed, which is what makes IBM what it is.'

## Sudip Banerjee

'Of all the things I can say with absolute conviction are critical elements, the absolute ingredient necessary is values and a value system. I think not just in the context of Wipro, but overall, in life, if you don't have values, there is no way you can make progress. You won't make progress as an individual, you won't make progress as a family, as a society, or as a company, so it is absolutely critical. In those days, to get a telephone connection you had to bribe someone, otherwise you would not get a telephone connection. I remember we were changing offices. I was area manager and I went to the chief general manager and said, "Look, give us the phone lines, we will not pay any money because we don't pay." We got a phone in two weeks! The CEO would often joke, and he even now says that there are some government tenders where people would give us a small part of the business just to see that they are not in trouble, because that is the kind of reputation we have built. I think values are definitely very important (but because multi-product lines are very conventional—lighting, vanaspathi, fluid bars), to be in those businesses in harder... Our medical system is one of the most corrupt, you know the racket with CT scans and such... In those days, our CEO was selling to government hospitals...we were often at the receiving end and received the lowest prices, we were technically the best, but we did not get the contract. You know the rest.'

**Rishikesha Krishnan**
'Values do define leaders, but I am not sure if there are universal values. I think people who are leaders normally do stand for some values they believe in. It would be difficult for me to imagine a leader who did not have some values, it is not necessary that he wears his values on his sleeve, and they are not necessarily values about which he or she talks all the time, but a good leader consistently demonstrates values through behaviour that follows certain principles. It would be very difficult to imagine a genuine leader without that. There are some values that I try to put into practice and I am quite conscious of them. One of these values is that I will not taking advantage of other people for personal corruption. So these are definitely things that I try to follow. It's not easy all the time. It's more of a personal improvement and loosely continuous improvement.'

Once the system has grappled with, and evolved acceptable definitions of purposes and values, the rational needs of the system—strategy, operations and tactics—come into focus. Strategy, operations and tactics are traditional concepts handed down from military theorists to corporate planners and serve well to define the needs of a system in its long, medium and short term, and in varying extents within its boundaries. In other words, the difference between the three sub-stages of the rational level—strategy, operations, tactics—is one of space and time; how much organizational and environmental space and time does one cover in terms of planning when one 'does' each one of these three sub-stages? One covers the largest orbit in strategy, lesser in operations and the least in tactics. Teleological and ethical convictions are not irrational, but operate on a complex composite of rational and non-rational levels. While all the levels described originate in a melting pot of differing levels of reality (ranging from verifiable 'objective' experiences to imagined states), the rational level covers the relatively 'objective' knowledge which has been arrived at through research, observation and experimentation. The level of values is often given a priori. They are amenable to rational discussions (hopefully), but their origins are not totally rational. They have unconscious and subconscious niches. Reason is only one of their many sources.

Let us emphasize a point we have implied in the foregoing description. Each one of the three levels—teleological, ethical and rational—are products of the negotiation between the system and its environments (internal and external). They are not decided unilaterally by the system, nor are they unilaterally thrust upon the system by its environment. They are evolved in a push-pull negotiation process between the 'candidate system' and the 'potential host' environment. The different levels of the model are not discrete entities; they are joined by a smooth curve. They are highly permeated by one another, and they are influenced by feedback. Strategies are influenced by inherent values and the results of executed strategies modify values. Purposes are prone to slower change, but they are influenced over a period of time by the other levels. There are, of course, very deeply held values which are not easily accessible to change by feedback. But on the whole, a system which survives and grows develops a healthy feedback circuit.

When the three sub-levels of the rational stage have satisfactorily negotiated between the system and its environment, the open system reaches the top of its peak. It achieves social acceptability, its place in the sun, its *lebensraum* (sorry for the use of a word which has acquired an odius connotation because of its association with Nazi philosophy), and is a citizen of its parent system, fully franchised with rights and responsibilities. The system has achieved harmony or **'vital balance'** between its internal and external environments. The environments accept and reward the system.

I will use the concept of vital balance all through the next chapter as the sign of the highest level of health, well-being and dynamic existence of any organization. The Goldilocks effect is just the right idea for our purposes. As Robert Browning wrote, 'God is in his heaven, all is right with the world.'

Now we come to the falling part of the bell curve. It is the mirror image of the rising part, except that it stands for **the fall of an open system**. At the peak is an area of **'suspended doubt'**. The system, till now, has experienced very little anxiety. There is no doubt about its utility or its integrity (or its potential and kinetic energy). The doubts about the system begin at the next level.

Doubt is neither the only nor the exclusive motivator. It is not always capable of singly motivating the creation of innovation and change. However, it is a powerful, and often necessary, but not sufficient factor in persuading creators to attempt transformational change. I will now discuss each level of doubt.

The levels of degeneration begin at the next level—**the area of 'rational doubt'**. This doubt may occur in any one or in many of the actors involved. This may occur at the tactical, operational, or strategic levels, that is, in increasing spans of time and space. An employee of a corporation may doubt the allocation of tasks on a particular day. He may doubt the packaging policies of the product. He may doubt the incentive schemes. These doubts are all at the rational level. Doubt may evoke annoyance and frustration. Great leaders have 'safety valves' designed to let off the steam, to vent, to find adjustments and small compromises. We call them 'rejuvenation'. At the level of strategic doubt, it is 'rehabilitation'. If the system does not respond and there is no assuaging or amelioration of the operational doubt, then, after a time, the doubts may grow deeper. After a certain period of dissatisfaction inflicted by operational doubts, and if no resolutions are provided, then the affected systemic element begins to probe deeper for answers. If something is rotten in the state of Denmark, where is it?

The next level for doubt to appear is at the level of values—ethical doubt. In the late 1960s, when a young American asked his father why he worked for Dow Chemicals when it was supplying terrible chemicals to kill poor, innocent Vietnamese, he was pitting his value doubts squarely against his father's values. His father may have subscribed to the belief that 'ours is not to question why, ours is but to do and die.' He may have believed that whatever his country did was right. Perhaps his loyalty was restricted to his family and to hell with everything else. Maybe he believed that his son's sources of information were of doubtful veracity and he could not be right. There may have been the thought, 'What is good for General Motors is good for the country and me.' The kid was neither questioning the way the family was run (operational) nor the need for the family unit (teleological). He was doubting the ethics of participating in an immoral act to gain a living. There are executives in pharmaceutical firms who declare that they would quit if their firms started producing biological warfare chemicals. Instances can be multiplied, but it is clear that the distinctive character of value doubts is that they act as the 'superego' of the system, the conscience which debates the 'dos' and the 'don'ts'. Just as values supply the vital strength of motivation when one thinks they are 'right', they detract from that strength when suspected to be in the 'wrong'. If values define the boundaries of the system, then value doubt is the debate sought on the propriety or otherwise of a boundary feature. In other words, it is not enough to live; it is needed to live 'right'. Value doubt is basically a debate on 'what is right?' and 'what is wrong?' Ethical doubt may evoke internal struggle and external anger. Scepticism deepens into cynicism about the organization and its leadership. 'Resuscitation'—an intense intervention at the level of the people, structures and processes may be needed to save the open system and restore health, or at least to stop it from sinking further to a stage where the options are stark and 'win-lose'.

The next level of doubt can occur either sequentially (when value doubts are not satisfied), or it can occur originally. It is the level of 'teleological' or 'absolute doubt'. It refers to the doubting of the very purpose of the system. The son who held earnest passionate dialogues with his father earlier may decide to 'drop out', rejecting family ties along with the 'establishment'. The feeling evoked here is anomie or alienation. The alienated ones may respond in two ways—'revolution' (attempting to overthrow the parent system) or 'suicide' (abandoning hope and withdrawing from the original vision).

So what do leaders and organizations do to cure these doubts? They rejuvenate, rehabilitate, resuscitate and reinvent the system to keep it going. I will describe in detail the pathologies of systems and their cures in the next chapter.

## Model 2: Roles Needed for a Fully Functioning System in a Turbulent Environment

In every fully functioning system, there are four kinds of leadership roles with their respective follower teams. These roles are represented as successive circles in the following model. The figure 3.2 represents a whole system. Outside the system is the environment. The system is represented by four concentric circles. The outermost circle is called the level of selection or sensors. The next level is called the level of interpretation. The third circle is called the level of strategy. The innermost circle is called the level of implementation.

This model proposes that the performance of these four roles is essential for a living system to be fully functioning. These four levels do not necessarily represent four distinct individuals; they represent communicative roles. Several of these roles may be filled by a single person. On the other hand, each role may be filled by a social group. The important thing to note is that regardless of the number of people involved, whether one or a million, these communicative roles are present in every fully functioning system.

The fuzzy swirls outside the system represent the turbulent environment. The turbulence from the environment is the turbulence of non-information. For any open system, there is always enormous activity going on in its environment which, initially, is incomprehensible to the system. There is no form to the environment, hence no information. No recognizable patterns are superimposed on the environment, hence most of it is non-sense (not nonsense). There are finite limits to the capacity of human systems to identify and absorb information from their environment. There is a minimal level of information needed for the survival of the system, but that permits only a low level of survival. For the fulfilment of a great 'present' and the creation of a glorious future, the system needs to be at a higher level, and there is a much higher level of optimum information needed for the system to be fully functioning. What is so special about information? Information is negentropic, that is, the acquisition of information (or, more accurately, the translation of the turbulence into useful information) is the means by which an open system delays 'entropic' death.[2]

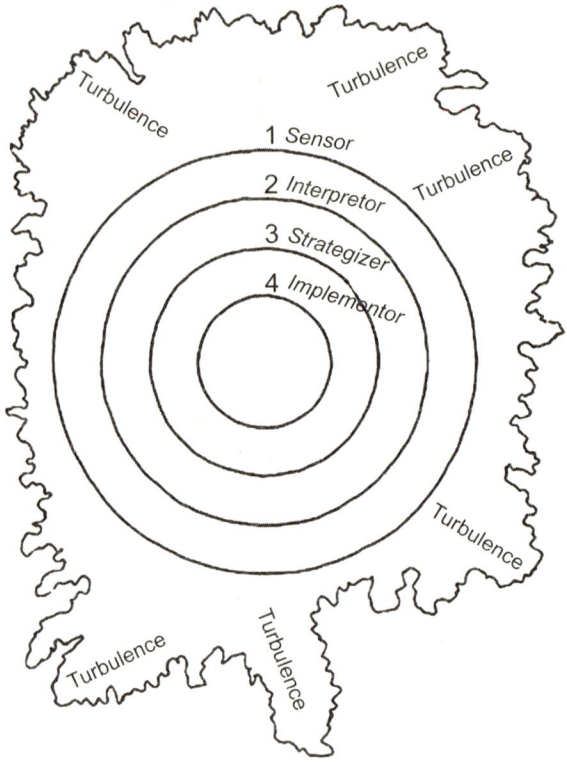

*Figure 3.2: Roles Needed for a Fully Functioning System in a Turbulent Environment*

Indeed, negentropy has been used by biologists as the basis to explain the purpose or direction of life, namely cooperative or moral instincts.[3]

For instance, a newborn 'knows' very little of survival techniques, let alone how to be a 'good citizen', spouse, parent or any of the many social roles that he or she can chose from in later life. A baby would not survive if left in an open street. By and by, the baby picks up information from various sources in its environment (starting from the mother primarily and gradually expanding its orbit of exploration) to 'grow up' through the stages of infancy, adolescence and young adulthood. What happens in between the two stages—the initial one of very little information and the later ones where the adult has sophisticated information? This dramatic transformation in the baby's ability to cope comes from its capacity to sense. This task is handled by the sensor. The capacity to derive information from the environment is the distinguishing characteristic of living systems. This fundamental and unique capacity is the ability to select and identify those parts of the environmental turbulence (or 'noise') which are essential for its growth. Sensors are those who mediate at the boundaries of open systems. They impose order on disorder and pattern on randomness to evolve 'meaning' for the system. The quotation marks around the word 'meaning' in the last sentence are deliberately used, for the sense that the sensor derives (or creates) from the external environment is a special kind of meaning, and in its raw and nascent form, is almost incompressible (or at least unacceptable) to the rest of the system. Why does this happen? It is difficult for the system to understand the information generated by the sensor, because the system cannot derive the same information out of its regular apparatus (elements or sub-systems or sense organs). In other words, the system is set up for status quo and on-going dynamics. Step-function adaptations in their fundamentals are impossible to achieve through the use of their homeostatic mechanisms.

Too much jargon? Let me explain. If I go for a 2-km walk every day and if my diet and life habits are adjusted to this level of physical exertion, I cannot hope to compete in the Boston marathon and complete the 29-km race. I will not be prepared for it. Hence, I will consult a marathon expert who is most probably a fitness freak and who will recommend a regimen which will seem totally scary to me. But if I want to run the marathon (let us say my job in my firm depended on a bet to complete the distance), then I better listen and follow.

Hence, the system delegates sensors—the special esoteric mutations—to do what the system is not set up to do. But this 'exporting of the freak' to the frontiers to gather special information creates the problem of acceptance once the sensor has derived information. The system finds it hard to accept the information, because the medium is the message—and the medium (that is, the sensors), is most often an unacceptable freak. There are two powerful forces at work here—one, the system's need to derive special information for its welfare, and the second, the 'dynamic conservatism' of the system which is suspicious of strangers bearing tidings, ill or well. Philip Slater describes this phenomenon of system dynamics excellently thus:

> There is a cybernetic law that states that the more probable a message is, the less information it provides. The information contained in a message, for example, decreases with its repetition. This creates a curious dilemma for any group; the longer its members are together, the less they have to say to each other, at least, about the group's own relational structure... The more effectively a group communicates about itself and its constituents, the more quickly it will stagnate in the absence of inputs from outside. Even with outside inputs, information will tend to decrease since the structure itself acts as a filter for screening out jarring information which it interprets as noise [...] A system needs occasionally to achieve a perception of the universe, including itself, through eyes other than its own, since its sense organs are designed to exclude most information from awareness. The only way to achieve this is to extrude a bit of circuitry which will evolve a perceptual apparatus different from the parent circuit and hence inhale a different vision [...] [But] the more information the segment acquires the less able the parent circuit will be to absorb it [...] A prophet is extruded into the desert, obtains a vision and returns. He is then either rejected or his vision absorbed and a new circuitry evolves in the parent system. A new prophet is extruded and so on. Clumsily, the parent system hunches along like an inchworm on the information provided by its extruded members—toward an ever receding and unattainable goal of total, perfect, and conscious circuitry.[4]

What the prophet sees in his vision is of trivial significance—it is how he sees that is important. He is not merely a scout exploring unknown territory—he is the territory. He is not the experimenter, but the experiment. Most innovations may turn out to be trivial, but occasionally the prophet actually evolves an inner circuitry that would confer a boon on the parent circuit if it were reintegrated with it. At this point a dilemma arises: how can a system absorb an external modification which came into being through a procedure premised on the system's inability to tolerate such a modification?

It is a little like the socially ambitious parents who send their child to an elitist school so that the child will follow a lifestyle uncorrupted by their own crudities. They want the child to be 'better' than they are, but when the child returns, they are dismayed and say, 'Who are you? I can't relate to you. How can you snub your own parents who gave you everything?' Parent and child will be able to maintain a close bond only to the degree that the child's attempted metamorphosis was unsuccessful.

The question then is, 'How is this curious and crucial dilemma resolved in a fully-functioning system?'

It is resolved by the creation of the next level of roles—**the interpreters**. The interpreters interpret the special act of sensors (or the sensors themselves). They perform the mediating role between the extruded sensors and the system. They 'translate' the sensor and the message to the language (value systems) of the system. They are the 'system brokers' engaging in transactions between the caravan merchants (in the desert and on the high seas) and the country folk who are in need of (or who are willing to buy) modified and processed goods. The qualifications for the role of an interpreter are clear. They should be able to understand the 'language' of both the system and the sensor. This is language in its broadest and most fundamental sense—the spoken and unspoken tongues. The interpreters should be able to filter the information from the sensor and give it to the system in a manner that can be used by the system to fulfil the original need which created the sensors in the first place. They should be able to maintain a rapport with both their constituencies. This does not mean that the interpreters can substitute for the sensors. In fact, quite the contrary. The role of the 'broker' cannot be maintained successfully if they go over completely to one side or the other. In most cases, the interpreter has neither the special ability nor the passion of the sensor. Hence they do not invent a new language, but they can learn it (at least enough to import the information into the system) once it is invented. The role of the interpreter-broker is an invaluable and indispensable one for a system to be fully functioning. None of these statements (including the metaphors) should be interpreted to mean that this is a narrow role. At its best, interpretation is the diffusion of innovation and bridging of differences. Apropos such a function, Geoffrey Vickers states,

> Since we depend absolutely on communication within societies, between societies and between generations, developments which

threaten these communications with failure are a lethal form of trap. By failure of communication, I do not mean failure in the means to transmit, store and process information. Of that we have already more than we can use. I mean, failure to maintain, within and between political societies, appropriate shared ways of distinguishing the situations in which we act, the relations we want to regulate, the standards we need to supply and the repertory of actions which are available to us.[5]

In the last decade, India has seen an increasingly conspicuous absence of those in the broker role, resulting in a deeply divided society with apparently irreconcilable dichotomous rationales, contesting for power and influence on the body politic. Those who could mediate between the system and its 'prodigal sons' are missing.

The third level of function or role is the **strategizer**. This is at the level of policymaking. The need arises for the system to make its choice(s) among the multi-valued options presented by the interpreters. Even when the system overcomes its dynamic conservatism and wishes to be responsive to the new information, it is still faced with the problem of particular (phenotypic) value formation. It has to analyse and work through issues such as the degree of applicability of the information, the feasible limits of usage, the standards of performance in use, the boundaries and structures to be imposed on the usage, etc. These are the issues of policymaking and form part of the 'appreciation process' (Vickers) by which the system decides whether or not the new information has any relevance, and if it does, what to do about it.

This is the arena of statesmanship and temporal wisdom. Political power and contemporaneous variables play an important part in the efficacy of this role. Choice, amidst an overload of information with dubious accuracy and varying degrees of reliability, is an extremely onerous task. The 'right' choice of policy or action is more often obvious only in hindsight and what appears as the glaringly appropriate advice to the 'Monday morning quarterback' may be one of a crowd of untested alternatives presented to the strategist or the policymaker. D.A. Schön quotes Tolstoy's *War and Peace* to describe the commander-in-chief on the Russian battlefield (analogous to that of a real-world planner):

> A commander-in chief never deals with the beginning of any event—the position from which we always contemplate it. (He) is always in the midst of a series of shifting events and so he never can at any moment consider the whole impact of an event that is occurring. Moment by moment the event is imperceptibly shaping itself, and at every moment of this continuous, uninterrupted shaping of events the commander-in-chief is in the contingencies, authorities, projects, counsels, threats and deceptions, and is continually obliged to reply to innumerable questions addressed to him, which constantly conflict with one another.[6]

The strategist (planner, policymaker) in probabilistic terms, makes decisions of 'uncertainty' at his most challenging profile and 'risk' at his least challenging. Uncertainty in decision-making arises when the set of domains (with which the decision-maker is dealing) changes as also the domains themselves. Also, the results of the interaction between the domains and between different systems are unpredictable. Hence, the possible consequences of decisions cannot be foretold. These cause uncertainty. However, when none of these phenomena occur and the field is stable, the situation reduces itself to one of risk, and a need arises to make a choice between the branches of a decision-tree whose certainty equivalents are known. These situations constitute the higher and lower limits of this role.

The fourth level is the level of **implementing or regulating**. The information has been identified, interpreted and adapted to context, yet all of this is in the inner world of appreciation. It still is to be tested in the realities of actual implementation. There are myriad details of an experimental nature that need to be worked out in the system. If the proof of the pudding is in the eating, this is the level at which the proof should be forthcoming.

I quote an illustration which describes a situation in biological sciences and medicine. It sets out the characteristics of the implementing level and contrasts it with earlier levels. Lewis Thomas in *Lives of a Cell* speaks of poliomyelitis,

> Once it had been learned (from basic research) that there were three antigenic types of virus and they could be abundantly grown in tissue culture, it became a certainty that a vaccine could be made.

Not to say that the job would be easy, or in need of any less rigor or sophistication than the previous research; simply that it could be done. Given the assumption that experiments could be done carried out with technical perfection, the vaccine was a sure thing. It was an elegant demonstration of how to organize applied science, and for this reason it would have been a surprise if it had not succeeded. This is the element that distinguishes applied science from basic. Surprise is what makes the difference. When you are organized to apply knowledge, set up targets, and produce a usable product, you require a high degree of certainty from the outset. All the facts on which you base protocols must be reasonable hard facts with unambiguous meaning. The challenge is to plan the work and organize the workers so that it will come out precisely as predicted. For this, you need centralized authority, elaborately detailed time schedules, and some sort of reward system based on speed and perfection. But most of all you need the intelligible basic facts to begin with, and these must come from basic research. There is no other source. In basic research, everything is just the opposite. What you need at the outset is a high degree of uncertainty, otherwise it isn't likely to be an important problem. You start with an incomplete roster of facts, characterized by their ambiguity. Often the problem consists of discovering the connections between unrelated pieces of information. You must plan experiments on the basis of probability, even bare possibility rather than certainty [...] you can measure the quality of work by the intensity of astonishment [...] There will be lots of disputing among the experts over what is certain and what is not. Perhaps the heat and duration of dispute could be adapted for the measurement of uncertainty.[7]

The mutual complementarity of the different roles is evident implicitly in this instance. A fully functioning system needs the regulating function to translate the genotypic information into phenotypic reality, abstract into concrete, dream into action. This not only serves the needs of the ongoing life of the system, but it also provides dynamic feedback to all the other levels about their performance. The consequences of sensing, interpreting and adapting are shown in the streets of the system and the marketplaces, and the regulators play an important role in recycling information to the rest of the system, and through them to the environment. Thus, the transactions and the interdependence within the system and across the system boundary are aided in a significant way.

This model is based on Arthur Koestler's work on creativity.[8]

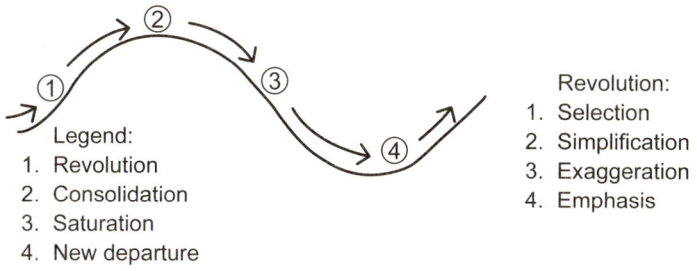

Legend:
1. Revolution
2. Consolidation
3. Saturation
4. New departure

Revolution:
1. Selection
2. Simplification
3. Exaggeration
4. Emphasis

*Figure 3.3: The Rise and Fall of New Movements (Or, What Happens When a 'New' Idea Meets an 'Old' System?)*

In this model, we are concerned with the dynamics of the development of a new idea or the development of innovation in any field of human endeavour. The purpose of including this model here is to provide an illustrative strategy that seems to be employed by new innovative settings to create themselves and gain resources for their survival. The model, which does seem to be extremely valid in the fields of art and literature, is presented here as a (and not the) scheme for analysing the phenomenon of emerging systems or settings. It helps, as one reads through the model, to choose and remember someone's historical innovation in art, literature, politics, religion, science or any other human activity (for instance, the anti-corruption movement in India in 2012–13, Dadaism or Surrealism in painting, the beatniks in the US and the Angry Young Men in Britain in the 1950s, rock and The Beatles in music, computers and operations research, statistics, behavioural science, the hula hoop—remember that? Or why don't you just think of anything Steve Jobs did? Seriously.)

There are four phases in this developmental cycle as we ascend the wave from left and descend on the right. The four phases are revolution, consolidation, saturation and crisis/new departure. Let us look at each stage in turn.

Revolution is the 'radical shift in turn,' according to Koestler, an activity that heralds a new movement into the social psyche or consciousness. Revolution is the strategy adopted by an ideator (the source of a new idea, concept, theory, system or movement) to explode through the dynamic conservatism[9] of the larger system or environment. The larger system fights back to maintain the status quo. A new emergent system, in attempting an entry, challenges (overtly or covertly) the established position or the integrity of the larger system. This creates resistance. To overcome resistance, the strategy is revolution. It is worthwhile to observe how each step involved in the revolution is designed with the express intention of 'exploding through barriers'.

Four steps can be distinguished in the course of a revolutionary innovation. They are selection, simplification, exaggeration and emphasis. While following these steps, it helps if one can think of a cartoonist producing a sketch. The first step, selection, is self-explanatory; it is the act of defining the limits or boundaries of the innovation or new movement. It is like turning on a spotlight in a theatre to light up a particular spot on a large stage. The subject is selected for the cartoon. The second step is to simplify the idea (a concept well understood by the Madison Avenue gurus, messiahs, dictators, etc.). It is recognition of the limits of psychological endurance that the environment (or a reader of this book for that matter) has for a new idea. It is also often an acceptance of and adaptation of the principle of bounded rationality, that is, it is the acceptance of the limits of human cognitive powers.[10] It is also important to keep the message simple from the point of view of broad diffusion, since simplicity aids memory and helps popularity (or notoriety). It is a basic tenet of the cartoonist's art to be able to draw a figure with as few lines as possible. The third step is exaggeration. George Bernard Shaw used to say, 'I told the British public once every six months I was a genius—and they believed me.' It is necessary to blow up or magnify the point in order to draw attention to it. This is not merely an idiosyncratic or freakish tactic. It is an eminently logical step because one of the most fundamental responses of an established system to a new system is to ignore it.[11] Hence, the emerging system overcompensates for the deliberate underplaying (by the audience) by exaggerating the point. In a limited analogy, the cartoonist uses exaggeration to draw the attention of the onlooker to a particular aspect of the character and fixes the idea in his memory (for example,

Nixon's Nose, De Gaulle's nose). In the final step of the revolution, there is emphasis. It is both quantitative and qualitative underscoring at the risk of redundancy. (It is like an ad for a new product that is in your face on TV eight times an hour). It is also essential in order to demonstrate the conviction with which the new idea is held by the authors. In other words, in a rapidly changing world where several concerns compete and clamour for attention, the credibility of a new idea is often judged by the system in terms of the conviction with which it is held by its authors (if time and tide wait for none—and there are lots of boats on the open sea clamouring to get into the dock—then it helps to distinguish yourself by unfurling a red flag). Again, in a limited sense, the cartoonist who repeats the same representation of a face day-after-day gains his reward when his audience begins to recognize the face with the least hint or suggestion. Selective and consistent emphasis is one of the keys to capturing hearts and minds.

Now back to the figure, the next major step in the bell curve is consolidation (parallel to the top of the curve in Model 1). Consolidation is organization. It is building a structure. It is usually intended to be semi-permanent at least. It is the phase in which the movement seeks stability by laying down foundations. Consolidation contrasts with its earlier phase—the revolution—in that the primary goal for the movement clearly shifts from one of seeding-propagation-diffusion of an idea to the establishment of a structure for the idea. True, there existed some organization in the first phase, but it had not been elaborate and was subject to rapid changes and fluctuations. Organization was not the main objective in the revolutionary phase. Also, the aim of whatever organizing that was done during the revolution phase is different from the aims during consolidation. Consider a military campaign. The invader may succeed in occupying a town or a district or a province of a country. During invasion, the needs of the organization are of war. Once the territory has been conquered, the needs of the organization are those of peace. Primacy shifts to governed mechanisms. The objectives of the group have changed from gaining *liebensraum* to conserving it for the longer run. To do the latter, the movement requires considerably different values and skills than what it needed to conquer the territory. There are, throughout history, repeated instances of invaders who wouldn't (or couldn't) rule over the territories they had conquered. Mohammed Ghori, and later Mohammed Ghazni, marched from the Middle

East and invaded South Asia repeatedly and vanquished vast territories, but each time they merely looted and plundered, whereas the later invaders of the sixteenth century dared to rule and built the renowned Mughal Empire. Similar instances of sharp transitions from revolution to consolidation can be found in most fields of human endeavour. Consolidation, in its later stages, most often is characterized by the larger system's acceptance of the movement. It may acquire respectability and become fashionable. At its zenith, the once-fledgling idea may become the prime force, for a time, to move the larger system. It may, in other words, become an 'idea in good currency'.[12] That is, it can become a powerful motivator of behaviour in the larger system.

The next phase, saturation, occurs when the parent system begins to feel suffused with 'too much of a good thing'. The new idea, by now quite dated, has been milked (probably) for all it is worth. (There are contrary situations wherein an idea 'saturates' without being milked fully). The environment, including the parent system, reacts with complacency, lack of excitement and even boredom. It also begins to entertain new 'suitors', other, more recent innovations, which clamour for attention and resources. What happens in the movement itself which leads to saturation and the loosening of its hold on the parent system? For this, Koestler has a succinct description. He describes the declining phases of the new movement thus,

> The new territory opened up by the impetuous advance of a few geniuses, acting as a spearhead, is subsequently occupied by the solid phalanxes of mediocrity, and soon the revolution turns into a new orthodoxy with its unavoidable symptoms of one-sidedness, overspecialization, loss of contact with other provinces of knowledge, and ultimately, estrangement from reality. The emergent orthodoxy hardens into a 'closed system' of thought, unwilling or unable to assimilate new empirical data or to adjust itself to significant changes in other fields of knowledge. Sooner or later the matrix is blocked, a new crisis arises, leading to a new synthesis, and the cycle starts again.[13]

Saturation is the inevitable price to be paid for the way in which the idea, in the first place, got into social milieu—through revolution.

Each of the steps in the revolution distort the 'real' message. To achieve an entry into the public psyche, the original idea was cut out of its natural 'set', shorn of its subtleties, nuances and necessary complexities by the needs of the simplification process. Tall claims (taller than can be sustained for long by anyone but a fanatical follower) were made glibly on its behalf through the process of exaggeration (quack medicine men in the country fair repeat to every group, 'Yes, folks, yes—this pill here can cure everything from the common cold to cancer—so hurry, hurry before the Sultan of Arabia buys up the whole supply which is really scarce and has to come from outer Mongolia...') and were repeated with such conviction and so often that 'wolf' was cried once too often. 'The greatest strength is the greatest weakness,' goes the Greek saying. The coin turns—and the other side of the revolution (even in total revolutions where power has been seized by the new idea), is saturation for the customers.

Continuing along the wave in the last figure, the last stage of the cycle occurs when the saturation deepens, precipitating a crisis for the movement. At the same time, newer innovations appear in much the same way as this particular innovation appeared earlier. That is, the newer ideas create their revolution by selection-simplification-exaggeration-emphasis. This is aided and abetted by the deepening crisis of the now 'old' movement. The public is sceptical (or even cynical) of the exaggerations—the pomp and ceremony of the old movement—and is willing to hear a new idea. The very steps that aided the fledgling movement to gather strength and impact the system now become the bane of its life—'the old man on the shoulder'. Its flexibility and responsiveness to the environment and its nascent vigour has vanished in the saturation phase and it has no more 'information' to give. Alfred North Whitehead, in *Adventures of Ideas,* sums it up succinctly, 'In its prime, each system is a triumphant success, in its decay, it is an obstructive nuisance.'[14] In fact, new ideas are generated out of the imperfections of the older idea. The seeds of a new rebel are sown by the mistakes of the old revolutionary. The price of admission into the establishment, as stated earlier, is diluted integrity or 'purity' of the original vision. This 'cop-out' (or overemphasis) then becomes the launching pad, the rallying cry for the new rebels to gather and launch their 'reform'.

It is to be stressed that this description is not the only way in which a new movement is born. There are, at any one time in a pluralistic system, many sources of innovations or rebellions that arise from the imperfections of the system or its environment or the discontent of the parts of either.

The dynamic described seems to be one of the major ways in which a new movement gets born. To summarize the last phase of the model, the movement passing through its crisis may either atrophy or make new departures. The withering away would happen if there is no capacity left for negentropy. Sometimes, there is just enough energy for mere sustenance. However, if it can summon reserves of energy from within, or if it can scrounge new 'information' from without, it can depart in new ways, giving birth to (and thus extending its longevity) new movements of influence.

# 4

# THE MANAGEMENT OF TRANSFORMATIONAL CHANGE

There is a tragic and painful affliction called 'Saint Vitus Dance', which compels patients to twitch and spasm continuously. It is named after Saint Vitus, the patron saint of dance and dogs. While this is involuntary and the patient is a victim, an entirely voluntary, religious and indeed very joyous celebratory dance by the Mevlevi Order, a Sufi sect also known as the 'Whirling Dervishes', involves vigorous continuous movement too. Whether forced upon oneself as an affliction, or chosen and practised entirely by one's own choice to attain one's spiritual dreams, continuous vigorous movement is the common feature in both these instances. These two represent a metaphor—a spectrum with these two states at either extreme—for our world and our lives in this world—of continuous change thrust upon us on the one hand and sought after by us on the other. But in either case we have to live with it and know how to manage it.

As the cliché goes, change has become the only constant phenomenon in the world. A consensus seems to have emerged some time ago and has become a core belief and conviction among those who lead and manage organizations and nations, or consult and advise them: If we are to survive as a species, we, individually and collectively, need to be ready, willing and able to change in significant, rapid and flexible ways—or else we will perish like the many other species before us. This statement is as true for a corporation competing for market share and profits as for a nation fighting for survival and prosperity and for the global community trying to preserve peace and develop higher civilizations. Here are a few instances of changes in corporations and economies in the last 50 years:

+ Xerox Corp saw its market share drop from a near-global monopoly to 18 per cent within a decade, owing to competition from new, hungry and nimbler-footed Japanese competitors, and yet it bounced back to its peak within a decade.
+ Apple went from being an iconic newcomer under Steve Jobs during his first stint as director, to near-bankruptcy under John Sculley, and then again exploded with innovation under Steve Jobs in his second stewardship.
+ In the 1990s, Florida Power & Light was considered thirteenth in a field of thirteen competitors (The company's CEO was reported to have said, 'Our employees would lie as to which company they worked for, since our performance was so bad.') It became the dominant player in the market and rose to the number one position and won the global Deming prize awarded in Japan for high quality.
+ The American can industry, once prosperous, was driven overnight to its knees because of the invention of a two-piece can technology that substituted three-piece cans.
+ The Indian IT industry snuck in on an opulent America and the West and created a low-price service industry which pioneered prosperity in India, only to find that it would have to face competition from the declining Western economies. Rich multinationals adopted the strategy of 'if you can't lick 'em, join 'em', and moved their operations to low-cost countries, thereby attempting to neutralize price arbitrage, but they faced hostility in their home countries for outsourcing domestic jobs and creating greater unemployment.
+ The Indian IT companies, which hired bright young engineers at low wages, found their employees no longer willing to accept salaries lower than their counterparts in the client companies, an instance of RORE among the middle-class well-educated youth.

Transformational changes continue to dominate every aspect of human life. Change is inescapable, sometimes for the better, often for the worse, but both need new leadership abilities. A principle akin to Newton's law of inertia (for elephants and for organizations/nations) is illustrated by the story in Box 4.1.[1] Organizational or systemic change is so difficult because the very factors that go into making an organization successful in a particular phase of its history become the albatross around its neck.

> **Box 4.1**
> **The Wise Men of Change: The Life of Karl Ludwigv Bertalanffy**
>
> Having spent most of his life in semi-obscurity, Bertalanffy may well be the least-known intellectual titan of the twentieth century. He was nominated for the Nobel Prize by R. Buckminster Fuller, though he was not considered for the prize due to his unexpected death. Today, is considered to be a founder and one of the principal authors of the interdisciplinary school of thought known as General Systems Theory. According to T.E. Weckowicz (1989), he 'occupies an important position in the intellectual history of the twentieth century. His contributions went beyond biology, and extended into cybernetics, education, history, philosophy, psychiatry, psychology and sociology. Some of his admirers even believe that this theory will one day provide a conceptual framework for all these disciplines.'[2] His General Systems' theory, especially the concept of open systems, has been immensely influential in diverse fields of human thought and action.
>
> He advocated the broadening of our individual loyalties from national to global and urged that we become patriots of the planet, and endeavour to think and act primarily as members of humanity. He suggested that we begin pledging our allegiance to humanity and to the earth on which we stand, one planet indivisible for all. He believed that 'we must begin protecting the individual and cultural identity of others'.
>
> He advocated a new global morality, 'an ethos which does not centre on individual good and individual value alone, but on the adaptation of mankind, as a global system, to its new environment.' He also believed that 'we are dealing with emergent realities; no longer with isolated groups of men, but with a systemically interdependent global community. It is this level of [reality] which we must keep before our eyes if we are able to inspire large-scale action designed to assure our collective and hence our individual survival.'[3]

## Rejuvenating and Transforming Organizations

For most organizations, the time to change was yesterday, the motivation to change is survival. It is no more a question of 'Should we change?' It is learning more of what to change and how to change.

When successful organizations try to achieve stability, they become totally wedded to the contemporary context and environment. When their environment changes significantly, they lose their ability to learn new things as well as their flexibility. A Spanish folk proverb goes, 'Take what you want, said God, take it and pay for it.' Our version of the law of inertia says that an elephant can run in a straight line at high speed, but as soon as change is asked for, the turn is difficult to make.

Why does our 'elephant' need to change direction at all?
The answer is VUCAI. Each one of these five factors has increased significantly, in quantity and intensity, over the years. The emergence of the global village and the 'flatness' of this village has lead to such unprecedented demands on the knowledge, skills and the wisdom of leaders and institutions that they struggle to cope with the changes thrust upon them, let alone muster the resources to transform their system to their desired vision. These five factors—the **volatility** (pace of change and unpredictability) of the environments as reflected in the markets, in international economics, and in the politics of nations; the **uncertainty** of not only outcomes but of all other factors—the 'why/what/how' of a situation; the **complexity** owing to the myriad factors influencing the fate of any one entity; the **ambiguity** involved in interpreting the 'intelligence information' from the direct stakeholders and larger 'influencers'; and the **interdependence** of a world opened up by every possible technology and policy—make the environment very difficult to predict.

How does a leader confront these five factors? This chapter is about change and a leader's ability to successfully transform an organization to the desired state.

## Why Is Change So Difficult?

There are four major reasons why change is difficult. Leaders who are responsible for transforming their system should avoid these 'tripwires' to

THE MANAGEMENT OF TRANSFORMATIONAL CHANGE ♦ 149

be successful. To do this, they have to transcend these essentially mental barriers.

1. Dynamic conservatism/planner's dilemma/ecological trap
2. Organizational agnosia: I don't know, and I don't know that I don't know
3. Lack of execution: Ignorance and ineptitude
4. Inability to multitask in real time

## 1. Dynamic conservatism, 'Planner's Dilemma' and 'Ecological Trap':

D.A. Schön, a great pioneering thinker on the pervasive issue of complex change, coined the term 'dynamic conservatism'. He talks about the dynamic conservatism of systems, a paradoxical juxtaposition of words, meaning roughly 'running like hell to stay in the same place'.

> **Box 4.2**
> **The Wise Men of Change: D.A. Schön[4]**
>
> D.A. Schön was born in Boston in 1930 and was raised in Brooklyn and Worcester. He graduated from Yale in 1951 (Phi Beta Kappa), where he studied philosophy. He was also a student at the Sorbonne, Paris, and the Conservatoire Nationale de Music, where he studied to play the clarinet and was awarded the Premier Prix. After graduating, he received the Woodrow Wilson Fellowship and continued his education at Harvard, where he earned his masters and doctoral degrees in philosophy.
>
> Schön pioneered the concepts of 'the learning organization' and 'the learning society', which Peter Senge (see later in the chapter) expanded upon in his influential book, *The Fifth Discipline*.
>
> One of Schön's pioneering ideas was to explore the extent to which companies, social movements and governments were learning systems—and how those systems could be enhanced. He suggests that the movement toward learning systems is, by necessity, 'a groping and inductive process for which there is no adequate theoretical basis.' A business firm, D.A. Schön argues, is a striking example of a learning system. He charts how firms move from being organized around four products toward integration around 'business systems'. He makes the

case that the technologies of particular products and the systems built around them are in a constant state of flux. Crucially, D.A. Schön and Chris Argyris further developed a number of important concepts with regard to organizational learning. Of particular importance for later developments was their interest in feedback and single- and double-loop learning.[5]

According to D.A. Schön, institutions are characterized by 'dynamic conservatism'—a tendency to fight to remain the same.[6] Belief in the stable state, he suggested, was belief in '[...] the unchangeability, the constancy of central aspects of our lives, or belief that we can attain such a constancy.'[7] Such beliefs are strong and deep, and provide a bulwark against uncertainty. However, with technical change continuing exponentially, the pervasiveness and intensity of dynamic conservatism becomes 'uniquely threatening to the stable state'. Schön's central argument was that 'change' was a fundamental feature of modern life and that it is necessary to develop social systems that can learn and adapt.

In his book *Beyond the Stable State,* Schön addresses the challenge of designing public policy in societies that are undergoing rapid change and are growing increasingly complex. Schön argued that we have to understand the shift from being a stable society to one which is fundamentally unstable due to the accelerating pace of change facing industrial societies. This calls for new ways of thinking for both individuals and society as a whole. He shows how the old command and control models will become increasingly inappropriate and that 'network' type organizational designs will replace hierarchical models. This would apply to the business world as well to the government. We had to redesign our organizations to facilitate learning.

'Social systems must learn to become capable of transforming themselves without intolerable disruption. But they will not cease to be dynamically conservative—not if dynamic conservatism is the process through which social systems keep from flying apart at the seams. A learning system, then, must be one in which dynamic conservatism operates at such a level and in such a way as to permit change of state.'[8]

Our systems need to maintain their identity and their ability to support the self-identity of those who belong to them, but they must

> at the same time be capable of frequently transforming themselves without intolerable threat to the essential functions the system needs to fulfil for the self.[9]
>
> As for policymaking, the implications of his analysis were clear: for governments to become learning systems, both the social system of agencies and the theory of implementation must change. The government cannot play the role of the 'experimenter for the nation', seeking first to identify the correct solution, then training society at large in its adoption. The opportunity for learning is primarily in discovering systems at the periphery, not in the nexus of official policies at the centre. The centre's role is to detect significant shifts at the periphery, to pay explicit attention to the emergence of ideas in good currency, and to derive policy ideas by induction. The movement of learning is as much from periphery to periphery, or periphery to centre, as it is from centre to periphery. The centre comes to function as a facilitator of society's learning, rather than as society's trainer.[10]

## Dynamic Conservatism in Action

*The case of the US Navy and the Telescopic Sight*

Schön narrates a fascinating instance from US naval history, wherein a revolutionary invention, later known as the 'telescopic sight' and thoroughly obvious in its utility, was held up by the navy for many years, till the president forced it down the navy's throat.[11]

Elting E. Morison, in his paper 'A Case Study in Innovation' describes the navy's resistance to change. He explains how 'the governing fact in gunfire at sea is that the gun is mounted on an unstable platform, a rolling ship.'[12] In 1899, five ships of the North Atlantic Squadron fired five minutes each at a lightship hulk at the conventional range of 1600 yards. After 25 minutes of banging away, two hits had been made on the sails of the elderly vessel. Six years, later one naval gunner made fifteen hits in one minute at a target 75-feet by 25-feet at the same range—1600 yards; half of them hit in a bull's-eye 50 inches square. [In those six years] many of the uncertainties were removed from the process and the position of the gun pointer radically altered by the introduction of continuous-aim firing.

And yet, the top brass of the navy refused to have anything to do with this potentially revolutionary invention till the President of the United States, Theodore Roosevelt, had to step in and have the navy test the telescopic sight. Why did the navy have this resistance to change? As Morison asks in more grand terms, 'Why should virtually all the rulers of a society so resolutely seek to reject a change that so markedly improved its chances for survival in any contest with competing societies?'[13]

Morison diagnosed the problem as below:

> [...] It is possible now to examine the evidence to see what light it may throw on our present interest: the origins of and responses to change in a society [...] Let us examine the reasons for what must be considered the weird response we have observed to this proposed change. Why this deeply rooted, aggressive, persistent hostility from Washington that was only broken up by the interference of Theodore Roosevelt? Here was a reform that greatly and demonstrably increased the fighting effectiveness of a service that maintains itself almost exclusively to fight. Why then this refusal to accept so carefully documented a case, a case proved incontestably by records and experience? Why should virtually all the rulers of a society so resolutely seek to reject a change that so markedly improves its chances for survival in any contest with competing societies? There are the obvious reasons that will occur to all of you—the source of the proposed reform was an obscure, junior officer 8000 miles away; he was, and this is a significant factor, criticizing gear and machinery designed by the very men in the bureaus to whom he was sending his criticisms. And furthermore, Sims was seeking to introduce what he claimed were improvements in a field where improvements appeared unnecessary. Superiority in war, as in other things, is a relative matter, and the Spanish-American War had been won by the old system of gunnery. Therefore, it was superior even though of the 9,500 shots fired at various but close ranges, only 121 had found their mark.[14]

The unexpressed reason, Schön analyses, for the navy's reluctance to accept this new 'firing mechanism' on its battleships, was that it would have totally destroyed (as it did later) a well-established social system built around the old technology. For instance, there were 12 sailors who 'managed' each gun and who would surely become redundant when telescopic sight enabled one sailor to do the job, and do it immensely better than the 12. In other words, the basic paradigm around which the life of the battleship was built, and the dynamic conservatism which fiercely defended it, could not absorb this new idea, which was antithetical to it. In many instances, unlike this one, there is no 'godfather' to help the idea along. Hence, the idea waits in the wings till the conditions in the prevailing ethos change to bring it within the acceptable range or make it 'an idea in good currency'.

*The Case of the American Industry and the Team Concept*

In the 1970s, an organizational innovation emerged called 'team concept' or 'technician concept' or 'socio-technical design'. Conceptualized by the Tavistock Institute of Human Relations, it was dubbed socio-technical systems (STS) by the British social scientist Eric Trist. STS was first applied in three different situations—a British coal mine, an Indian weaving mill and a ship in the Scandinavian merchant fleet. The bottom line of each organization showed such great improvement that within a decade US companies such as General Foods, Procter & Gamble and Cummins Engine had teams in factories located in Topeka, Kansas; Lima, Ohio; and Jamestown, New York, and the results were far superior to any traditional organizational design. More was to come in terms of astounding results in every metric of a firm's performance.

In his book *Megatraps: The Team Killers,* Steven Rayner comments on the results and their shocking aftermath,

> [...] The extraordinary story of the Tektronix portable oscilloscope division. Having sustained a brutal attack from overseas competition in the early eighties, the division had fought back, regaining market share and profitability. Over a two year period, the division went from the company's number one loser (rated last among Tektronix's 29 divisions with a $23 million loss on $170 million in sales) to its premiere group. The secret to success, according to the division's then vice president Fred Hanson, was remarkably simple: get your people involved. [...] Onlookers were astounded by the success of the

portables division and were anxious to replicate it. The Vancouver, Washington facility became overrun with tours, serving as a source of inspiration for senior managers from such companies as Martin Marietta, Allied Signal, Texas Instruments, TRW and Fisher Controls.

Today, the portables division no longer exists due to a massive consolidation effort. Nearly all of the senior managers who were part of the turnaround have long since left the company. Even the Vancouver, Washington facility is gone—leased, ironically, to a Tektronix competitor. [...] The experience of the portables division is by no means unique. Digital's Enfield Connecticut plant, once referred to as the "Mecca of new organization design," was shut down during a recent consolidation effort. It was one of the most publicized and well-documented examples of a team-based work system in action—a book and countless articles described its innovative management approach. When DEC announced the shutdown, people who had toured or read about the facility wrote over 1,000 letters requesting the plant be kept open.

Martin Marietta's Space Launch Systems group, which in a mere 18 months documented a savings of over $10 million through employee involvement efforts, saw its attempts to transform the organization stumble when lay-offs were announced. The list could go on and on. [...] Procter & Gamble, Kodak, IBM, ABB and Monsanto are but a few additional examples of companies that have seen the dramatic impact of the new management perspective.[15]

There are competing hypotheses as to why the team concept elicited this strange, even bizarre, reaction. Why did these firms' management shut down the programmes or plants which were yielding far superior results in every way to anything they had tried before? The author goes on to diagnose three reasons. He identifies, 'Strategic blunders, careless consolidation efforts and the inability to transfer learning,'[16] as the reasons for what Tektronix, DEC and Martin Marietta and every other firm named in the earlier paragraphs experienced.

I would humbly like to argue that though this is the right description of the consequences, it is a wrong diagnosis because the adjectives and nouns used are too benign and avoid ascribing accountability!

**Strategic blunders**: The 'mother system' did not commit a blunder, strategic or otherwise. A blunder connotes ignorance, ineptitude and unintended mistake—'They did not mean to but they erred'. No, I believe that exonerates the guilty and ignores the deep intent behind the act of abolishing the innovation or transformational change. The parent system is very consciously killing the 'foreign import' which is destabilizing the stable system.[17]

**Careless consolidation efforts**: The system is not careless in its consolidation efforts, but is very deliberate and clever in using the one approach which is politically correct in a large corporation to negate a wildly successful local effort. After all, who can dispute the merits of consolidation which will, it will be argued successfully, lower costs or keep industrial peace in the long run? 'Yes, we may lose this fancy-schamnzy innovation in the short-term and suffer a bit of loss, but in the long run it is the tried and tested and true traditional methods that will stand in good stead.' 'Let us lose the battle to win the war,' is the battle cry, but no one will be there to see if the war is won ultimately, let alone won cheaper and earlier. Once the innovation or change is removed from the scene, there is nothing to compare it to, or challenge the existing system.

And the third 'trap'—the inability to transfer learning—would be better rephrased as the 'unwillingness to transfer'. It is the system's lack of acceptance of the change agents who have neglected to 'woo' the old system, in fact, they may have flaunted their spectacular successes and thumbed their noses at the 'old fogies'. The old has its revenge, as the saying goes, 'The forest will claim the village unless the villagers are willing to negotiate with the forest.' The old system has a lot at stake in preserving the status quo; the change agents have to 'sell' the idea and convince the system that the change they propose will outweigh the losses the system will suffer in letting go of old practices.

There are other lessons to be learnt from the failures of once-exciting firms. Look at People's Express (remember them?):

> No organization structure is immune to the strains and pressures of market conditions, competitive threats or technological change regardless of how well its internal management structure operates. People Express airlines painfully realized this during the 1980s. Having

the most highly participative organization in the industry meant little in light of a major strategic error: failing to go after the business traveller market. A highly involved work force that was the envy of their competition did little to improve the company's financial position. Teams cannot cover-up for bad fundamentals or strategic blunders.[18]

Recall the 'five pillars' of transcendent leadership. The TCL is not partial to any of the five pillars—she does not embrace one at the cost of the other. People are an organization's greatest assets, but so are its customers, communities and the ogres out there called competitors and the government. Everything matters, even though at different times they have different weightages. Every time a TCL thinks one factor is being given more importance in the strategy as a whole, she asks herself what the impact of it is on the other factors, and what the impact will be on the whole system. The joint optimization of the whole system may require the sub-optimization of many sub-systems.' As the ancient Sanskrit prescription recommends, 'For the sake of a family, sacrifice an individual; for the sake of a village, sacrifice a family; for the sake of a society, sacrifice a village...' you get the drift. Let me remind you of two of my favourite proverbs, 'The greatest strength is the greatest limitation,' and, 'Take what you want, said God, and pay for it.' People's Express, and all those great firms which made the team concept such a profitable strategy for a period of time, paid for it bitterly because they neglected the other factors. The third pillar in our mantap—'our people'—cannot make up for the fifth pillar—'the world'.

## The Turbulent Environment

The most significant concept to be appreciated by the leaders of the new age with regard to the environment in the contemporary post-industrial age is the concept of the turbulent field, as set forth by Emery and Trist in 1965.[19]

First, what do we mean by 'environment'? Ackoff defines the environment of a system as a set of elements and their relevant properties which are not part of the system, but a change in any of which can produce a change in the system.[20] Thus, a system's environment consists of all the variables which can affect its state.

## Box 4.3
## The Wise Men of Change: Eric Trist

Eric Lansdown Trist, the father of the concept of the socio-technical system, was a British social scientist and leading figure in the field of organizational development. He was one of the founders of the Tavistock Institute for Social Research in London.

Emery and Trist, in their book *The Casual Texture of Organizational Environments*, emphasize at the outset that the environment itself is changing at an increasing rate and towards increasing complexity. This phenomenon can impact a system on three levels—it can impact (1) the internal relationships, (2) the interrelationships between the setting and its environment, and (3) the interrelationships between elements of the environment. The third is termed 'casual texture' by Emery and Trist. Four types of causal texture are identified which form a series in which the degree of causal texturing increases.

- Type I—The placid, randomized environment in which goals and standards are relatively unchanging
- Type II—The placid, clustered environment in which goals and standards hang together in certain ways. Strategy as distinct from tactics, emerges for the critical survival needs of the organization and centralized control is the norm;
- Type III—The disturbed-reactive environment in which several organizations compete in the environment and operations emerge as the intermediate organizational response between strategy and tactics. Decentralization is encouraged. Unlike the static types I and II, type III is dynamic
- Type IV—The turbulent and dynamic field environment, where the interdependencies and the interrelationships between environmental domains increase. The complexities are high and the impact of organizational activities tend to persist in the environment. Values emerge as organizational coping responses.

In our age and in the future, the Type IV environment will become increasingly prevalent. The high degree of uncertainty and complexity, and the emergence of values as coping responses, will make 'sensing'

> and 'interpretation' critical for making effective transactions in a Type IV environment. Time-flow adds increased uncertainty to the environment. When we view the environment as the energy-information source for the creation of any innovation or change, then the passage of time becomes a critical variable.

Heraclitus said, 'You can't step into the same river twice.' Cratylus, a disciple of Heraclitus, took is a step further and said, 'You can't step into the same river even once.' In another similar moment, Marshall McLuhan, when told of a communications conference, remarked, '...very obsolete premises by definition...by the time you can get a thousand people to hold such a meeting, conditions will already have changed. The principles will be useless.'[21] Smith and Keith sum up the problem of time-flow succinctly in the passage below,

> In the environment as information position there is an irrevocable tie with a time dimension. At time one (T1) the environment presents itself to the organization. The organization processes the information and then acts at time two (T2). Meanwhile, the environment changes through its dynamics, insofar as it is composed of organizations and individuals, and changes also because of its scanning of organizational action at time two. Consequently, the environment may be different at time three when the organization scans again. The handling of processes, changes over time, is an important and difficult methodological, theoretical, and practical problem.[22]

If we look at complexities from this perspective, we see both McLuhanesque implications and Heisenberg's 'uncertainty principle' in them. The ground shifts from under the observer (the setting) between observation and action. Also, the observation itself distorts that which is observed, so the information that one gets is already biased. Finally, one's actions on the basis of the information gathered changes the environment in ways that are unpredictable, and so the next observations (after the action) may reveal unanticipated consequences. These are complex problems that hinder a leader if she wants to forecast the future for her new or transformed setting in the environment.

The phenomena described here lies at the heart of what Emery and Trist calls '**the planner's dilemma**'.[23] Since the concept of planning itself is crucial to everything that a leader does, I now deal with the complexities of planning in the midst of a turbulent environment.

## Planner's Dilemma and the Ecological Trap

'The planner's dilemma' deals with the complexities of planning in the midst of a turbulent environment. As Emery and Trist observe:

> [...] Turbulence arises from the increased complexity and size of the total environment, together with the increased interdependence of the parts and the unpredictable connections which arise between them as a result of the accelerating but uneven change rate. This turbulence grossly increases the area of relevant uncertainty for individuals and organizations alike. It raises far-reaching problems concerning the limits of human adaptation. Forms of adaptation, both personal and organizational, developed to meet a simpler type of environment no longer suffice to meet the higher levels of complexity now coming into existence.[24]

On the basis of this analysis, he describes a 'planner's dilemma' as: '[...] The greater the degree of change, the greater the need for planning, otherwise precedents of the past could guide the future; but the greater the degree of uncertainty, the greater the likelihood that plans right today will be wrong tomorrow.'[25]

According to Emery and Trist, such dilemmas lead to what Geoffrey Vickers calls 'ecological traps'. An 'ecological trap' is what a species (or a setting) gets ensnared in, when there begins to occur 'a wild and growing disparity between the least regulation that the situation demands and the most that it permits.'[26] According to Vickers, we now seem to be approaching a point at which the changes generated within a single generation may render the skills, the institutions and the ideas which form that generation's principal heritage inept for the future.[27] This is an ecological trap whose determinants are social and cultural rather than biological.

The relevance of the concepts 'planner's dilemma' and 'ecological trap' to the management of transformational change are clear and obvious. If change calls for careful planning based on reliable data, then the VUCAI factors, which make the plans of today at best redundant and at worst wrong for the changed future, make the job of the change agent/planner more difficult. If all I can do is improve my horse and buggy when an automobile is at my door, then I have a bigger problem than just my ability to plan. My basic theory of change and the institutions that I need to create will have to change significantly.

## 2. Organizational Agnosia: 'I Don't Know, and I Don't Know that I Don't Know'

Neurologist and celebrated essayist, Oliver Sacks, writes in his book, *The Man who Mistook his Wife for a Hat*, of a patient, Dr P, a wonderful musician. Dr P could describe with excruciating detail a rose or a glove and yet could not recognize these most familiar things for what they were—he could not see these everyday objects as a whole and associate the correct word with them. But the punchline is—Dr P did not know that he did not know these articles.

This is 'double-loop ignorance' in contrast to the concept of 'double-loop learning' as formulated by Chris Argyris.[28] The US automotive industry, for the longest period of time, refused to accept or 'know' that the American consumer's love affair with big, gas-guzzling cars was over and that small cars were now their choice. This gave the Japanese the chance to swamp the US market with small fuel-efficient cars and win a large chunk of the market from the once-invincible Detroit.

American leaders and 53 per cent of the public (according to the latest polls) refuse to acknowledge such '400-pound gorillas in the room' as the deep divisions between the top 1 per cent and the 99 per cent, sky-rocketing medical care costs, declining education standards, rising gun violence caused by lax gun laws and the impending bankruptcy of a social security system which could put American senior citizens at serious risk, just when America is 'greying' at a rate faster than ever before. The list of such wilful self-deceptions is long. Europe has its own tales of woe; problems are escalating to crises.

This 'double loop' of ignorance, when a system doesn't know something, and doesn't know that it doesn't know it, make decision-making in a turbulent environment even harder.

## 3. Ignorance and Ineptitude

What do these terms mean and what do they imply for the process of change, adaptation and innovation?

Atul Gawande, a surgeon and author, explains these terms in his book *The Checklist Manifesto*,

> Gorovitz and MacIntyre point out we have just two reasons that we may nonetheless fail. [...] The first is ignorance—we may err because science has given us only a partial understanding of the world and how it works. The second type of failure the philosophers call ineptitude—because in these instances the knowledge exists, yet we fail to apply it correctly [...] Sometime over the last several decades—and it is only over the last several decades—science has filled in enough knowledge to make ineptitude as much our struggle as ignorance.
>
> Here, then, is our situation at the start of the twenty-first century: We have accumulated stupendous know-how. We have put it in the hands of some of the most highly trained, highly skilled and hardworking people in our society. And, with it, they have indeed accomplished extraordinary things. Nonetheless, that know-how is often unmanageable. Avoidable failures are common and persistent, not to mention demoralizing and frustrating, across many fields—from medicine to finance, business to government. And the reason is increasingly evident: The volume and complexity of what we know has exceeded our individual ability to deliver its benefits correctly, safely, or reliably. Knowledge has both saved us and burdened us.
>
> That means we need a different strategy for overcoming failure, one that builds on experience and takes advantage of the knowledge people have, but somehow also makes up for our inevitable human inadequacies.[29]

This pair of obstacles to change is, in our analyses, a part, but not the whole of the set of reasons why humans fail in their attempt to change. The other three 'obstacles' that we will discuss in this section are deeper systemic factors which may often masquerade as ignorance and ineptitude. The lack of political will owing to dynamic conservatism, the practice of old values such as 'divide and rule' when new values of cooperation are needed to beat the planner's dilemma and ecological trap, the inability to create learning communities and organizations, the inability to create institutions that embody the gains of successful change—all of these may be the more intractable roots of feigned ignorance or unconscious ineptitude. Yet, Dr Gawande makes a good contribution to this discourse standing on the shoulders of the two philosophers.

### 4. 'Urgent' Overwhelms 'Important'

Among the four obstacles to transformation, Number 4 is the most familiar and self-explanatory. Hence, a brief explanation would suffice. Most organizations in which executives are asked to take on change processes also expect the executives to run the organization at its best or near best—they are not allowed to slack off on targets and are still asked to champion the change process. It is like a pilot being asked to fly a Boeing 747 at 35,000 feet and, while flying, crawl onto the wings and repair the engine.

The 'urgent' most often overwhelms the 'important'. Adrenalin flows best when there is a crisis. A man goes to a doctor complaining of a common cold. The doctor examines him and says, 'I would like you to stand outside all night and come back in the morning.' The patient says, 'But it is supposed to rain all night.' The doctor replies, 'Exactly. I don't know how to cure the common cold, but I can cure pneumonia.' To catch problems young we need to learn 'how to read the tea leaves', but most often governments and corporations alike let the problems escalate into crises before scrambling for what then would inevitably be sub-optimal solutions.

### Change Leadership Mini-Cases

The success or failure of transformational change leadership is largely dependent on the wisdom of the men and women who lead, manage or consult and advise organizations and nations.

In each of the mini-cases presented here, ask yourself as you read what is the 'pain' and what is the transcendent leader doing to alleviate the pain. In each case, when they were able to go beyond their own system boundaries in their minds, they survived and even hit the jackpot; when they did not, when they defined their world narrowly, they failed or they gave away the golden opportunity to someone more prescient, or yes, transcending. As you read, please reflect upon a TCL's change strategy to transform her systems many times by transforming the environment(s).

*The Case of the Company which Never Knew How Good It Was: The Missed Opportunities—Ineptitude in Action*

Amazon introduces the book, *Fumbling the Future: How XEROX Invented, Then Ignored, the First Personal Computer* by Douglas K. Smith and Robert C. Alexander (New York: William Morrow, 1988) with the following blurb:

> Ask consumers and users what names they associate with the multibillion dollar personal computer market, and they will answer IBM, Apple, Tandy, or Lotus. The more knowledgeable of them will add the likes of Microsoft, Ashton-Tate, Compaq, and Borland. But no one will say Xerox. Fifteen years after it invented personal computing, Xerox still means 'copy'. *Fumbling the Future* tells how one of America's leading corporations invented the technology for one of the fastest-growing products of recent times, then miscalculated and mishandled the opportunity to fully exploit it. It is a classic story of how innovation can fare within large corporate structures, the real-life odyssey of what can happen to an idea as it travels from inspiration to implementation.
> 
> More than anything, *Fumbling the Future* is a tale of human beings whose talents, hopes, fears, habits and prejudices determine the fate of our largest organizations and of our best ideas. In an era in which technological creativity and economic change are so critical to the competitiveness of the American economy, *Fumbling the Future* is a parable for our times.

Computer Desk Encyclopaedia notes:

> Xerox owned the famed Palo Alto Research Center. For more than a decade, from the early 1970s into the mid-1980s, PARC yielded an astonishing volume of ground-breaking hardware and software innovations. The modern mouse, windows, and icons style of software interface was invented there, and so was the laser printer and the local-area network. PARC's series of D machines anticipated the powerful personal computers of the 1980s by a decade. Sadly, the prophets at

PARC were without honour in their own company, so much so that it became a standard joke to describe PARC as a place that specialized in developing brilliant ideas for everyone else.

The stunning short-sightedness and obtusity of XEROX's top-level suits has been well anatomized in *Fumbling The Future*.

*Xerox: The Case of the Company which Fumbled*

Anthony Bianco and Pamela L. Moore write of Xerox's fall in *Businessweek*,

> Once-hot stock. Less than two years ago, Xerox looked to be a company on a roll. Earnings were rising smartly, and investors were bidding up its shares in a market enthralled with all things tech. Xerox hit a record high of nearly $64 a share in May, 1999, just three weeks after Thoman replaced Allaire as CEO. Today, the stock trades around $7, a few dollars above the price at which it listed on the New York Stock Exchange in 1961. The evisceration of $38 billion in shareholder wealth already qualifies Xerox as a corporate catastrophe of the first order. And the company's woes are not over yet—not by a long shot.
>
> Xerox's failures to commercialize the breakthroughs made in its famous Palo Alto Research Center (PARC) in the 1970s and 1980s—including the personal computer—have been thoroughly documented […] Over the past few years the company fumbled the digital future yet again by badly underestimating the inkjet printer, a deceptively humble device around which Hewlett-Packard Co. (HWP) has built a profitable division larger now than all of Xerox […] This is the story of the management fiasco at Xerox, based on exclusive interviews with …other company executives, past and present.[30]

'The stunning short-sightedness and obtusity of Xerox's top-level suits', 'the management fiasco'—these are rather harsh words in the prosaic, staid world of business. Surely it 'is a tale of human beings whose talents, hopes, fears, habits and prejudices determine the fate of our largest organizations and of our best ideas'?

Those human beings are called leaders. The inability to look beyond their current product lines and their profitability and see the potential of what they had at PARC is at the heart of the concept of transcendence and transformational change. Though Steve Jobs and Bill Gates, and indeed the leaders at HP, could see the ideas and prototypes at this frontier of knowledge called PARC at Xerox's outpost and discern a world of dreams, Xerox could not. Leadership and the ability to envision change—this is a parable of those who had them and those who did not.

*Xerox: The Case of the Company which Triumphed*

But there has been another Xerox, very much the opposite of the fumbler described earlier. Like a phoenix rising from the ashes, Xerox lost and found itself in the early 1980s. In an interview with Joe Flower, Robert Camp remarks,

> In 1979, Xerox had a problem: it was rapidly losing market share in the copier business. Lower-priced, high quality Japanese competitors were squeezing Xerox out of an industry it had created and had always dominated. If the company that made them could not figure out something fast, Xerox copiers would go the way of Hupmobiles, Kaiser cars and Reo trucks. So Xerox Manufacturing Operations started a process they called, 'Product quality and feature comparisons.' They bought competing products, catalogued their features and claims, then tore them apart.
>
> It was the first formal 'benchmarking,' and it worked. The knowledge that the Xerox managers carried back to Rochester brought the company's costs down rapidly, without compromising quality. By 1981, the success of the manufacturing operation was so obvious that the top brass declared benchmarking to be standard operating procedure throughout the company. From Xerox, the practice spread through the 1980s, first to other manufacturing giants such as Motorola and du Pont, and later to the service sector.
>
> Robert Camp, Ph.D., who introduced benchmarking to Xerox's logistics operation in 1981, writes, 'From that moment, the annual productivity increases of Xerox's logistics rose from two or three percent to more than 10 percent—and stayed there throughout the mid-1980s.'[31]

*Genius Is a Golden Cage: The Story of Polaroid and Organizational Agnosia*

As you read this excerpt from *Yale Insights*, by Andrea Nagy Smith (November 2009) replace the word 'Polaroid' with 'Polaroid's leaders'. It is the quality of thinking, the 'theory of change', held by the leaders of Polaroid over three decades that brought down a monopoly firm to extinction.

> Polaroid went from ubiquity to obsolescence as digital photography replaced print. But as early as the 1960s, Polaroid had been researching digital imaging. Did mistaken assumptions keep the company from making the transition to the digital world?
> 
> Founded in 1937 by scientist Edwin Land, Polaroid was one of America's early high-tech success stories. In 1948, in response to a question from his young daughter, Land invented a camera that produced finished photographs in minutes. The invention was an immediate success, and over the next two decades, the instant camera became widely used. By the 1960s and early '70s, Polaroid held a monopoly in the instant photography market [...] In October 2001, Polaroid filed for bankruptcy.
> 
> Why was Polaroid unable to make the transition to digital photography? The key may have been some fundamental assumptions that did not allow the top management to adjust to new market realities [...] The leaders of Polaroid were unable to transcend the early world they had created—of chemical films and paper prints—and it's phenomenal success to a new world—of electronics and digital imaging—that was sweeping across the globe.
> 
> First, Polaroid leaders believed that customers would always want a hard-copy print. Gary DiCamillo, CEO from 1995 to 2001, said in a 2008 interview at Yale, 'People were betting on hard copy and media that was going to be pick-up-able, visible, seeable, touchable, as a photograph would be.'
> 
> When customers abandoned print, Polaroid was taken by surprise. 'It's amazing, but kids today don't want hard copy anymore,' said DiCamillo. 'This was the major mistake we all made...'
> 
> Even though it had performed thorough market research, Polaroid was unable to foresee that the photo album would be replaced by the

digital slide show [...] The leaders believed in chemistry and that 'in spite of its early research in digital photography, the company culture had a bias against electronics that went back to the days of Edwin Land.' According to former vice president Sheldon Bucker, Land was sceptical about investing in electronics [...] He, and his successor leaders ignored the 'the physics side, in contrast to instant photography, which was heavily founded in chemistry.'[32]

'The sheer profitability of film sales created another obstacle to thinking.'[33] Equally, or more probable, is the reality that lots of jobs would have been lost and careers would have been destroyed at Polaroid if the overwhelming number of chemistry experts would have to be replaced by electronics whiz kids. As in the case of the US Navy and telescopic sight, the 'dynamic conservatism' of the old leaders prevented them from seeing the writing on the wall. They did not, perhaps could not, think outside the box. They could not transcend their past selves and their once-successful creations.

According to Andrea Nagy Smith, 'When Edwin Land first invented his camera and film, he imagined that instant photography would change people's lives. He said that the camera should "go beyond amusement and record-making to become a continuous partner of most human beings... a new eye, and a second memory."'[34]

(Sadly, he, the genius who invented instant photography, came to lack a 'a new eye, and a second memory' when radical change caused by a technology revolution replaced chemistry as the way to the future of photography, and people abandoned print for an image on a screen).

*'No, You Can't Have My Cow Dung': The Case of an Idea without a Leader*

On a mellow winter morning, a group of us visited a sleepy village in Karnataka, India, to see the gobar gas plant that was supplying cooking gas to every home in the village.

The plant had been designed and set up by a famed national scientific institution. An idealistic professor had set up an NGO to find ways to use technology to aid rural development. He and his team of students trained village youth to operate the plant. It had been six months since the start of the plant and we were the 'pilgrims' seeking to see the model village.

Alas, it was not to be. As soon we arrived at the village, we realized something was amiss. No one would tell us where the headman of the 'panchayat' (village council) was. People avoided our eyes and some turned away rudely. Finally, when we reached the plant, we found it to be in a dilapidated state. It seemed barely operational. We decided to seek an explanation since we had come all the way from the big city to see the innovation which is supposed to have transformed the village. Finally, we found the chief's home. We could see the cooking gas from the plant. After being seated and fed coffee and snacks we asked, somewhat impatiently, 'What is happening with the gobar gas plant?'

The old man said, 'Were you not told? The plant is to close by the end of the week, permanently.'

We were nonplussed. The lady of the house, who seemed very intelligent, took pity on us and emerging from the kitchen, told us, 'You see, you can't run the plant without the raw material, cow dung. And only the rich people have cattle, the sources of dung.'

'So, what is the problem? You just have to ask a few of those youth who were lounging under the banyan tree to collect the dung by walking behind the cows when they were grazing and when they were in their sheds…'

'Oh, collection of dung is no problem,' said the man of the house, picking up from where the lady left off, 'but the plant was refused permission to pick up the dung.'

'But why?' We were confused. 'It is just dung, and anyway there would be this valuable gas that you will all get.'

'See, that is the problem,' said the chief, offering us beetle leaves and areca nuts, 'You city guys don't understand! It is not JUST dung—it has value as fuel in our homes and as plaster for the floors, and it even has medicinal value. We can't just give it away and let those who have no cattle get the benefit of OUR dung.'

The truth emerged in a torrent. The rich householders of the village had begun protesting the collection of dung from their cattle when they realized that the gas produced in the plant was being distributed to every home in the village, rich or poor, to everyone whether they had cattle or not.

The rich got together and decided that they couldn't let this unfair 'exploitation' of their assets be allowed to continue, the famous people from the big city notwithstanding. They forbade the collection of dung from their cattle, except for a small chunk which they felt was adequate to produce what gas they needed. Of course, this fell far short of the 'critical mass' needed to run the plant. The scientists, after making a painful attempt to persuade the 'dung capitalists', decided to close the plant for the lack of the precious raw material.

What had happened here? After all, the gas was very useful to everyone and it transformed the homes and the streets of the village. Why would the rich pull out?

As it turned out, there was a wise old man in the village who walked in just in time to enlighten us. 'You see, sirs, when the professor and his people came and proposed the idea, we were all excited and let it start. But then, there are "proper" ways to organize the leadership and the distribution of benefits. You understand, don't you? If I came to your home and said, "I see that you need food. So, all of you, domestic servants included, sit at the table and we will serve you." Will you agree? How can you sit with your servants? How can you get the same food and the same quality and quantity as those who are inferior to you? I'm sure you would have said, "I would rather not have your food than be insulted in this manner." What do you say, chief?' he asked, turning to the big man who was listening intently while chewing paan.

'You are absolutely right, uncle. We can't let tradition vanish just because of some gas or whatever. What will the world come to if we let everyone have everything? The gas should have been only for those who gave the dung; we should have been on the committee, and when the minister came, we should have been the first ones to garland him. He should have been told that it was our dung which made the plant run, not those "darlings" of the city folk.'

Let me explain this event from a theoretical angle. All systemic change is socio-technical, not just social or just technical. Transformation requires, in fact demands, the 'joint optimization of the whole system', both the technical and the social. 'The joint optimization of the whole system may require the sub-optimization of many sub-systems'. What does that mouthful of a sentence mean in this case for instance?

The new 'technical' idea (production of gas from cow dung) has to work within the existing 'social' system (class/caste). The city scientists ignored the existing social structure, its power distribution, pecking order and the culture of the village which had been shaped through times immemorial. Most importantly, the 'change agents' did not understand the 'dynamic conservatism' of the village as a system. This does not mean that they should have been a party to injustice or class prejudice or should have curried favour with the power holders. However, it does mean that in order to achieve their noble mission of improving the quality of life for the villagers by providing them clean and cheap gas for cooking and bathing and such, they needed to have factored in the sources of resistance, especially those which could prove fatal to their noble intentions. If they had included the leaders in the village in their change strategy before they launched the plant and had made them part of the solution, they would not have become part of the problem. Joint optimization here means paying close attention to the social system—the class divisions in the village—and the technical system—the collection of the raw materials (the dung) and the conversion process—and respecting the power structure in the village. To achieve this goal, the value 'all are equal', which may have been the values of the scientists from the city, had to be sub-optimized. If the leaders of the village had been asked to give inputs on the design of the whole system instead of being made to feel that they were the 'dung sources' and the passive recipients of the benefits of the innovation, if the village as a whole could have been the 'owner' of the project, the plant may have flourished long after our visit. As such, the well-meaning efforts of the good Samaritans went waste and the village went back to cooking with polluting smoke and used lanterns that deepened the darkness around them.

*The Case of an 'Almost' Leaderless Factory*

A new laundry detergent plant was set up in Lima, Ohio, a small city about 100 miles north of Cincinnati in the US. The plant featured the latest and the best computer systems and the factory was completely automated. But its truly distinguishing feature was the human systems around the technology. Lima represented a major step forward in the empowerment of the workforce.

In this instance, Procter & Gamble also valued a location near, but not too near, Cincinnati. Lima was close enough to enable corporate and division managers to keep a watchful eye on the plant, but far enough to remain independent of the company's traditional way of operating. It was protected from the imposition of existing P&G policies and the procedures or staffing models that might have threatened a new way of operating.

Planning for Lima's work system began in 1966 under a recently established corporate organizational development group formed to assist with the implementation of the technical system in the new plant and the implementation of change initiatives elsewhere. This group was a proponent of 'open systems', the notion that organizations are living, organic entities that grow through constant interaction with their environments and adapt to them. As an observer later put it, an open-system organization 'would never be "finished"; it would never stop learning and evolving during its lifetime.' The Lima plant came to embody these concepts.

Like Augusta and other new plants, Lima did not have an union, and employed salaried technicians who were assigned to relatively autonomous work teams. These work teams formed the fundamental units of organization. The only non-operating (off-line) positions were the plant manager, the managers' administrative assistant, the personal manager and the accounting manager.

The plant was divided into separate businesses for Downy and Biz, two laundry products, with work teams of technicians and managers running each. Roles within the teams were based on mastery of skills. These skills were divided into three levels: operation of equipment, maintenance of equipment, and improving the business and providing leadership to the teams. The technicians received no operating and maintenance overtime and no incentive pay. There were no first-level supervisors—just managers acting as resources to the teams. There were no barriers to stop the technicians from cooperating with each other inside the business, or outside with suppliers, or with customers or other parts of P&G.

Any technician could perform any job consistent with safe operations. The teams chose new members, decided who would do what work, what training might be required, and how it would be obtained (even on the outside), and which projects to pursue. They even interviewed prospective managers. Rotation included both on- and off-line assignments. A technician could perform not more than two non-operating jobs before returning to an operating position. Team leadership roles changed as required. The teams handled their own disciplinary matters, a responsibility they took very seriously and with standards stricter than those in traditional plants.

Lima began production in 1968 and quickly established itself as by far the most effective and productive plant in P&G's system. The plant also recorded outstanding results in quality, safety and control in absenteeism. Stories of breakthrough performance became legendary inside the company. Some of these stories were amusing. One time, a team of technical people from a supplier visited the plant to install some equipment. They were met at the gate by a technician. One of the supplier group indicated that they were supposed to meet with an electrician, a machinist and a pipe fitter from the plant to help them. 'You are looking at her,' said the technician.

On another occasion, in the early 1970s, Downy became a major success and was to be sold throughout the United States. Retailers complained about short shipments and the company promoted top division managers to look for ways to expand capacity quickly. Some believed that the Lima workforce simply lacked the skills, especially in electrical and mechanical work, and could not be trained fast enough. The division managers began making plans to hire extra technicians and skilled tradespeople in the community to help ramp up production. However, Seitz, from P&G, would have none of this. He made a two-hour drive to Lima and held a meeting with the Downy technicians to explain the situation and describe the necessary actions. Then he arranged for production to shut down for a week while the technicians made plans to run the lines faster and acquired the training to do the work themselves. After a week, the plant went live again and ran flat out to meet Downy's orders.

On still another occasion, a determined technician developed a revolutionary new process that changed the liquid fill industry. According to Seitz, the technician had watched the inefficient way that Downy bottles were filled. Bottles came in from suppliers in cases, from which they were removed, filled, capped, and then put back in cases for shipping. The technician made his proposal to the Downy team and in turn to P&G. The project was funded, and the technicians oversaw the installation and the operation of the new equipment. The process worked as designed, resulting in significant savings for P&G.

Such performance garnered widespread attention inside P&G. As a result, many other P&G operations sent visitors to observe and appropriate as many techniques and lessons as they could from the Lima plant.

*'Leaders from the Bottom? No Way!': The Case of the Schizophrenic Hospital*

Two psychiatrists, Nick J. Colarelli and Saul M. Siegel, write in their book, *Ward H: An Adventure in Innovation* (D. Van Nostrand Co., 1966), that they were despondent about one class of patients under their care in a famous mental hospital in Boston. They had a good success rate in curing or controlling every kind of mental affliction except chronic schizophrenia (CS). Whatever treatment course they adopted, the CS patients had the highest recidivism rate, meaning they returned every time they were sent out cured. They just couldn't cope with the stress of life outside the hospital. This was professionally seen as a failure for the hospital and specifically for the two psychiatrists. Equally troubling was the repeated and wasteful expense the hospital incurred every time a patient returned. Budgets were limited and there were many in the waiting list for the services of the famous hospital.

Then they hit upon an idea; a theory of change, one could call it. They hypothesized that the CS patients had failed to manage their everyday lives in the outside world because they did not know how 'normal' people lived and the rules of their world. What if they were provided 'role models' of behaviour inside the hospital who could guide them in the ways of the outside world, but more indirectly through their own savvy and natural ways? The two psychiatrists became obsessed with the idea, especially since they were at their wit's end with regard to this seemingly intractable problem. But who would be these role models who would be empowered to do everything (from drug administration to toilet routines to teaching thrift, cooking and prayers) for these CS patients in Ward H? Whoever they were, such individuals must be available to the patients for the most of each day and night. This ruled out all the higher elite of the hospitals, the psychiatrists and even the nurses. Then the eureka moment arrived. The only and obvious solution was to make the ward workers at the bottom of the totem pole part of the treatment. They were all African-American middle-aged women who were mostly single mothers with absentee husbands. Many of these ladies worked two jobs and brought up their children under the toughest circumstances. They were hard-working, honest and tough. No better role models could be found. With great excitement, the two psychiatrists proposed this major change in the treatment process. The hospital bosses agreed reluctantly since everything else had been tried.

To cut to the chase, the experiment succeeded beyond anyone's wildest dreams. The role models took their jobs and their responsibilities very seriously. In two years, the recidivism reduced spectacularly. CS patients moved out and were found to hold their own in the big bad world out there. So the hospital must have been ecstatic at this new 'treatment' strategy which solved one of the thorniest problems it had, right? Guess again. At the end of two years, when the special grant from the federal government for this project expired, the hospital administration decided not to continue the experiment. Soon the recidivism returned and it was business as usual.

You must be exclaiming, as I did the first time I read about this incident, *Why, for God's sake? How could they do this?* The answer lies in the dynamic conservatism of the hospital system. In simple English, the hospital had established a structure with rigid defined roles and hierarchy. Each role was defined by specific formal qualifications and professional experiences, and boundaries and privileges were jealously guarded. This new experiment focused on the cure of CS patients and ignored this fortress of structure. Nurses were the first to resign because they thought it undermined their position to have semi-literate orderlies, those whom they viewed as their 'social inferiors', be given this authority over the treatment of patients. The doctors (except the two 'change agents' psychiatrists) were next. To get a call from an orderly at 3 a.m. for the exact dosage of a drug for a patient in pain was just too…weird. The central kitchen was angry because patients were encouraged to cook their own food in the ward so that they learnt life skills, instead of eating in the central cafeteria. The chapel was upset because the patients had set up a shrine in their 'home' and prayed together.

The design of the change experiment 'won the battle but lost the war' because it failed to understand that the hospital as a fully functioning system had its own priorities and any sub-system under its umbrella had to accommodate those priorities. Negotiations should have been engaged in before launching the experiment and compromises should have been arrived at. Or the two good change agents should have politicked and found a 'godfather' to serve as a buffer and eventually get them enough legitimacy in the hospital to gain a place at the budgeting table.

*The Case of Failure to Sustain Change*

A young Peace Corps volunteer was posted in a Mexican village to do her internship. In a day she had found her mission—she taught everyone to boil water before drinking it. At the end of a month, she returned to her home in California. Next year, she fondly returned to the village and was welcomed with open arms by everyone. Sitting in the chief's hut, she asked for a cup of water.

When she was handed a cup of cold water she immediately asked, 'What is this, father? Why is the water not boiled?' Everyone was embarrassed.

Then the chief said, 'We will boil it right now, dear child.'

The young woman protested, 'But friends, why didn't you boil the water earlier?'

The chief explained, 'My dear child, we boiled the water when you were here because you seemed so particular and we all like you so much and we didn't want to hurt your feelings. But when you were not here, you couldn't be hurt. Now that you are back, we will boil our water again.'

Needless to say, the young 'change agent' who had felt so proud and gratified that she had helped put the village on the path to better health through her simple intervention felt bewildered and disappointed. She wondered, 'Where did I go wrong?'

Where, gentle reader, do you think she went wrong? Maybe she could have spent time with the village elders and shared her rationale for heating the water every time before drinking it (killing bacteria and such). She could have engaged them in debates so that when finally the time came for the decision ('Do we boil water or not?'), the villagers, and not the young 'un from distant California, would be the ones who would decide. And if they had been convinced and had said, 'Yes, we must all boil water before drinking,' it would have been their decision, not an outsider's, however well-meaning the do-gooder was.

Let those who have to implement the change and 'suffer' the consequences of the change, good, bad or indifferent, be intimately involved in the implementation of the change.

**Learning Organizations and Systems Thinking**

According to Peter Senge, 'Learning organizations' are those organizations where people continually expand their capacity to create the results they truly desire, where new and expansive patterns of thinking are nurtured, where collective aspiration is set free, and where people are continually learning to see the whole together.'[35] He argues that only those organizations that are able to adapt quickly and effectively will be able to excel in their field or market. In order to be a learning organization, two conditions are mandatory: the first is the ability to design the organization to match the intended or desired outcomes, and second, the ability to recognize when the initial direction of the organization is different from the desired outcome and the flexibility to follow the necessary steps to correct this mismatch. Organizations that are able to do this are exemplary.

---

**Box 4.4**

**The Wise Men of Change: Peter Senge**

Peter Michael Senge, born in 1947, is an American scientist and director of the Center for Organizational Learning at the MIT Sloan School of Management.

According to Peter Senge, there are four challenges in initiating changes: There must be a compelling case for change. There must be time to change, there must be help during the change process. Lastly, as the perceived barriers to change are removed, it is important that some new problem, not considered important before, or perhaps not even recognized, doesn't become a critical barrier.

Senge also believed in the theory of 'systems thinking', which has sometimes been referred to as the cornerstone of learning organizations. Systems thinking focuses on how the individual who is being studied interacts with the other constituents of the system. Rather than focusing on the individuals within an organization, it prefers to study the interactions within the organization and in between organizations as a whole.

## The Process of Transformational Change in Nine Steps

In this book, I present two sets of ideas: 'Ways of Thinking' and 'Ways of Doing'. This section is about the ways of doing. I present a 9-step process for the life cycle of a transformation process. (Figure 4.1)

I will NOT discuss each step; instead I define the first three steps in detail because they lay the foundation of the transformation process. The next six steps are self-explanatory, and I would not insult your intelligence by defining the obvious. However, they are concerning the implementation of change and for these cyclical steps I present the major factors which influence the birth of change—the communication processes before and during the change process, change as a helix, the 'journey through hell', the phases of five feelings for the people in a change process, which is 'change of the people, by the people, for the people', resistance to change, and organization culture. Now, back to the first three steps: We need to change; we want to change; this is what we want to change. These three steps are the 'iceberg underneath the water'—the critical prerequisites for effective change. We need to ask ourselves these three questions: do we need it? Do we want it? Are we willing to be committed to it?

We start with a generic organization structure for the management of change. What are the roles and relationships that need to created for the change process? (Figure 4.2)

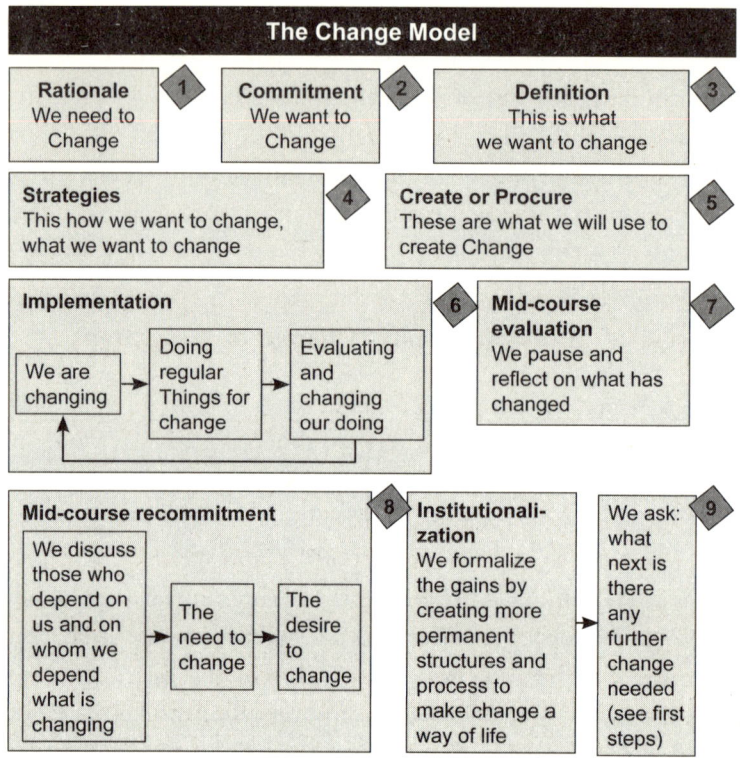

*Figure 4.1: The Change Model*

## Designing Change—Content and Process
## Structure of the Change Management System

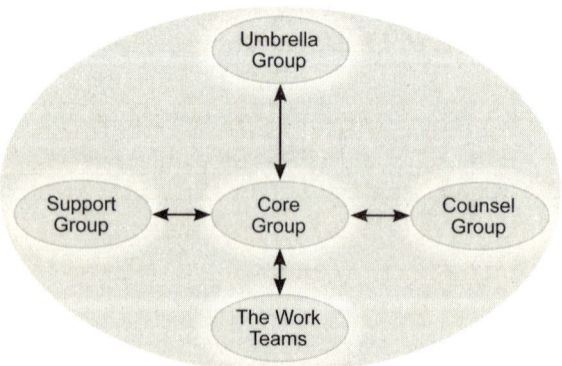

*Figure 4.2: The Structure for Participative Design*

## The Participative System

The leader ought to first formally create a group that could be called an icon, a blessing group or the 'holy water' group, those who need to say, 'We agree with the concept of this change, and we believe there are resources.' They are the resource givers, and these are also the people who would be willing to be the senior partners in the change journey. They provide the vision, the inspiration, the resources and the mandate; they don't give it unilaterally—it may come from here to there—but ultimately the approval of the vision, the resources and the inspiration should come from there.

Second, the core group: this should be a combination of consulting resources and key people in the organization (typically the top management of the unit that is being changed, but not necessarily so) and internal and external consultants, if any. This core group will aid the facilitation of the change process itself. It is the group that integrates data, the group that synthesizes efforts and, most important of all, it is the group that is the conscience of the organization in terms of telling somebody that tomorrow is the deadline for that report. The group should also be able to point out that the emperor is wearing no clothes, and it should be able to serve as an umbrella group, a formal group which keeps the execution of the change process on track.

The other two groups here are support groups. It is important to formally create the kind of support resources you need and to have a contract with them, so you don't get stuck as the process goes up. Advisory groups, though often ignored, are equally important. They are usually not formal groups, but every organization needs wise old birds (old and young) who seem to know where it is at, and what it is all about. They are the politically savvy who have the wisdom to say, 'Don't step on these toes; you won't even know what hit you.' These are the people you talk to after the day is over, saying, 'Will you have a beer with me, I want to sort something out?' I call this a therapy group. It is wise for a good TCL to have personal therapy groups with whom she can let her hair down. Finally, and most importantly, the proof of the pudding is readily in the implementation groups. I call them cylinder groups because many a time they go down into the organization, across all sectors of the organization. This is where the real game happens, and all of these are support groups.

## Implementing the Change Process

It is worth quoting Charles F. Knight, Chairman and CEO of Emerson Electric Company,

> When I meet with people outside Emerson, I'm often asked 'What makes Emerson tick?' [...] We believe we can shape our future through careful planning and strong follow up.
>
> Our managers plan for improved results and execute to get them [...] We adhere to few policies or techniques that could be called unique or unusual. But we do act on our own policies, and that may indeed make us unusual.[36]

The emphasis on doing (execution, follow-up and implementation) is clearly important for successful change efforts. The best vision and design can fail because of the lack of effective implementation.

Let us now start with the steps in a transformation process, the first two of which influence the other eight steps:

## 1. Rationale: 'Why Do We Need to Change?'

Most successful change processes, for better or for worse, seem to arise out of fear rather than out of a positive need or out of the desire for growth. It may be an inherited reaction—'fight or flight' was the reaction of our ancestors. It still seems to be that if things are going well, 'if it ain't broke don't fix it,' is the norm.

There are at least three major conditions under which organizations seem to change rapidly, willingly or unwillingly:

### a) Significant Market and Customer Change

Any organization's survival is closely tied to its ability to respond to its market's needs. The market is the master in a modern free-market economy and the business organization is its shadow. This means that when its market—the quantity and quality of customers—changes in a non-trivial manner and affects stakeholders, then the organization has to change to cope with the market change, or else fail or disappear.

*The Case of the Poor Programmer and the Rich Computer Owner: India and the West*

In the 1990s, American industry felt the pinch of costs and the lure of cheap services from India's information industry was too good to ignore. Competitively, it was a domino; once one player in an industry outsourced his IT projects, the others had to follow suit, or else the higher costs drove them out of the market. Hence, a whole new industry grew in a very poor country—India. In fact, this development was the precursor, harbinger and the symbol and substance of India's move onto to the world stage as the world's fourth largest economy. The trend reversed recently when the political wind shifted, and US companies were forced to rethink their outsourcing policies in terms of rising unemployment rates in the US. Generating more jobs for Americans became the new slogan. The impact of this change—the loss of business from the US—may be wrenching for India and may also drive many US firms out of business owing to higher costs.

*The American Civil War and the 'Mini-Indian Industrial Revolution': The Case of the 'No Permanent Friends but Only Permanent Interests'*

In 1860, the American Civil War erupted and Northern ships blockaded the Atlantic passage to prevent British ships from importing cotton from the Southern states. Mills in Lancashire were starved of their raw materials and Britain had to rethink the supply chain.

As the saying goes, 'Britain had no permanent friends but only permanent interests.' At the time, the jewel in the crown of the British Empire was India, which had just emerged from the Sepoy Mutiny (as the British called it) or the First War of Indian Independence (as the Indians called it). The western state of Gujarat saw high cotton production. Queen Victoria had taken over the colony from the English East India Company and the Empire needed to continue the exploitation of India for the good of Britain. (Enough partisan polemics, get on with it, man). So, the British contracted cotton farmers in Gujarat to supply their mills and lo and behold, the first modern Indian industry was born. Overnight, enterprising Gujarati entrepreneurs sprang up, rose to the occasion and created the textile industry in India. Indian cotton was coarser than American cotton, but beggars can't be choosers, and the British mill owners substituted Indian cotton for the American variety for the most part.

Never before had the Empire permitted the fruits of the Enlightenment and the Industrial Revolution to trickle to India from Europe. The new industry spawned a robust free market for every product under the sun, including speculation. Millionaires were born overnight in the cotton state. But alas, the sudden bonanza for India did not last long. In a mere four years, when the Civil War ended in 1864, Americans lifted the blockade in the Atlantic. Eager, even desperate, to recover the lost business and rebuild the South, now that there was no more blockade in the Atlantic, America began trading with the British again. The British instantly dumped Indian cotton and went back to buying cotton from the Southern States. But the story did not end there.

The withdrawal of British business from Gujarat was disastrous for almost, but not all, the new entrepreneurs. Most were ruined and many probably jumped off tall buildings (as in the tulip crisis in the Netherlands in 1637) barely four years after India had acquired the infrastructure and the technology. However, a few hardy Indians held on to their resources and sowed the seeds of a modern industrial state. Ahmadabad in Gujarat (Gandhiji's home state—his caste, the baniyas, were said to be savvy merchants) and Bombay in Maharashtra became the centres of the modern textile industry in India.

*The Case of the Milk Cans in Chicago*

'From 1885 to 1966 the Bowman milkmen were a familiar sight to Chicagoans as they delivered dairy products to homes, first by horse-drawn wagons and then by trucks. During these years the Bowman Dairy Company grew rapidly, becoming one of the largest dairies in Chicago [...] At one time, Bowman Dairy Company was the largest home-deliverer of milk in the world.'[37]

The company was hit with serious problems 'resulting from a fundamental shift in consumer patterns of purchasing milk. Bowman, the largest deliverer of milk to homes in Chicago, found consumers increasingly abandoning home-delivery in favour of grocery store purchases.

The problem became acute when the Teamster (a labour union in the US and Canada) adamantly opposed any cut in the number of home-delivery routes in order to protect the jobs of unionized milk deliverers. In 1959, the parent firm, Bowman Dairy, began to lose money.'[38]

The cost of home delivery was calculated on the basis of the number of cans delivered to that household, a legacy left over from the days when horse-drawn wagons carrying milk cans were used and the delivery man would walk up to the door and place the can at the door of the customer.

Once the grocery store around the corner started stocking milk, housewives began to pick up milk at the store, along with their other groceries and for a lesser price. Without the additional cost of home delivery, store-bought milk was cheaper. On the other hand, because of their 'dynamic conservatism', the Teamster's Union insisted on keeping the home delivery routes unchanged in order to preserve the income levels of its members. This was a 'zero-sum game', a lose-lose proposition in which both the company and the union lost finally, the company closed and the union members were left unemployed or were forced to accept lesser wages.

Let me get on my soapbox here.

Transcendent leadership, anyone? Gentle reader, do you see my point that true leadership in this case on the part of both, the Bowman Company and the IBT, would have meant transcending their insular parochial vested interests and creating a joint plan to save the business and save jobs? Any idea what you would have done if you were the supreme leader in this case?

And finally, '...eventually losses in the home delivery sector of the business forced the company out of the dairy business, which was sold to Dean Foods in 1966.'[39]

## b) Change in Technology

Significant technological change in the environment may make the organization suddenly wake up, or if it does not wake up early enough, sleep forever. Instances abound. In the can industry, technology changed and people moved from making two-piece cans to three-piece cans. What had been an enormously complex technology had become so simple that customers could afford to own their own facilities to make cans. The canmakers woke up late and were left 'holding the can' (pardon the pun). They paid a steep price for not preparing for this momentous change in technology. Similarly, Polaroid lost its pre-eminent position when the SX film technology proved increasingly costly and uncompetitive, and newer technologies in every aspect of photography overtook and overwhelmed Polaroid.

The can industry moved from 3-piece cans to 2-piece cans, from glass to aluminium, the introduction of 6-packs, and the battle for supermarket shelf-space...what next for cans?

Bear with me. If you can, then I can tell you about a can. What are cans like? To find out more, read about the history of the can below, as provided by the Can Manufacturers Institute.

*The History of the Can*[40]

The can's distinguished history began in 1795 when the French government, led by Napoleon, offered a prize of 12,000 francs to anyone who could invent a method of preserving food for its army and navy. In 1809, Nicolas Appert, 'the father of canning,' received the prize for preserving food by sterilization.

Major cans are classified into two types. Three-piece cans consist of three components: (1) a bottom lid, (2) a cylindrical body and (3) a top lid (with an opening for a beverage can). Two-piece cans consist of two components: (1) a body integrated with a bottom lid and (2) a lid with an opening. A technique called double seaming is used to attach the can lids to the can body in such a way that the contents are protected from external contamination. Three-piece cans are made of a rectangular sheet rolled into a cylindrical body and lids are attached either by soldering or electric welding.

Welded cans dominate the market while soldered cans have almost disappeared from the market. Two-piece cans are further classified depending on their body processing method: drawn cans, DWI cans (draw and wall-ironing cans) and TULC (stretch-draw-ironing cans).

Notice the evolution since the invention of a can by the can industry:

The beverage can itself was not developed until 1930. Made from tin plate, it was due to technology changes that this invention became possible. British producers introduced beverage cans shaped like bottles that were constructed from three pieces of metal and featured a cone shaped top. In 1964, the two-piece draw and wall-ironed (DWI) can was developed in the United States. This was an important step forward, since it used less metal than the traditional three piece can. The 1960s also saw the rise of the motorcar. Big changes took place in the automotive industry and more and more people and families owned cars. This meant that days out were also becoming more popular. Road trips, day trips and picnics were on the rise and cans were the most suitable way to transport beverages while out and about.

The 1970s saw the demise of the returnable system, a deposit structure for take home beer and soft drinks, which had been primarily sold in bottles. This system largely disappeared in the 1970s due to a rise in family incomes, resulting in people being less incentivised by small deposits as well as wide-scale recognition of the convenience of one-way packs to both consumers and retailers.

Social attitudes had changed, but so had supermarkets. There were a larger variety of products available, and therefore, less space on shelves. Beverage cans were right for the time and place, as they could be stacked and displayed easily and in different ways. The large surface area for printing designs was perfect for on-shelf display. The result escalated growth in the use of drinks cans.

The 1970s also saw multipacks become increasingly popular, specifically in beer. Consumers were offered greater convenience with the rise of the multipack and unit purchases saw an increase.

The two piece DWI cans were launched [...] Ringpull ends, developed in the 1960s, became readily available in the 1970s, meaning the drinks can became much easier for consumers to open.

Canned soft drinks were first dispensed in vending machines in 1961, joining glass bottle and paper cup machines, and by the late 1960s, dominated the vending market. Some years later, in a popular series of national television ads, both space aliens and supermodel Cindy Crawford would choose cans of Pepsi from a vending machine.

By 1985, the aluminium can was the most popular beverage package in any market. Today's consumers buy soft drinks from their grocery stores in aluminium cans four times as often as in plastic bottles, and thirty-eight times as often as in glass bottles.[41]

We can multiply the examples. Would you, reader, adduce examples? Please send me your examples for all three categories, if you do not mind. Here are more:

*Polio Society—From Death to Resurrection*

The universal killer, polio, was overnight declared cured with the discovery of Jonas Salk's vaccine. With the vaccine, the central mission for the world's largest voluntary organization, the Polio Society, vanished. There was no more reason for it to exist. Two years later, and after intense community involvement, there appeared 'Multiple Sclerosis Society', a new avatar for the once-Polio Society. With a new cause, and the journey began once again with the three Is—integrity, intensity and intelligence.

*'Telescopic Sight' and the US Navy (Dynamic Conservatism)*

See the case of the US navy and telescopic sight described under 'dynamic conservatism'. It is a perfect illustration for change forced on an organization by the change in technology.

*Computerized Printing for the* New York Times *and* Washington Post

The two most famous newspapers in America, the *New York Times* and *Washington Post*, were the last to enter the age of computers in terms of printing. The opposition by the union prevented this radical change till the management negotiated a contract which paid printers a free in return for letting the papers launch computerized printing. One of the 75 workers who was part of this golden handshake is supposed to have done a PhD in Sanskrit at Columbia University.

c) Leadership (Internal)

Change in leadership: organizations seem to get unfrozen when the top of the house changes. That is why new presidents have honeymoon periods. Within organizations, in terms of organizational design and power distribution, we are at the stage that the medieval world was in, in terms of politics. The power to make decisions is restricted to the top of the power hierarchy, and therefore, all of us who have spent large parts of our careers in organizations realize that there is no such concept or practice as organizational democracy. No, what we have in the world of organizations are oligarchies. True, there have been experiments in 'industrial democracy' (as seen in the significant work by Trist, Emery, Rice, Thorsrud, Davis, Cherns and others from institutions such as the Tavistock Institute, London, UCLA, and Work Institute, Oslo), but from personal participation, one observes that even when these experiments have had spectacular results, they have needed the prerequisite of the top management's full commitment. When there is a shift in the power structure within a company, there are fundamental changes in terms of the rational visions of the organization. When this happens, this is the most propitious opportunity for change. It will not last long—most leaders realize that six months to a year is the honeymoon period, beyond which they have to earn their stripes.

As for examples to illustrate this cause for change, all the cases in the chapter on 'transcendent leadership' are just the ones for this category. 'The Case of Little Jack who Suddenly Grew Up' is an instance wherein the firm was saved and prospered because of leadership change. The list of '10 Great Companies that Lost Their Edge' are negative examples of the disproportionate impact a leader can have on the change process—its vision and its execution. Xerox, Polaroid and any number of cases that you can think of in your experience belong in this change category. However, two critical central points are to be made here:

a) A leader of an organization is not omnipotent, nor is she omniscient. The proposition presented here is just that a leader can be the major source of transformational change, but it does not by any means imply that she will succeed or fail just because she initiates change. There may be other 'actors' in the drama of change. In fact, the central theme of this book is that an organization is a socio-technical system and that there are many domains, in and out of the system, which directly and indirectly act on it, sometimes in collusion, and sometimes independently of one another. The author's article, 'Open Systems Planning',[42] offers a strategic planning process for a holistic and integrated diagnostic and execution plan.

b) None of the above causes for change—market/customers, technology, leader—act alone; most often the forces use each other for greater impact. Wisdom, that quality which distinguishes a TCL from the rest, is not some mysterious gift bestowed upon a chosen few, but can be learnt by studying and practising systems thinking. This book repeatedly emphasizes the need to look 360 degrees at any issue before honing in on the specific domain, or aspect of a domain, which deserves special attention at that moment. Like the director of an opera in a great theatre who uses the spotlight to draw attention to different characters at different times but always knows, in his mind's eye, where everyone is and who next and next and next must be spotlighted, a TCL does her 'five pillars homework'—work on self, work on key interpersonal relationships, work on the team(s), review the strategies at the level of the firm, and finally asks, 'What does all this mean in the larger scheme of things? What is that relevant larger scheme? How are we faring in that larger world where we are but a speck (but a speck with a vision)?'

*CEMEX and the Cement Revolution (IT and Organization Design)*

In 2004, CEMEX received the Wharton Infosys Business Transformation Award for its creative and efficient use of information technology.

CEMEX is one of the world's largest building materials' suppliers and cement producers. Founded in Mexico in 1906, CEMEX has operations all over the world, with production facilities spanning 50 countries in North America, the Caribbean, South America, Europe, Asia and Africa. Lorenzo Zambrano is the company's current Chairman and CEO. About one-third of the company's sales come from its Mexico operations, a quarter from its plants in the US, 15 per cent from Spain and smaller percentages from its plants around the world.

A Stanford graduate, Zambrano, transformed a third-world manufacturing system into a world-class process with the use of information technology and a team-based organization design. At the height of the boom in CEMEX stocks, Wall Street analysts attributed its success to these two radical innovations. Zambrano's vision and execution has made CEMEX a global giant in its industry.[43]

Do you remember some of the cases we reviewed earlier—the case of little Jack, Steve Jobs, and India before and after Gandhi? The closest to a law of change in systems seems to be as follows: for creating change, there ought to coalesce an optimal mixture of frustration and hope.

Yes, you recognize this vaguely? You have seen this 'formula' before? How right you are! This is the same potent mixture I presented as one of the major causes for the unleashing of RORE.

There are those who say that if there is enormous misery in the organization, it would give rise to change, but below a certain level of hope, people do not have the energy to contribute to change. In a hopeless situation, each person looks out only for himself or herself; there is no momentum or motivation. The battery just won't charge. On the other hand, why do so many children of enormously rich parents never become greatly successful? Partially because there is not enough frustration or pain.

In most societies, it is the middle class which is the source and fountain of accomplishment. The ones in the middle truly have frustration ('I am as good as that richer boss; why am I not in his chair?') and because they have climbed the ladder of success and have caught glimpses of the 'promised land of prosperity', they have hope. ('I am as good as he, and I will make it up there.') The middle class believes, based on their experience, that they can make it.

While creating a strategy for change, if a leader does not find enough frustration or hope, she has to create them. A leader who wants to transform—or else she is not a leader but an administrator—her system must find the rationale to convince people that change is needed. It is never difficult to find pains and problems! She must diagnose the situation and come up with reasons as to why there are pains and problems and why they ought to be addressed. On the other hand, it is necessary to create hope too! A leader must seem to hold out the manna from heaven. From Moses leading his people out of Egypt to a CEO trying to save her company from the ravages of the stock market and globalization, and the political leader of a nation (developing or developed) trying to deliver the millennium development goals to her people while preserving her power base, the maxim is the same: create a vision of a better future based on an optimal mixture of frustration and hope. 'When a job is undertaken, not only will the consequences have to be examined; what will be the consequence if it is not done is also to be determined,' says the ancient scriptural wisdom in the Hindu epic, *Vidura Smrithi*.

## 2. Commitment: 'We Want to Change'

For major change efforts, 'needing the change' is the first step, a necessary but not sufficient condition for launch. The 'pain' or the 'gain' needs to be felt. The question, which needs to be answered, is set, but the answer has not appeared yet. This need has to be 'owned' by the stakeholders (the management and shareholders of a company, and the leaders and citizens of a country). They must want the change. This step is not by any means inevitable. Just because I may need to change does not mean I may not want to change. A smoker may have all the medical evidence to convince him that he must quit smoking or else he will suffer, but as vouchsafed by millions of smokers, there may be no will to change. Every kind of addict (drugs, food, sex or gambling) would rather pay the price of their addiction than motivate themselves to quit.

Here we have to distinguish between not wanting to change and wanting to but being unable to change. (As Mark Twain said, 'It is easy to quit smoking. I have done it hundreds of times.') Here we stress the former, 'not wanting to change'. If there is a genuine desire to change, then the real transformational journey begins. The rest of this chapter is focused on that journey. But the question is, how do you create a 'want' in those who are to be either a) sponsors (the power-holders in the system to be changed, the resource-givers, the vision-creators)' b) the implementers of change (the ones who have to 'do it', who have to deliver the change in its nitty-gritty); or c) its 'victims' or beneficiaries (those who would be affected by the change in direct and indirect ways)?

The role of the 'sponsor' is described in detail earlier in the section on 'Structure for Change'. All serious transformation processes absolutely require the involvement and commitment of the top management of the system to be changed. Whether the impetus or incentive for change comes from the middle or from the bottom of the hierarchy, the support of the sponsors is absolutely necessary. It is the understanding and enthusiastic support of those who hold organizational power to withhold resources or 'open the spigot' that is the key determinant to the fate of the project. The ushering in of the tele-communications age in India happened almost solely because a 'prophet'—a man called 'Sam' Pitroda who had an obsessive idea to sell—was given a blank cheque to 'do his thing' by the most powerful man in India at that time, the Prime Minister of India, Rajiv Gandhi. Without such a sponsor, even the most brilliant of change agents would fail and the change effort will be stillborn, as countless thinkers, inventors and innovators know to their utter grief.

The 'prophet' is the one with the 'bee in her bonnet'. In fact, the prophet has, and is, the bee. She is the Steve Jobs of every change effort, perpetually, obsessively, even irritatingly steeped in the core idea of transforming some specific thing in the whole wide universe. Most importantly, the prophet supplies the energy to push the idea to the forefront with her commitment and dedication. As D.A. Schön observes, 'At the root of most innovations significant enough to precipitate a change of state, there are individuals who display irrational commitment, extraordinary energy, a combativeness which enables them to battle established interest over long periods of time, and a remarkable skill at guerrilla warfare.'[44] The role of the 'prophet/sensor' at the periphery in the figure 3.2 is the embodiment of the individual described in the foregoing statement.

**Whose Problem Are You Solving, the Company's or Yours?**

Once the leader/change agent has confirmed that there is a 'felt need' on the part of the stakeholders, once the 'why' for the change has been answered, she must confirm that they in fact do want 'it'. But what is 'it'? (One is reminded of the sophistry of the most colourful of Presidents of the United States who famously replied to a special prosecutor, 'It depends on what "is" is.') The leaders must attempt to accurately and objectively define the problem which the change effort intends to resolve. In the next step, the change agent would have to create a definition for what has to be changed. Unless there is a clear 'first definition'[45] shared, understood and accepted by the key sponsors and the prophets, change would be impossible.

## Communicate, Communicate, Communicate—The Principle of 'Optimal Redundancy'

If the people affected by a process and responsible for the implementation of it do not feel empowered to give their inputs, the change falls through as soon as the external influences which provide the motivation for it are withdrawn.

Doris Goodwin, in her book *Team of Rivals,* comments, 'Lincoln understood that the greatest challenge for the leader in a democratic society is to educate public opinion. With public sentiment nothing can fail; without it nothing can succeed. Consequently, he who moulds public sentiment goes deeper than he who enacts statutes or pronounces decisions.'[46]

More recently, two top leaders (chairman Paul Allaire and CEO Anne Mulcahy) of the famous Xerox Corporation, faced with a severe downturn, engaged in a turnaround strategy. Here are a few excerpts from a case study by ICMR:

> Xerox Corp. (Xerox), the world's largest photocopier manufacturer had been in trouble since the late 1990s. Between April 1999, when G. Richard Thoman became CEO, and May 2000, Xerox lost $20 billion in stock market value. […] 'I'm 100 per cent confident in this company's ability to return to financial health and build a growth trajectory,' [says] Anne Mulcahy, CEO, Xerox Corp in August 2001.[47]

Here is how they responded to the situation:

> Even before the reorganization plan was revealed to the public, Allaire and Mulcahy spent a lot of time travelling in the US and overseas to meet and talk with as many Xerox employees as possible and prepare them for the changes that were going to happen. They held meetings, teleconferences and even large town meetings to help employees

understand the situation Xerox was in, what the leadership planned to do, and how that would affect them. According to Mulcahy, keeping the communication lines open with employees and maintaining high visibility built employee confidence in her leadership and her ability to execute the turnaround strategy. Mulcahy said, 'It was pretty wearing, but if people understand your leadership style and you earn credibility, you get permission to take a lot of actions. When you're in a situation like ours, that confidence dramatically affects your ability to pull off change.' Mulcahy started sending out a regular memo called 'Turnaround Talk' to keep employees informed about the changes taking place in the company [...][48]

The communication has to be about the why/what of the change process. It encompasses VISTAR—the vision, strategy, structure, action plans and review—of the organization.

This strategic planning process is described below. If we, and the 50 leaders I interviewed, are convinced that vision is a necessity and a leader ought to create one in collaboration with the key stakeholders, then it is time for a 'how to' manual. What follows is the introduction to a process used with great effectiveness for the transformation of more than 500 organizations in corporate, development and political sectors. In the time-honoured and contemporary tradition, I have provided slides from a PowerPoint presentation from an initial workshop. (A digression: why are these called 'power points'? Does it mean the presenter has power and he is pointing us towards something? Why only power? How about meaning, clarity and insight…? I seek to be enlightened about the etymology of this near-ubiquitous corporate term).

## VISTAR

In simple terms, VISTAR attempts to answer three fundamental questions on the existence and functioning of organizations through deliberate and intensive processes. The three questions are as follows:

1. Why: Why does an organization exist? What is its purpose? The answers to this question will be the vision and the goals of the organization.
2. What: What has the organization to do to reach its vision? The answers

to these questions will be the goals/objectives or the project with metrics.
3. How: How will the organization achieve its goals? The answer to this question will provide the necessary strategies, structures, processes and action plans.

The process of VISTAR helps create an overall diagnostic, planning and execution blueprint to maintain a sustained effort to achieve optimum results. To create a VISTAR process suitable to your organization, first put together a workshop which will be attended by the chief stakeholders in the change process. Collect data and feedback from all the participating functionaries in the workshop through a well-designed questionnaire with open-ended questions. The answers to the questions are collected and collated well ahead of the workshop and these form an important input for the workshop. During the workshop, the participants systematically answer the three questions mentioned earlier and the outcome will be a blueprint or roadmap of the vision, goals, strategies, structures and review parameters and mechanisms. The workshop will assign responsibilities to different groups by people to carry out the action plans by creating a number of task forces.

The entire process of VISTAR is made highly participative and action-oriented through an intensive and professional facilitation process.

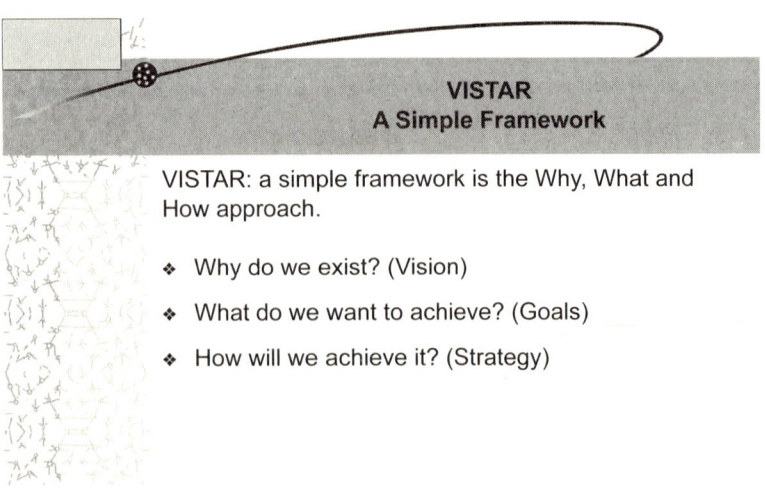

**VISTAR
A Simple Framework**

VISTAR: a simple framework is the Why, What and How approach.

- Why do we exist? (Vision)
- What do we want to achieve? (Goals)
- How will we achieve it? (Strategy)

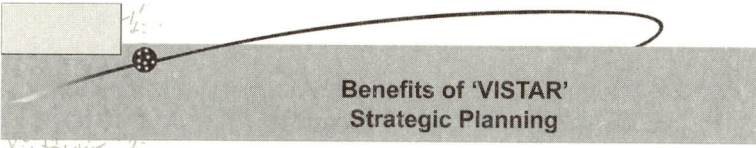

### Benefits of 'VISTAR' Strategic Planning

1. To clearly define the vision of the organization, to establish realistic goals and objectives congruent with the vision
2. To communicate goals and objectives to the organization's stakeholders
3. To ensure the most effective utilization of the organization's resources by focusing on priorities and implementing
4. To provide a base from which progress can be measured and establish a mechanism for informed change when needed
5. To ensure synergy of everyone's efforts in building a consensus about where an organization is going

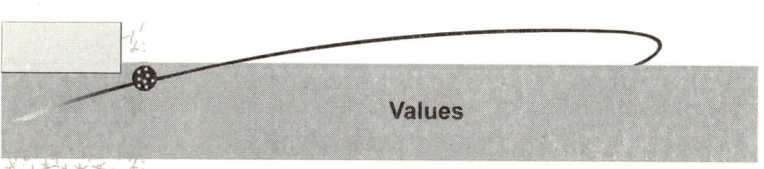

### Values

- An organization's value system is its guiding light in hours of darkness, confusion and self-doubt, and when faced with moral dilemma, it provides clarity and confidence in such situations.
- A leader should create and nurture a common value system.

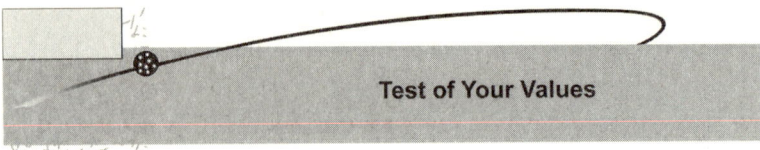

### Test of Your Values

- The importance you attach to your value system is reflected in the cost you are willing to incur for your beliefs and convictions.

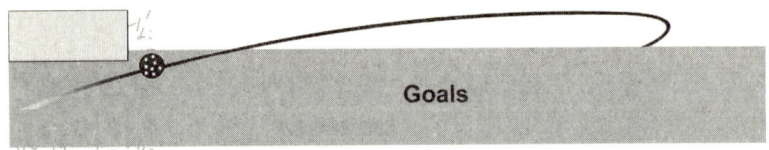

### Goals

- A goal is the pragmatic translation of the idealistic vision.
- It answers the question: 'What should we do?'
- Many goals may need to be accomplished in order to fulfil a vision.
- S.M.A.R.T. Goals
  - Specific
  - Measurable
  - Actionable
  - Realistic
  - Time-bound

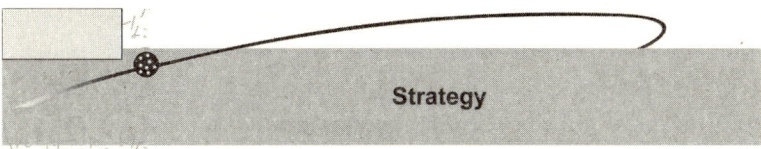

- Strategy is the action translation of the goals.

- Strategy answers the question: 'How should we achieve our goals?'

- Strategy is broad both in terms of time and space.

- Action plan is to strategy what strategy is to goals.

- Every goal may have one or more strategy. Every strategy may have more than one action plan.

- Action plan translates strategy into specific activity, with accountability, deadlines and metrics included.

- An action plan must clearly state the answer to the question, 'Who does what, when and how?'

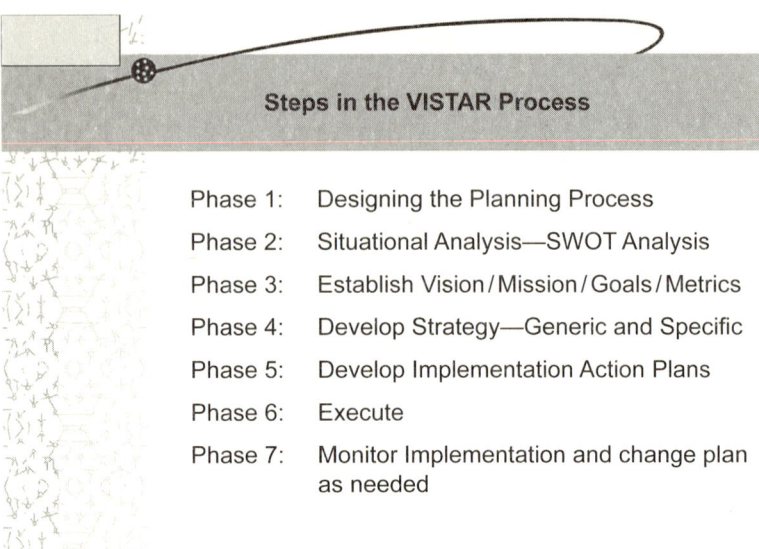

### Steps in the VISTAR Process

Phase 1: Designing the Planning Process
Phase 2: Situational Analysis—SWOT Analysis
Phase 3: Establish Vision/Mission/Goals/Metrics
Phase 4: Develop Strategy—Generic and Specific
Phase 5: Develop Implementation Action Plans
Phase 6: Execute
Phase 7: Monitor Implementation and change plan as needed

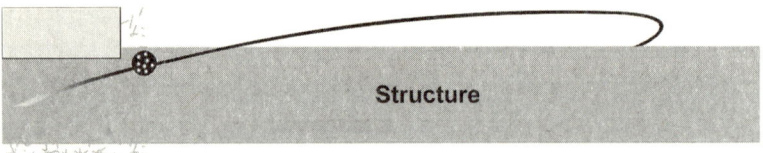

### Structure

- Structure is the way in which roles and relationships are created and used to achieve strategies.
- Structure is a major strategy.
- Structure is a major answer to the question, 'How are we going to achieve the goals?'

## Review: Metrics and Evaluation

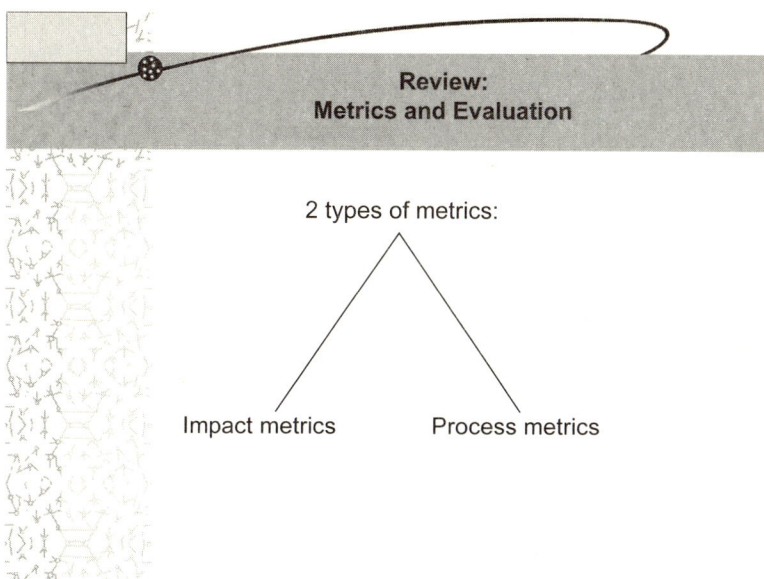

2 types of metrics:

Impact metrics     Process metrics

## Review: Metrics and Evaluation

- Metrics are already embedded in VISTAR process.
- Each goal statement must include one or more evaluation measures.
- Impact metrics help us answer the question, "are we doing the right things?" (Effectiveness)
- Accomplishment of every step of the action plan, as verified in the monthly, quarterly review, offers process metrics.
- Process metrics answers the question, "are we doing things right?" (Efficiency)

All good communication must be participative. However, we need to ask an important question about the participative process: 'What information is "right" to be shared by the leaders with whom, and to what intent and purpose?'

There are three levels of sharing:

1. Information: The leader shares information on decisions already made on certain issues. This is non-negotiable and merely informs followers. It is the lowest level of participation.
2. Involvement: The leader shares an important issue, concern, problem or opportunity with the team for discussion and input, but the decision-making is still the prerogative of the leadership.
3. Co-creation: The leadership shares the total problem-solving cycle with the team, from problem identification to analysis and strategy-building and from zeroing in on the best option to execution of the optimal strategy.

The degree of participation deepens as the leadership moves from level 1 to level 3. The more an organization believes in PROBE and wants to give its people opportunities to grow themselves and the organization as well, the higher it must invest in level 3. One does not need to be a devotee of 'organizational democracy' to practice what would be a 'win-win' for the individual and the organization.

**Change as a Helix**

Change implementation is not a linear process. It is more like a helix. Any organization which initiates a major change process at a certain point in its history needs to, as it were, climb a series of peaks rather than climb the sheer face of a single mountain. At each stage, there is a pause to collect energy and recharge, an opportunity for retrospective learning and the chance to review the vision and strategy of the process based on that learning, followed by a re-planning for the next 'ascent'. People in the organization (and the external stakeholders) need this step-function change process for the learning to be internalized.

# THE MANAGEMENT OF TRANSFORMATIONAL CHANGE ♦ 201

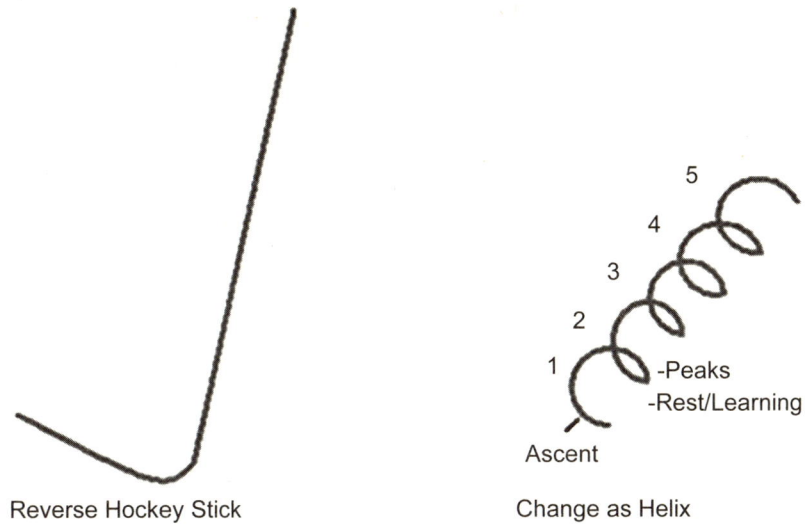

Figure 4.3: *Reverse Hockey Stick: change as Helix*

When water is heated, even when it is at 99° Celsius, there may be little indication of any 'action', but at 100°, the lid is dancing. Any major change in an organization requires ultimately a cultural change—a change in the way people relate to other people, to processes, to tools and to equipment. This cultural change needs a critical mass of time and change energy to gather before results in the form of improvements in performance or in the 'bottom-line' are seen. At the bottom of the 'reverse hockey stick' where the change process begins, a ton of effort may produce only an ounce of results, and worse, there may actually be negative results and productivity may dip. There is often a significant dip in the productivity of an organization during the initial months of a change process.

If the change agents and the citizens of change persist and persevere, then the curve reaches the tipping point, after which it rises. Now, for an ounce of effort, a ton of results may be obtained. Once the curve starts rising, the slope of the curve indicates that high results are possible in a brief time.

Once the momentum picks up, the system becomes self-motivating and the acceleration of the change process is remarkable.

The so-called 'journey through hell' (see figure on the following page) is a painful experience for the people in the organization. Self-doubt, scepticism about the change agents, anxiety about the change strategy and general insecurity fill the organization and there rises a thick fog of gloom. There is a need for faith and patience until the change gains credence and experience, before the light at the end of the tunnel becomes visible and the train whistles out into the open. There is also a need to plan for the possible dip and not panic when it happens nor punish the victims, which would squelch any potential for successful change.

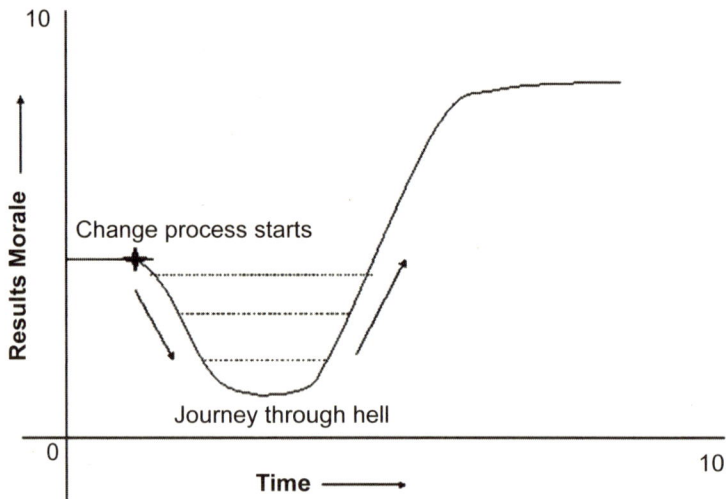

*Figure 4.4: Resistance to Change—the Journey*

What if no dip can be tolerated? Then plan a slower pace of change if you can afford it, so that the price paid for the change is tolerable to the overall system.

People in the organization, regardless of the levels at which they are working, find themselves reacting to major change in one of several ways, as seen in the figure below. There is no monolithic support or resistance to change. Instead, there is a 'distribution of motivation'.

The minority of those who are highly positive and 'gung-ho' at one end, and the minority of those who are highly negative at the other, are the exceptions to the large majority who lie along a spectrum ranging from sceptics to sympathizers of change.

# THE MANAGEMENT OF TRANSFORMATIONAL CHANGE ✦ 203

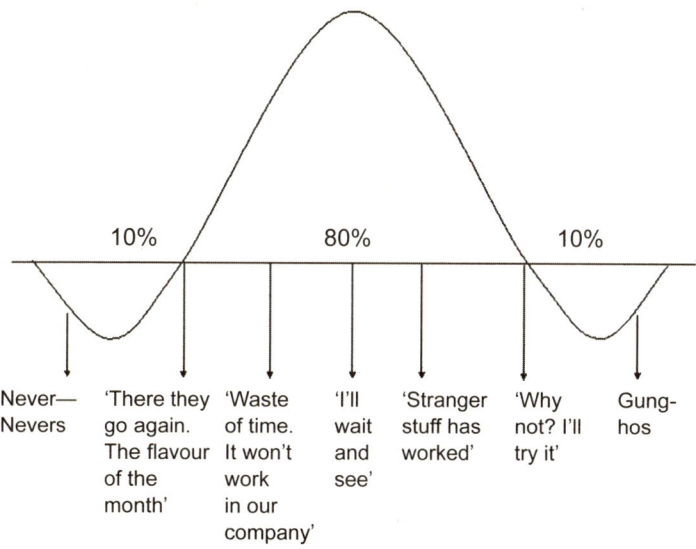

*Figure 4.5: Resistance to Change—Attitude Towards It*

The energy that it takes to 'break the ice' while introducing a new change comes from the right-hand side of the curve. There is no need for the entire organization, or even a majority, to be highly enthusiastic at the beginning. However, mobilizing the energies of the 'naturals' through task forces, pilot programmes, demonstration projects, etc. are some of the 'trail-blazing' techniques used to introduce change in a diversely motivated employee world.

What are the kinds of people that one comes across during a change process—what kind of positions are the employees of the organization likely to take with regard to the change? As seen in the above figure, at any time during a significant change process, there are two extremes. For personal reasons, some people are gung-ho about change—they love it and they are the kind of people who will say, 'I have been saying this for ages, and thank God now you people at the top are saying the same thing. Where do I start?' The 'gung-ho' people are the most important. If anything, you may have to hold them back because sometimes they might press the pace of the system too much, and therefore the backlash might actually deter the change process. At the other end of the spectrum, there are the 'never-nevers', who are likely to say, 'I would rather die. Over my dead body! If this is how the organization is going, my resignation is ready,' and so on. It may be a unconscious or very conscious resistance on the part of the never-nevers.

In between lie most of us—from the mild-to-moderate positive people to the mild-to-moderate negative people. A mildly positive person is one who asks the safe questions in the first meeting and who will say, 'At least they are doing something now. I wonder what their case is, but now at least they are doing something,' and then there are those who will say, 'Listen, let's wait and see. I am four years to retirement, and I am not going to jeopardize that by jumping on the bandwagon. You know how these people are, they'll attend one seminar and they'll want to change everything.' Then at the most negative, there are those who say, 'There they go again with the flavour of the month—this too shall pass.'

This is the kind of distribution that we find. The aim of change management is to win the hearts and minds of a critical mass of this population so that you really have the momentum for change. The leadership needs to learn to harness this energy, and to get enough people to contribute not just their minds, brains and guts, but to put their hearts into it—they have to give not just their 'intellectual' labour, but also their 'emotional' labour. This is where a leader's challenge lies.

In the history of change processes, it has been observed that there are five phases (Figure 4.6) in the emotional climate of an organization undergoing change. At any point of time, one or more of the phases may dominate the cultural landscape of the population.

**Organization Culture**

The iceberg underneath the water is the culture of the organization. How does culture—the values, beliefs and traditions that make us what we are—originate? It is the shared experience of the community. It is to believe in shared values and practice as a group certain kinds of norms and behaviours, both important and non-important. Now, when change unfolds, the basic challenge is as follows. Culture has given the group stability. The old culture is inevitably, appropriately and justifiably resistant to change and one of the fatal mistakes in the change process is for the change agents to disrespect the old culture and to say, 'You are old fogies—go away. The new modern and new-fangled ideas are here.' There is a need to mourn the passing of the old culture. Bob Tannenbaum calls this 'holding on and letting go', where you institute processes of change in the organization which identify the good parts of the old culture and respect them, as though to say, 'We are not changing everything. In no change process is everything changed, we are changing certain policies, but certain of the old things are valuable, and these are the things we are going to keep.' Like the Greek God, Janus, who has two faces, one facing forward and the other facing back, we all have two faces when change happens. One looking back at the past with nostalgia and saying, 'Those were the good old days, how great we were,' and the other facing forward and saying, 'You don't know how it was, it will be better now.'

What are the 'emotional phases' (see figure below) that a majority of people go through and the leaders/change agents have to manage? We have a lot to learn from Elisabeth Kübler-Ross's research on dying. When a loss is suffered by an individual, the five stages of grief are: denial, anger, depression, bargaining and finally, acceptance. There is something akin to this that happens in organizational change.

As with Kübler-Ross's five stages of grief, the five stages of reactions to change are not meant to be complete or chronological. Not everyone who experiences a significant transformation feels all five of the responses, nor will every person who does experience them do so in any particular order. But a change agent can expect a majority of the participants in the change process to go through these phases in the first 18 months to three years.

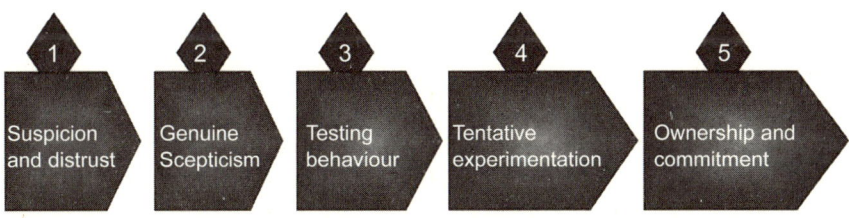

*Figure 4.6: Resistance to Change—From Cynicism to Commitment*

*Suspicion and Distrust:* The majority, or at least a significant minority, will suspect and distrust the change process, and/or the need for change, and/or the change leadership, and/or the motives of change agents. Whatever the cause, the feelings are negative towards change.

*Genuine Scepticism:* Those in this phase may not feel any dark cynicism, but they will lack conviction in this proposed change as well. The scepticism may be expressed variously as:

- We have tried this before and it didn't work.
- Top management is not committed to real change.
- This is a new fad and this too shall pass.
- They mean well, but they don't know what they're doing.
- Their ideas are good, but they won't be able to pull them off.

*Testing Behaviour:* Many people graduate to, or even start out with, a 'man from Missouri' attitude. They will say, 'Show me why I should trust you', or 'Show me that it can really work,' or 'Show me that I won't get hurt by this.' Testing behaviour can be provocative, especially between labour and management. It is a period when the faith and conviction of the top and middle managements are tested, and the time to win the confidence of the implementers (middle management all the way to the workforce on the shop floor). The lack of patience or understanding may abort the change process at this stage.

*Tentative Experimentation:* Insiders move through the first three stages to arrive at an attitude wherein they are willing to experiment with new behaviours, processes, roles and relationships, but only tentatively. 'I can try it once,' or 'I don't know yet whether it will really work, but I'm willing to try,' or 'If you will keep the door open, I'm willing to walk in and play,' are some of the common positions taken.

Barriers such as the fear of change and nostalgia about the past may be lesser here, but there is not yet the conviction born out of personal experience of the new way of life.

*Ownership and Commitment:* This is the 'nirvana' sought after by the designers of change. A majority of the people in the organization come to 'own' the change—the need for change, its goals, objectives and strategies. They are willing to commit to the vision and the changes needed to achieve the vision. This is the stage where the whole organization works as one team.

## Elephants, Humans and Organizations

Three questions in a particular sequence—Why? What? How?—will help us analyse and plan any system. Let us now recapitulate at this stage of our dialogue where we started.

**Proposition 1**: We need urgently, importantly, even desperately, new kinds of leaders. We call such a new breed of leaders as 'transcendent leaders' (TCLs).

**Proposition 2**: TCLs are needed at every level of an organization.

**Proposition 3**: A TCL is a systems thinker. This means that a TCL believes that everything depends on everything else and hence her every action is planned such that it benefits the whole system.

**Proposition 4**: The central job for a TCL—the raison d'être —is to create and lead transformational change (TC).

**Proposition 5:** TC needs many types of leaders with different talents for different outputs. A TCL evolves systems and processes, and above all a culture, to create, or transform existing leaders into the right kind of leaders for each task of TC.

**Proposition 6**: The process of creating new kinds of leaders is a complex, multi-strategy process and ultimately it is up to the individual to develop or recreate oneself into the right kind of leader.

I hope the first four propositions have been well-presented and defended with enough theory and evidence in the previous chapters to make you a believer, tentatively at least. Now, to complete our self-appointed task—we need to answer not only the 'why' question and the 'what' of leadership, but also the 'how'—we need to present the defence for the last two propositions. I shall do so with an 'operators manual' in the next and the last chapter. (I heard that sigh of relief. That is not nice).

But before we move on to a detailed model of a leader's development process, we need to remember the place we started—our dear elephants. Let us pause for a moment and read a few research findings about elephants.

Elephants have empathy and can recognize themselves in mirrors, according to research conducted by Joshua M. Plotnik, Frans B.M. de

Waal, and Diana Reiss.[49] According to Think Elephants International,

> Recognizing oneself in the mirror is an ability humans take for granted... Interestingly, this ability is actually a cognitive capacity that few animal species possess. The only species to have passed this test of mirror self-recognition are the Great Apes, dolphins, one bird species (a corvid), and elephants. Recognizing oneself in the mirror demonstrates that an animal is able to see itself as separate from others, one of the main traits underlying empathy and complex sociality.[50]

**Elephants understand humans in a way most other animals don't, according to the latest research from the University of St Andrews.** The new study, published on 10 October 2013 by *Current Biology*, found that elephants are the only wild animals that understand human pointing without any training to do so:

*Elephant Know When They Need a Helping Trunk*

> In this study, we show that elephants wait for a partner in a task that requires two individuals to pull two ends of the same rope to obtain a food reward. The elephants learned not only that a partner was necessary in the rope-pulling task, but also that it was the partner's behaviour and not just their presence that was needed for success. Such an understanding of cooperation has only been shown in a small number of species.[51]

The researchers go on to ask:

> Why are elephants so social? Why do they live in such complex family groups? Do they have empathy, and how can we test this? How do elephants 'see' their world—with their eyes, their ears or their trunks? These questions lead us to testable hypotheses and hopefully exciting answers about the evolution of intelligence in this remarkable animal.[52]

Substitute the word 'humans' for 'elephants' in all of these research findings. If a Martian researcher were to come to earth on a research project, she may ask exactly the same questions. (Well, not about the trunk, but all the rest). For that matter, if an elephant was a scientist studying humans, she would ask those questions about us.

These questions are the ones that concern the foundation and the first three pillars of our TCL bandstand. Let's take a look at the model of transcendent leadership again so that we can refresh our memory.

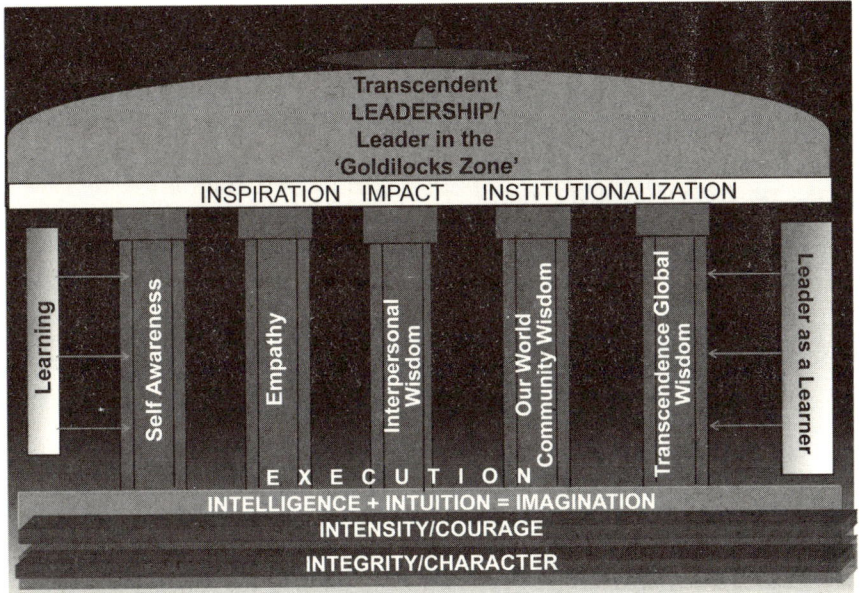

*Figure 4.7: '3+5 Transcendent Leadership' model*

Do elephants have transcendent proclivities? Do they sense the larger system? On the basis of recent studies, some believe they can.

> Amazingly... elephants, both male and female, show (often synchronized) moments of stillness where they all stop simultaneously with whatever they are busy sometimes accompanying with raised trunk to smell the air. They listen, smell and look around them using their senses to the fullest at these moments to become aware of each other, their surroundings and the activities and direction of the herd. Being around these magnificent animals at that time gives you a glimpse of their raised awareness, calmness and great determination. Elephants show us that [there is] time to stop, step back and reconsider or reflect if the activities that keep you and your team busy all day are

the right ones and really do contribute to reaching the business and your personal goals.[53]

Even if you discount the breathless gushing in the concluding sentences (As Freud said, sometimes a cigar is just a cigar), the behaviour described looks like the elephants take stock of their environment regularly as a herd, not just as individuals or as a lone leader. It is tempting to interpret this as 360-degree data gathering for planning future food forays and predator avoidance. But, just for a moment, could there be a more profound collective purpose than mere self-preservation in this striking interlude in the life of the elephant herd?

We may never understand the deeper meaning this behaviour has for the elephants, but we can certainly use this as a metaphor for our species. It is necessary for us to review our systems from a holistic perspective regularly. If elephants can do it, so can we.

Finally, another similarity, this time in social organization,

> Within family groups, which range in size from two to more than 20, the oldest, most experienced female takes the lead. But the group size is constantly changing, responding to the seasons, the availability of food and water, and the threat from predators. An adult female elephant might start the day feeding with 12 to 15 individuals, be part of a group of 25 by mid-morning, and 100 at midday, then go back to a family of 12 in the afternoon, and finally settle for the night with just her dependent offspring [...] The elephant family unit [...] known as a fission-fusion society, is a complex social dynamic relatively rare in the animal kingdom, but not uncommon in primates, including humans.[54]

Enough about elephants.

## What Is the Next Chapter, and the Concluding Presentation?

The next chapter provides a model to help set up leadership development as a formal and important activity in the organization. Why do we need it? If you are convinced that your organization needs to develop leadership of the kind described in this book, namely transcendent leadership, then it is incumbent upon me to provide a roadmap to assist in such a developmental process. It needs the creation of an 'institution within an institution', a corporate university for the present and the future leadership of the organization.

But can one really teach transcendent leadership? Even if one concedes that TCLs are not always born but they can become TCLs, still the question remains, how do we encourage people to become TCLs? How do the specific '3+5' qualities evolve in such leaders? How much of it is externally induced and which ones are internally acquired?

We will address these questions in the next chapter, through a succinct discussion on the '3+5' qualities and how they are developed. But to create an institution within an institution, an a structure ('the anatomy') and processes ('its physiology') are needed. The chapter also provides a 'manual' on creating an institute on leadership.

But before we embark on Chapter 5, we interrupt this broadcast to bring you breaking news from a few leaders:

## LEADERS SPEAK

### On Leadership Development

**Vivek Mansingh**
'What is your brand? Mine will be transforming people and making sure that the people who work with me are challenged and reach their potential. Everyone does not have the same potential.'

**Manish Sabharwal**
'It's unclear to me [how exactly we develop good leaders], but obviously we need to do it through interpersonal skills training and leadership. To my mind, the best way we can train them is to expose them to high pressure situations. The most fighting and screaming we see in the office is about whether the target for the year has been achieved. If a person just reaches 35 per cent of their target, then we have to measure what happened to the remaining 65 per cent. Some will survive, some will not. It works for leaders who are below the P&L level, nothing but many years will prepare you for being number one, that's the best, first give them a small fish to fry and

then give them a bigger fish. We used to have three P&L verticals, now we have eight P&Ls [...] some of them are smaller P&Ls, but they take wall-to-wall responsibility.[...] Yes, those people who have spent a considerable amount of time in the company can teach them lots of stuff, how to manage operations, how to handle a meeting, design effective MIS.'

**Rishikesha Krishnan**
'I think one of the problems that I see is that most of these corporate guys expect leadership development to be like a magic show. They would ideally like to take this guy, do some magic, and six months later he should suddenly become this whiz. I don't think they actually provide a supportive environment for leadership development on the job. According to all these fancy studies [...] 70 per cent of leadership development has to happen on the job and I'm actually inclined to believe that. But the problem is that, that 70 per cent of the process is very poorly done and nobody wants to give you a more challenging role and allow you to try something out and fail and learn. They want you to tell them what you exactly want them to do. And in the 30 per cent, either Dr Jayaram or Rishi or somebody else is expected to create a miracle and make it happen. I think there are far too many inconsistencies and wrong assumptions embedded in this whole thing and that's one of the reasons why leadership doesn't get far enough.'

**Sudip Banerjee**
'I think you have to see it in three perspectives—leadership development as in having the next generation of managers take over from you in the business context, leadership development in terms of building expertise, and leadership development in terms of building or sustaining your values and culture. I think in most organizations there is an attempt to develop leaders on the technical side, so if I have good factory processes I have them documented and educate my employees, or if I have got good software, people are taught how to use it. All good organizations try to improve the technical skills of their leaders, but only some organizations try to do it for leadership talent [...] We used to have what is called an annual belief session in the old days... We used to have a values booklet that was distributed to every new employee and (the CEO) would take a one and a half hour class on values. He would tell people why values are important, why you should do the right

things, and why you should not do the wrong things. Then the company grew and it was impossible for him to take those classes and we used to do it and it became a part of us. Every time we received communication about the annual plan, we used to hold a belief session, and this continued till at least 2005-06. I don't know whether those sessions still happen now or not, but very few organizations would do that and I think that it's necessary and those who do it make their people better, not better as in technical people but better managers and better human beings and it's a part of leadership development because ultimately leadership development is not only about building more skills, it's about building skills, values culture and everything else...only then it's leadership development.'

## Kishan Anantharam

'I get a 360-degree evaluation from all those I interact with. We are putting into place a mechanism so that each employee can give feedback to us on the level of trust that they have in the company and in each of the senior executives (including myself). [...] We conduct tech-talks on a variety of subjects, including leadership, personal development, teamwork, people management, project management, customer management, trust, excellence and innovation to develop leaders within our organization. These efforts are taking shape now, and we do have a long way to go before we can confidently say that we have a programme for developing good leaders within our organization.'

## Mali Mahalingam

'Budgets were always a constraint while designing a formal training system. (We) had instituted a mentorship programme and a career coach programme. I look at development opportunity as two-fold—development through coaching and mentoring based on relationships, and development through experiences by providing potential leaders with varied opportunities, different geographies, different projects, etc., And then there is the knowledge-based or education-based development programmes created because I could not invest enough in them to send them to good leadership programmes.'

# 5

# LEADERSHIP DEVELOPMENT—HOW?

Can the following '3+5 Transcendental Leadership' values be taught? What do you think?

- Integrity/Character
- Intensity/Courage
- Intelligence + intuition = imagination
- Self-awareness
- Empathy
- Interpersonal wisdom
- 'Our World'—community wisdom
- Transcendence—global wisdom

It is obvious to the meanest intelligence that every single quality listed here is only partly 'teachable' by an external agency—an institute, a mentor, etc. Hence, I will not insult your intelligence by discussing each quality in detail in terms of how one acquires it. Instead, let me illustrate this point using the most fundamental of the above values as an example.

## Can We Teach Integrity?

Wait, wait, before you declare that it is impossible to teach a person to have integrity, please consider that every major—and minor—religion has attempted to do this since the dawn of time. Every religion contains at its core central tenets that prescribe the 'right way to live', the definitions of 'right' and 'wrong', and a code of ethics to guide human life.

Similarly, the best business corporations of the modern era have prescribed and seriously enforced their definitions of integrity. The 'HP Way' at Hewlett Packard and the 'J&J Credo' at Johnson & Johnson are just two examples drawn from a long list of companies that practise a 'code of conduct', including IBM, Proctor & Gamble, General Electric, Matsushita and Tata. These companies have leadership development academies where they 'teach' the code of conduct, but just as religions can vouchsafe and corporations concur, I'm sure no one has as yet invented a sure-fire way of inculcating integrity in every leader. While some companies take the 'code of conduct' very seriously and encourage leaders to 'own' it, other companies are more ritualistic and half-hearted about their stated values. From personal observation (I have no proof to adduce), I would like to conclude that integrity can be 'taught' 49 per cent of the time, and the rest has to be learnt.

Similar conclusions can be drawn about each of the other qualities. It may seem that intelligence can be tested through IQ tests, but serious detractors point out there are kinds of intelligences. Howard Gardner has identified 'multiple intelligences' and Daniel Goleman's 'emotional intelligence' has led to EQ tests. However, on the whole, the qualities of a TCL should be learnt rather than taught. 'In 1964, Justice Potter Stewart tried to explain "hard-core" pornography, or what is obscene, by saying, "I shall not today attempt further to define the kinds of material I understand to be embraced [...] [b]ut I know it when I see it [...]"'[1] Most managers and mentors of future leaders would empathize with the good Justice and say about these qualities, '[b]ut I know it when I see it.'

All is not lost, though. From experience, as a species, we have many insights about this process of leadership development even if we can't teach it fully. What are these insights from research and best practices?

Below, I present a set of propositions that help me think about each of these and act upon them.

- To become a leader from within, change must not be externally imposed but internally acquired. The qualities have to be earned. You can't make me a leader. Only I can do it for myself. The qualities of a TCL cannot all be taught; some can be and that would constitute the curricula of a leadership development institute, but the rest have to be gleaned by each individual who aspires to be a leader. As the cliché goes, 'You can take a horse to the water, but you cannot make it drink.'

+ The good news is that we, as a species, have shown ourselves to be capable of learning without being taught. According to a 'learning theory' found in mathematics and computational sciences,

> Humans appear to be able **to learn new concepts** without needing to be programmed explicitly in any conventional sense [...] We regard learning as the phenomenon of knowledge acquisition **in the absence of explicit programming** (emphasis mine).[2]

+ Learning means changing oneself. If no change happens, then no learning has taken place. In the context of TCL development, change does not refer to trivial or cosmetic changes in oneself; it is changing one's vision and values (refer to the bell-curve in Figure 3.1)
+ Personal change is necessary to become a leader, especially if one wishes to become a transcendent leader. The following equation presents the two variables that are the 'actors' in the change drama:
**Changeability = (ability to change) x (willingness to change) = (I can change) x (I want to change)**

## The Questions—Why Change? What to Change? How to Change? (Table 5.1)

If we can measure two variables in a potential leader (or an existing one)—the ability to change and the will to change—we can develop a 'leadership deficiency quotient' based on which an 'individual development plan' can be created for that individual. These two variables can be used to quantify the individual's overall leadership capabilities (for example, a sort of Hamlet, the reluctant leader) or can be used to pin down specific qualities (for example, 'this person has intellect and experience, but is unwilling to use them to be strategic').

Now for the operator's manual. Since it is a 'structure and process' manual, we deliberately do not refer to the contents of the curricula. You may assume safely, after reading these four extensive chapters, that the leadership development institute will design its curricula to help people learn 'the qualities' of a TCL. You can bet that the lesser leaders—TFLs—can be developed through this process as well. A TCL needs to be versatile, not just a 'jack of all trades', but a master of many. The model of the 'nine pillars' provides the different kinds of learning that the TCL needs to be the master of many.

**Table 5.1: A 2x2 matrix**

|  |  | 'I must change' ⇩ ⇨ | I have the 'will to change' | 'Unwilling to change' |
|---|---|---|---|---|
| A B I L I T Y  T O  C H A N G E | | And I am 'able to change' | What are you waiting for? Go change. The rest of us have bigger problems.<br>Easy—A<br>'I envy you. Go away, you lucky…chum.' | Self-awareness is needed, as is self-diagnosis and the ability to trace the roots of the unwillingness.<br>Difficult but doable—C<br>'What's wrong with you?! Are you a masochist, or something?' |
| | | 'Unable to change' | It is necessary to enhance the ability to change by building knowledge and skills through training programmes and mentors and role models.<br><br>Less easy but doable—B<br>'Poor chap; hope you get lucky.' | Deep therapy is needed, at the level of values and vision of life.<br>Most difficult—D<br>'Lost & not found' |
| | | Willingness to change ⟶ | | |

## 'Nine Pillars of Wisdom' Leadership Development Manual

Leadership Institute **(LI)**
Your Corporation **(YOCO Inc.)**

In the next few pages I will provide a template for an operations manual for a hypothetical leadership institute. You may use it to create a formal mechanism for leadership development in your own organization if you agree with my concept of the 'Nine Pillars of Wisdom'. Along the way, I will add my comments in parentheses, which are not part of the manual, but my dialogue with you. Remember we started with that agreement; why break a good habit?

In the figure below you'll see, what else, another bandstand (You believe in love, truth, beauty; I believe in bandstands). There are nine pillars standing on four layers of foundation. Why have I chosen this model with nine pillars? What are these pillars, and what do they represent? How does one go about designing and executing this model of a leadership development institute?

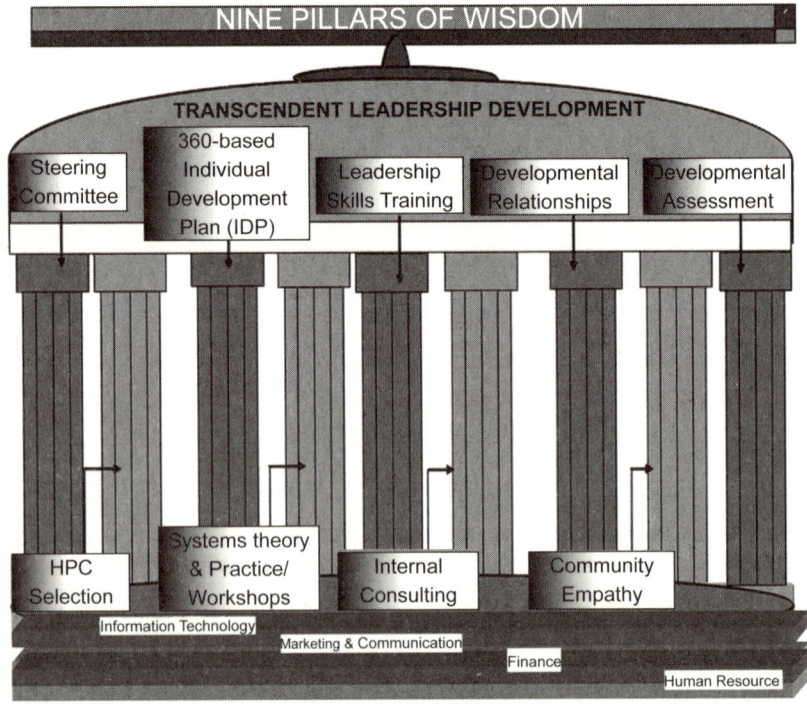

## TABLE OF CONTENTS

| TITLE | PAGE |
|---|---|
| Vision and Mission Statements, Philosophy & Objectives | |
| Message from Chairman | |
| Message from CEO | |
| Introduction | |
| Structure of the Leadership Institute (LI) | |
| Pillar 1—Governance Structure | |
| Roles and Responsibilities of the Board/Top Management | |
| Roles and Responsibilities of the Steering Committee | |
| Scope of Activity | |
| Pillars 2: 5-Tier Structure | |
| General Guidelines | |
| Pillar 3—Individual Development Plan (IDP) | |
| IDP: Process | |
| Pillar 4—'Leaders Teach' Knowledge and Skills Seminars | |
| Pillar 5—Internal Consulting | |
| Pillar 6—Developmental Relationships | |
| Pillar 7—Developmental Assignment | |
| Pillar 8—Community Empathy | |
| Pillar 9—Developmental Assessment | |
| Annexure 1: Development Assessment | |
| Annexure 2: Post course Evaluation | |
| Annexure 3: Module Outline Format | |
| Annexure 4: Model Session Plan Format | |
| Annexure 5: Report On External Training/Seminar Attended | |

**(Here start the contents of the manual. Please remember that this was created for another organization, a real one, but you would have your own vision, etc. I am sure you would, otherwise this book is love's labour lost).**

| VISION |
|---|
| To create an institution that is a strategic instrument of growth and transformation by developing three types of leaders—Transcendent (TCL), Transformational (TFL) and Transactional (TAL)—and by promoting a culture of continuous learning for the organization's development and the personal development of the individual. |

| MISSION |
|---|
| To enhance the quality and quantity of leadership and follower-ship for long-term success.<br>To create versatility in the leadership cadre by encouraging the use of different kinds of leadership, such as TCL, TFL and TAL, according to the needs of the situation and demands of the role. |
| To constantly endeavour to raise expectations for the self and the unit in achieving customer delight.<br>To instil the 'right' values in the organization.<br>To promote a culture of proactiveness, agility and quality.<br>To create a cadre of leaders as part of a succession plan. |

| PHILOSOPHY |
|---|
| To encourage staff to take ownership and responsibility for the achievement of individual and organizational goals.<br>To improve knowledge, develop business skills and inculcate the right attitude for the organization's progress.<br>To provide an environment of participative learning and knowledge management.<br>To build a better organization to achieve competitive advantage.<br>To imbue a spirit of entrepreneurship in the individual. |

| LI OBJECTIVES |
|---|
| To create learning opportunities in alignment with the business needs of the organization.<br>To assist the staff in taking responsibility for their personal development in tune with the business needs and growth of the group. |

> To help leaders and experts impart and disseminate information and share knowledge across the group.
> To provide opportunities for higher learning and to empower employees to shoulder higher and greater responsibilities.
> To provide and facilitate up-to-date and comprehensive training for all staff.

**Introduction**

The leadership development institute (LI) has been established with the principal objective of identifying, developing and preparing future leaders, with special attention to TCLs. The LI's main aim is to prepare leaders for the YOCO group of companies with a single-minded focus on one standard of performance—excellence! The effort, the expertise and the investment in this institute are to ensure that in a relatively short period of time it becomes the standard of leadership development for corporate executives everywhere.

YOCO, by setting this high standard and deploying quite considerable resources to facilitate the learning, growth and preparation of its future leaders, is sending a clear message to its promising young leaders that YOCO is willing to invest in helping them reach their highest potential. Through LI, YOCO hopes to carve out a competitive advantage in the marketplace and sharpen its leaders to aid the YOCO group to prevail and be very successful against whatever challenges the competition may throw up.

The persons who will be chosen for the LI will be those with proven academic, professional and intellectual achievements seasoned with common sense. They will also have proven managerial experience and they will have recorded measurable successes in their performance over the years. The persons who will be chosen must display a strong sense of integrity, clear commitment to hard work and excellence in performing their jobs, and must have displayed courage in dealing with the difficult issues. Consideration will be given to those individuals who have sufficient time left in their possible careers with the YOCO group so that they will be able to display the benefits of the training and their experiences at the institute. The strength of LI nominees is at 400 (about 1 per cent of the total staff) in 2014, and we expect the number to increase proportional to the growth of the company.

It is emphasized that being chosen as a LI nominee, a high potential candidate (HPC), is a privilege and not a right. YOCO insists on offering equal opportunity to compete for a berth in LI, but does not offer equal entitlements for the same. It is a meritocracy and let the cream rise to the top if you like clichés. It does not confer on any candidate a permanent place in the institute. Rather, it is an opportunity to continue to prove oneself as a future leader of the organization, and unless candidates in the institute continue to perform to the highest measured academic and managerial levels, they will lose their place in the institute as a result of periodic evaluations at the institute. The excellence that we require at the institute is a standard that requires continuous vigilance and diligence. The highest quality cannot be maintained otherwise. The world out there—the markets, the customers, the shareholders and the stakeholders—they do not accept excuses; they just relentlessly expect excellence if they have to accord their highest rewards to the winner.

Just as important, candidates' performance at the institute will be considered during each person's corporate performance evaluation and will therefore affect their recognition, promotion and bonuses when these are being awarded. Again, it is one of the surest ways to ensure that the standard of excellence is maintained at the institute. Any ambitious candidate who asks why she should compete and what's in it for her has her answer: Your career as a whole in YOCO.

Workshops and seminars at the LI will be conducted partly through classroom lectures, and also at the workplace through supervised assignments and shall include projects that will require research outside the parent division, and some out of YOCO in the relevant domains of the external environment.

LI is being established to stretch, burnish and sharpen the skills of the group's most valuable asset—people—so that we can continue to be successful and win in perpetuity in the markets that we operate in by focusing on and serving our customers excellently well.

The Leadership Development Programme is built on the 'Nine Pillars of Wisdom' below:

## Structure of the Programme: 'Anatomy'

- Governance Structure
- High Potential Candidates—Selection & Structure

## Processes of the Programme: 'Physiology'

- Individual Development Plan (IDP)
- Leaders Teach—Knowledge and Skills Workshops
- Internal Consulting
- Developmental Relationships
- Developmental Assignment
- Community Empathy
- Developmental Assessment

# THE NINE PILLARS OF WISDOM— BRIEF DESCRIPTIONS

## Pillar 1—Governance Structure

This section defines the roles and responsibilities of the following groups towards achieving the vision of LI:

1.1 Board and Executive Management
1.2 Steering Committee
1.3 Leadership Institute (LI)
1.4 LI Nominee-Leaders
1.5 High Potential Candidates as LI Nominees
1.6 Human Resources Group

### 1.1 Roles and Responsibilities of Board and Executive Management

LI shall have the commitment and support of the board and the executive management.

## 1.2 Roles and Responsibilities of the Steering Committee

The steering committee is the ultimate authority for all matters relating to LI.

The initial members of the steering committee should be:

- Chairman and Managing Director
- Vice Cairman
- CEO
- Director
- Consultant

**Why Steering Committee? Why These Members?**

Leadership development at the highest levels of the organization and the creation of TCLs, TFLs and TALs works if, and only if, the candidates (and the rest of YOCO) realize that this effort has the active, committed and involved blessing and participation of the top management of the company. If the 'buck stopper' says that she believes in the necessity, desirability and feasibility of such an enterprise, and if her actions follow through, then the rest of her followers have a choice to make—they can either, at the very least, give it an honest try, or they can give up on the vision, YOCO's and one's own. This is the 'psychological contract' between each candidate and the topmost leaders of the firm.

The steering committee will be responsible for guiding and supervising LI activities, in particular relating to:

- Setting the strategic direction
- Providing guidance for making each of the 'nine pillars' operational
- Reviewing progress and performance
- Directing the institutionalization process

## 1.3 Roles and Responsibilities of LI

The roles and responsibilities of LI are as follows:

- Advise and make suggestions to the steering committee about specialized training and developmental needs.

- Formulate and finalize the training and developmental activities calendar in consultation with the steering committee.
- Prepare and implement an annual training and developmental calendar.
- Guide and counsel LI nominees on IDP preparation and execution.
- Assist leaders in the dissemination of knowledge and information through 'Leaders Teach Series' programmes.
- Organize and conduct specialized training programmes in line with business needs.
- Coordinate assessment and evaluation of LI nominee performance.
- Ensure high quality of training and developmental activities.
- Evaluate and measure the impact of training and other developmental activities.
- Collect, maintain and analyse training and development data.
- Guide and support nominees in their internal consultancy and project assignments with divisions/units and take an active role in research and development of new ideas, products, processes, etc.
- Contribute to the image building of the group and act as a vehicle for conveying the strategy and vision of the management across the organization and outside.
- Advise on faculty selection/succession plan.
- Any other responsibility assigned by the steering committee.

## Scope of LI Activity

*Assisting in Selection of Nominees for LI*

Based on the criteria specified from time to time, the performance of staff will be assessed and evaluated and based on the results, staff shall be inducted into LI. LI will assist HR and the steering committee in the 'processes'.

*Assisting in Individual Development Plan (IDP) of LI Nominees*

LI shall provide the necessary support and counselling to nominees to prepare their IDPs and to implement the plans. LI will keep in mind the organization's needs while assisting the nominees to draw up their IDPs.

*Assessment of Training and Developmental Needs for LI Nominees*

Training and development activities should complement the vision, mission and strategy of the YOCO group. Training requirements, particularly relating to the focus areas of development, shall be collected from the unit heads, IDPs and 360° feedback at regular intervals and will be used as the basis for drawing up the training plan.

*Assessment of Individual Development Needs of LI*

The assessment of the training and development needs of LI nominees shall be conducted by LI to ensure that a learning path is defined for each LI nominee.

## LI Workshop Design

The LI faculty, with inputs from the functional and operational personnel of the LI group, shall design suitable workshops. The design process involves:

+ Preparing course and content outline
+ Preparing a lesson plan with learning methods
+ Preparing course material, hand-outs, case studies, assignments, PowerPoint presentations. etc.

## LI Initiatives Management

The LI faculty shall be responsible for leading and facilitating the initiatives of LI.

The faculty's role is grouped under learning, development and assessment.

*Learning Activity*

+ Conduct workshops for LI nominees to sensitize them on their roles and responsibilities in LI.
+ Conduct skill development workshops and seminars in line with the learning objectives defined in the training plan; assist in conducting

'Leader Teach' series workshops.
- Guide nominees on IDP preparation and execution for achieving IDP objectives.
- Guide nominees on the methodology for conducting internal consulting assignments.
- Guide nominees for their workshop presentations.

*Assessment Activity*

- Maintain and provide periodic feedback on the LI performance of each nominee.
- Ensure maintenance of database.

*Internalization*

The LI faculty shall ensure that all LI activities are internalized in such a way that smooth hand-offs and transitions occurs at all levels. It shall be the constant endeavour of the LI faculty to conduct specialized and need-based training programmes.

## 1.4 Roles and Responsibilities of LI Nominee-Leaders

- Assist LI in assessing and evaluating performance of nominees.
- Ensure participation of registered persons for training.
- Supervise, coach and evaluate nominees during the post-training course phase.
- Give effective, constructive and periodical feedback to LI on the impact of training and developmental activities.
- Motivate and encourage LI nominees to follow the path of self-development and achieve their set IDP objectives.
- Conducting 'Leaders Teach' series.
- Provide key inputs for annual training need assessment. Validate the course content.
- Coach and guide nominees in their internal consulting assignments and encourage nominees belonging to other units.
- Sponsor candidates for nomination to LI.

### 1.5 Roles and Responsibilities of LI Nominees

+ Nominees shall display full commitment to their own development process with LI guidance.
+ There shall be active participation in training sessions and honest and objective evaluation of the training courses offered.
+ The LI nominees shall endeavour to attain their IDP objectives as well as ensure that the defined learning and development activities are undergone within the stipulated timeframe.

### 1.5 Roles and Responsibilities of LI-HR

+ Collaborate and support LI in its initiatives and activities.
+ Compile a list of sponsored employees and provide a brief profile of each.
+ Prepare and mail welcome letters to LI nominees.
+ Periodically guide and support LI in keeping to the direction envisaged by the steering committee.
+ Support and facilitate LI and the LI faculty in resolving operational issues.

## Pillar 2—High Potential Candidate Structure

The second pillar, 'Membership Structure', defines the members of LI and reflects the LI philosophy that each member of the staff in the LI group should 'earn the privilege of being nominated to and associated with LI'. In creating a select group of high potential individuals, the management wishes to convey that these select positions are available to all high potential and performing employees.

### Sponsorship to LI

LI-HR shall create a list of all employees eligible to be inducted into the LI programmes based on their performance appraisal ratings and levels. The list shall be circulated to all unit heads. The unit heads shall sponsor the proposed employees from their units to LI-HR. It is expected that the unit heads consult the employee concerned regarding his willingness to participate in the LI programme.

## Selection to LI Courses

Following the approval of nominations by the select committee, the employees selected for the LI programmes shall be informed by LI-HR by way of a welcome letter, which will list out the activities to be completed by them for formal induction into LI.

## Induction to LI

Every selected LI nominee shall undergo/undertake the following activities before being formally inducted to LI. Failure to comply with any of the requirements shall result in automatic cancellation of the selection, which shall be communicated to the employee in writing by the HR department outlining the reason.

The nominee shall have the right to appeal and any appeal made regarding the cancellation process shall be adjudicated by the LI steering committee.

*List of Activities Needed for Induction:*

- Respond to the learning path survey conducted by LI. This activity will inform all LI nominees of the mandatory courses being offered and will enable each employee to select the desired learning path, in consultation with LI faculty.
- Participate in the 360-degree feedback exercise.
- Submit first version of the IDP.

After completing these, every nominee will receive the LI welcome kit comprising of the following key elements, among others:

- List of expected activities during the tenure in LI with the rating and evaluation matrix for each activity (when developed).
- Planning calendar, with scoring sheet, to help the nominee to plan her learning and development milestones.
- List of compulsory and elective courses for the LI nominee.

## Voluntary Cessation

If a nominee decides to opt for voluntary cessation from LI and makes a request for the same, then such requests shall be considered by LI and an appropriate decision will be made. This will not prevent the employee from being considered for future nominations into LI.

## Course Requirements

The following represent the core activities under LI. The outline of the activity map is given, which is followed by a detailed activity map.

*Learning Activity*

- Attendance and submission of assignments, if any, in the compulsory, selected and optional courses.
- Successful completion of the compulsory and optional courses.

*Development Activity*

- Participate in the 360-degree feedback process.
- Submission of IDP within the stipulated time.
- Complete internal consulting assignments.
- Contribute to LI activities by handling sessions in LI courses (faculty/ LTS/Knowledge Sharing Seminar).

## General

*Learning Activity*

Before beginning learning activities, every nominee shall be required to respond to the learning path survey wherein they will indicate their choice of elective training courses during the LI programme. The LI faculty shall review this and shall inform the nominee of acceptance of the same. This shall be in line with the requirements of the position in which the LI nominee is at the time of admission into LI. By adopting the aforementioned process, we will ensure that the right people attend the right courses which are relevant to their development needs or organizational requirements. The participant's chosen courses will be checked against the agreed learning path of each nominee as well as the requirements for completing pre-requisite courses. The workshops and seminars shall be at intermediate and advanced levels.

*Knowledge and Skill Seminars*

Each LI nominee will be required to undergo four compulsory courses per year initially, based on the learning path. The elective courses shall be faculty programmes, Leaders Teach series or knowledge and skill seminars.

## Pillar 3: Individual Development Plan (IDP)

Individual development plan (IDP) is the central tenet of LI. It is the single most powerful pillar, designed to create a culture of change and lead to the development of the individual. IDP is a means of translating intellectual property into reality. IDP aims to create capable individuals who can surmount professional challenges; every person has potential, and given the right opportunity, he/she can change and bring out the best in him/her. It is a proactive process which is initiated, nurtured and completed by the individual. Though the responsibility for change rests with the nominee, the LI faculty shall act as the facilitator in the process. The entire process of IDP is mandatory and compliance is required by tier-1 and tier-2 nominees.

IDP takes a proactive approach to planned individual development. Development goals shall be set based on the suggestions for improvement from the 360-degree feedback process. Given the critical value of IDP in the LI model, it is presented in greater detail and a separate comprehensive document is attached.

## Basic Concepts for Reflection by the Designers of IDPs:

The overlap between an individual's and an organization's core values, vision, mission and activities needs to be high. An increased overlap in terms of values and work and time commitment would be required. The lines between organizational development and individual development would need to be seen as closely intersecting aspects which facilitate organizational growth as an outcome.

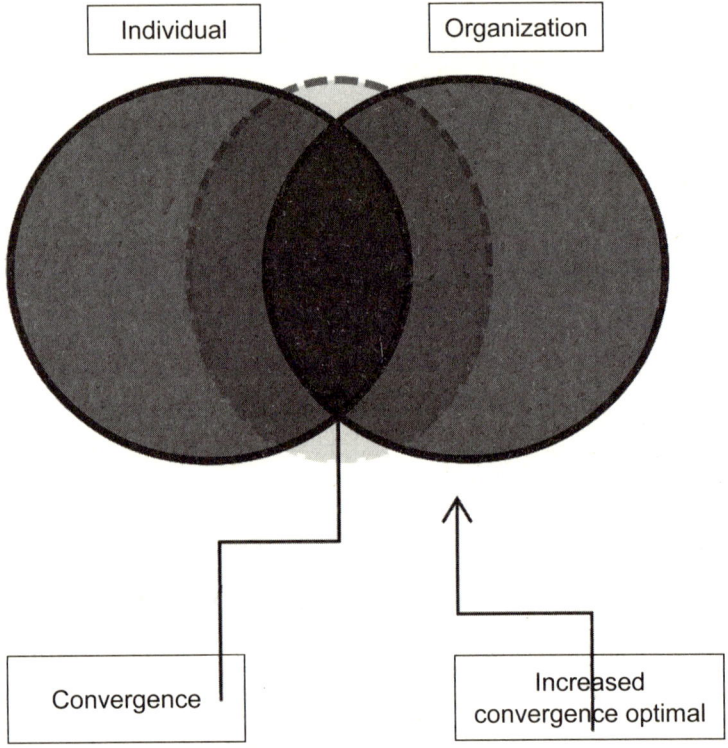

*Figure 5.2*

## Steps towards the creation of the IDP:

The objective is to build skills/competencies across roles spanning broad functions.

| Strategic | Administrative |
|---|---|
| Behavioural | Technical |

This can be done by referencing this matrix to ensure all four aspects of a role are considered.

- A 360-degree feedback process for individuals identified with potential which would become the input for the IDP.
- Identifying activities (job rotation, grassroots programmes, technical training, etc.) that would constitute the IDP.
- Ensuring activities are not just a reflection of the nominee's current role, but are experiences that facilitate growth and learning.
- Achieving an understanding and formulating individual development plans through a joint negotiation exercise between the individual and the organization.
- It is important to note that the development programme has to be a self-managed process by the individual with the management being available for guidance and consultation.
- IDPs should be individual-focused but would 'care' (reflect the priorities of) about the team each one leads, and ultimately, the whole organization.

## Internal Consulting: Learning by Consulting

Internal consulting (IC) is a key developmental activity. It helps in improving and developing the practical skills required for the identification and resolution of problems and the creation of business opportunities. Any change, modification or improvement in business activities consequent to the execution of an IC assignment which results in a tangible or intangible benefit to the lead LI group shall be construed as an IC. The IC process shall be undertaken by way of the following steps:

- A project proposal shall be developed which shall be signed off by the unit head. IC can be done in groups by LI nominees. IC done outside the division shall be reviewed by the unit heads from the parent and beneficiary units and signed off by the beneficiary division.
- IC done outside the division shall be construed as activity under the LI pillar 'developmental assignment'.
- The data relating to the potential or actual financial implication of each IC shall be made available to LI for creation of Developmental Assessment Metrics.

## 'Leaders Teach': Learning by Teaching

Learning by Teaching is yet another key LI activity. These activities could be by way of:

+ Handling sessions during the LI-LTS or knowledge and skill seminars either independently or jointly with a faculty, dean or fellow.
+ Handling sessions in general training courses which are facilitated by LI faculty or unit heads.
+ Supporting faculty sessions by preparing course materials and lesson plans.

## Developmental Assessment: Review Activity

This seeks to determine the impact of LI on the individual as well as on the organization. Individual assessment will be by tracking the change in the nominee's performance appraisal rating as well as by assessing the extent of achievement of the change objectives in the IDP. The LI impact shall be assessed by way of qualitative and quantitative assessment of the internal consulting assignments done by the LI nominees and the tangible and intangible benefits to the organization. This review of both the individual and LI shall be done at regular intervals.

## The Steps in the Creation of an IDP

IDP Process: The roles and responsibilities of the persons involved in the IDP process are:

*A. Nominee*

The role of the nominee is grouped under five distinct areas of activities as below:

1. Preparatory Stage:
    + Complete the 360-degree feedback process.
    + Get objective feedback from the appraiser as provided in the online performance appraisal system.
    + Prepare individual SWOT.

2. Deciding on the Change Goals and Objectives

    The nominee has to make SWOT analysis based on the 360-degree process results. Since there will be one IDP subsisting at any given point of time, if there is a pending action plan as per the previous IDP, it has to be brought forward. The change goals relating to such an action plan is treated as the on-going change goals and objectives. Besides these, the nominee can choose any number of change goals.

3. Preparation of IDPs
    + Defining the change goals/objectives.
    + Developing a detailed action plan for each of the change goals and objectives.
    + Identifying potential obstacles.
    + Developing a 'preventive' and/or 'contingent' solution for each potential obstacle.
    + Relating each change goal to the business need.
    + Identifying class of support persons and type of support persons.
    + Getting the IDP approved by the LI.

4. Fine-tuning of the IDP
    + Submitting the IDP to the designated LI faculty.
    + Seeking their observations.
    + Attending counselling sessions with the LI faculty if needed.
    + Modifying the IDP.
    + Submitting the revised IDP to the LI faculty.

5. Implementing and Following Up
    + Creating the action plan.
    + Measuring progress periodically.
    + Realizing the goals and objectives.
    + Preparing a fresh IDP.
    + Repeating the above processes.

B. *LI Faculty*

+ Assisting the nominee in preparing the IDP.
+ Counselling the nominee where and if required.

*C. Unit Heads*

+ Acting as the guide and counsellor in helping the nominee achieve his/her goals and change objectives set in the IDP.
+ Giving timely and honest feedback to the nominee regarding the progress/status of the change goals/objective.

## Pillar 4—'Leaders Teach'

### Knowledge and Skill Seminars and Workshops

LI, through its knowledge and skills seminars offering, shall address the needs of the LI group by:

+ Providing soft skills training to enhance the quality of leadership.
+ Providing functional skills in technical areas.
+ The knowledge and skills seminars are classified under three major heads, with sub-offerings under each head.

### Knowledge and Skills Seminars and Workshops

*Leaders Teach Series (LTS): Facilitated by Members of the Top Management of LI, Functional Specialists and LI Faculty*

The objective is the transfer of knowledge. The values and the beliefs that leaders have in their professional and personal lives can motivate others down the line. The leaders share their professional knowledge as well as their vision for the organization. Leaders can teach many subjects, not necessarily those confined to their areas of specialization. Leaders can also become advisory faculty to LI. The leaders and functional specialists would be encouraged to present their knowledge, vision and values through the medium of the Leaders' Teach series. The LI faculty would support the leaders in the smooth conduct of such programmes.

*Leaders Teach Series (LTS): By Other LI Nominees*

LI nominees based on their placement and expertise shall be encouraged to share their knowledge and skills by supporting leaders in their LTS programmes and by supporting LI faculty in their seminars

*By LI Faculty*

The LI faculty will also hold sessions for LI nominees. For the course design and methodology details, refer to the annexure.

*Business Needs Seminars (BuNS).*

These are special need-based programmes designed to meet the specific business needs of the LI group. These would be based on the business demands and requirements of the various units.

## Pillar 5—Internal Consulting

The fifth pillar—internal consulting—is organization development at its best. It is a highly refined form of process consulting. The process of internal consulting may be described as 'continuous improvement through employee involvement'. The unit heads shall identify problems or issues and offer them to LI nominees for internal consulting. Alternatively, LI nominees shall research existing processes and procedures and come up with process improvement proposals. This process helps supplement workshop efforts by resolving issues in actual work situations.

LI nominees will be encouraged to complete internal consulting assignments in other divisions. This will help LI nominees gain valuable information on the working of other divisions and make them more rounded in their knowledge and skills. This will facilitate cross-functional learning which can hold the nominee in good stead while trying to move to other divisions in search of better prospects.

| **Project Name:** | |
|---|---|
| LI Nominee/s: | |
| Employee ID/s: | |
| Division/Department: | |

| | |
|---|---|
| Division where IC done: | |
| Date: | |

**1. Business Need:**

Define the specific business need or problem being addressed. Include current and future needs. (A short phrase may be used to describe the current problem/difficulty/issue and the affected business unit or client group).

*Strategic Alignment*: Emphasize how this project aligns with corporate strategic objectives.

Note that a project can be advantageous but extraneous if it does not benefit the end customer or fit in with business initiatives.

**2. Project Purpose/Objective:**

Describe specific project objectives, for example, reduction of existing costs, operational efficiency, customer satisfaction, or improved communication. Identify key deliverables during the life of the project and at the completion of the project. Define, in as much detail as possible, what service, product or result is to be delivered by the project.

**3. Assumptions and Methods:**

*Key Assumptions*: Identify key assumptions for this project.

*Proposed Solutions:* Give an outline of possible solutions.

For example, is a new system required or are you proposing a change to an existing system?

—Is a new process to be adopted or an existing process to be modified?

—What process and/or tool currently exists and how is it managed?

**4. Project Impact Analysis:**

*Target Audience:* Define the users (internal/external) of the project deliverables. Identify which business units need to be involved in the project. Define areas of organization (business units and processes) will be impacted when the project is completed.

**5. Preliminary Estimates:**

(Use approximations—bear in mind that you are completing a financial analysis before any requirements analysis. These estimates will be refined as the project progresses and more detail analyses can be conducted).

**5a. Time Estimates:**

Provide the expected project duration, for example, six months or two years. Also identify any project phases and their timelines, for example, Phase 1—Eight months.

| 5b. Cost Estimates: |
|---|

Identify internal and external costs. Consider one-time implementation expenses, capital costs and on-going operational costs, including:
- Salaries, over-time expenses, travel expenses, vendor fees and consulting fees
- Training of staff and external resource costs
- Conversion costs and re-structuring costs
- Hardware and software costs (purchase costs and upgrade costs)

| 5c. Resource Estimates: |
|---|

Estimate the resources (equipment, people, etc.) needed to complete the project

| 5d. Benefit Estimates: |
|---|

Indicate expected financial benefit(s), its magnitude, and timeline(s) for the realization of such benefit(s).

Indicate expected non-financial benefit(s), its magnitude, and timeline(s) for the realization of such benefit(s).

*Notes/tips:*

State benefits in precise measurable terms. For example:
- Reduce average X process time from four days to one day.
- Eliminate X position(s) by day/month/year.
- Increase sales for X product by 10 per cent by day/month/year.
- Justify cost savings where possible and use cost avoidance carefully.

Define the work being eliminated. For example:
- Identify the role(s) that currently perform the work.
- Calculate the percentage of time currently spent performing the work.
- Identify the location of workers and determine whether it is actually possible to reassign work such that the headcount can be reduced.

| 6. Target Delivery Date and Consequences: |
|---|

Provide the specific time (if any) by which the project must be completed (for example, to comply with new government regulations which take effect May 2005).

Identify any consequences of the project being delayed, if applicable.

## Pillar 6—Developmental Relationships

'A person cannot lead others without first learning how to lead oneself. A mentor cannot mentor others without first having been mentored successfully. It is in "knowing thyself" and recognizing your own strengths and weaknesses that authentic leadership begins. It is in the experience of "seek and you shall find; ask and you shall receive" that we learn the wisdom of life and powerful strategies to help others.'[3]

## Introduction: What is Developmental Relationship/Mentoring?

The word 'mentor' reaches back to Greek mythology. When Odysseus went to war, he entrusted a mentor with his son's education and development. The mentor's wise counsel, teaching, parental concern and protection are evident in current interpretations of the mentoring process. Developmental relationship (DR) is effectively used in many organizations as a way of passing down values, beliefs and practices, thus implanting the organizational culture. It also contributes to leadership development, successful retention, career satisfaction and better decision-making.

Research indicates that too often, people are asked to take on a leadership role with little or no training. Although they devote time to fine-tuning management skills, they rarely spend time developing leadership skills. Mentoring is referred to in the literature as an interaction between a senior and junior member of an organization wherein the senior person takes an active role in the career development of the junior person. Blackwell has defined mentoring as 'a process by which persons of superior rank, special achievements and prestige instruct, counsel, guide and facilitate the intellectual and/or career development of persons identified as mentees.'[4]

## The Benefits of Mentoring

There is a substantial body of literature that demonstrates the benefits of mentoring to the mentee, the mentor and the organization as a whole. Through mentoring, mentees gain an understanding of the organization's culture, can access informal networks of communication that carry significant professional information, and can receive assistance in defining and achieving career goals.

Mentoring also benefits the mentor. Mentors gain satisfaction from assisting junior colleagues, improve their own managerial skills and benefit from working with bright and creative mentees. The process may also boost the mentor's self-esteem from being seen as successful and as having something to offer junior colleagues. Mentors also benefit from joint projects leading to shared grants and authorship as well as increased revenues from clinical practices. Mentoring has proven to be valuable to the overall stability and health of an organization. It plays a vital role in the development of leadership skills in both mentors and mentees.

## Mentoring Types Compared

There are two types of mentoring: informal and formal (Table 5.1). The traditional form, referred to as informal mentoring, is viewed as spontaneous, exclusive and reliant upon the 'chemistry' between the mentor and mentee. Formalized mentoring represents a paradigm shift that is more conducive to the organizational environment and is better able to prevent potential obstacles.

When combining the best features of these types of mentoring processes, we end up with what is called 'assisted' mentoring or development relationship (DR). Assisted mentoring is a formal programme which does not rely on a perfect match of personalities/chemistries as in the case of informal mentoring. The characteristics of informal and formal mentoring are as follows:

*Mentoring*

| INFORMAL | FORMAL |
|---|---|
| Spontaneous | Planned |
| Lifetime commitment | 4 months to 2 years |
| Comprehensive impact | Intentional impact |
| Relationship evolves | Matched pairing |
| 'Special chemistry' | Signed contract |
| No training | Programme assisted |
| Post-hoc evaluation | Pre-monitored, refined |
| No defined end | Designated end |

Exclusive                                    Inclusive
Mentor-driven                                Joint ownership of the process

*Developmental Relationship—Initiating the Programme*

This type of mentoring takes full advantage of the benefits of formality while maintaining the flexibility derived by tailoring mentoring objectives to meet the specific needs and goals of the mentee, based upon an inventory of desired skills and competencies. The procedures for matching pairs as mentors and mentees will include but not be limited to:

1. Selection of a specific senior participant to serve as a mentor (outside mentors?)
2. Assess needs and styles of mentor-mentee
3. Identify a process for matching the mentor-protégé (designated vs. voluntary)
4. Contract signing
5. Conduct mentoring workshop
6. Assist mentor/mentee pairs in reaching an acceptable level of comfort and deal with any interpersonal issues that may arise and help them develop realistic and achievable action plans
7. Document experience
8. Establish a review mechanism
9. Conclude relationship

*Roles and Responsibilities of Mentors and Mentees*

It is important to define mentoring roles in order to appreciate the significance of the commitments a mentor may be making. For simplicity, a list of key roles and their meaning is necessary:

- Trusted counsellor: A fellow participant, usually senior, to whom the mentee may go for advice. The counsellor listens to and reflects on the mentee's ideas and plans and shares his or her insights, practical experience and may recommend specific steps.
- Teacher or tutor: The mentor instructs or guides the mentee in learning

specific information or concepts. The mentor may provide specific information and some 'how to' guidance.
- Coach: The mentor may go over the mentee's training and background, assess the experience level, and where deficiencies are identified, teach these skills to the mentee. Then the mentor would let the mentee try out these new skills for which the mentor provides feedback at various stages.
- Motivator: The mentor encourages and pushes the mentee to assume additional responsibilities when the time appears right. She urges the mentee to test his or her capabilities.
- Sponsor: The mentor supports and represents the mentee to the organization. He or she may champion the mentee's request to attend developmental courses or full-time education or provide strong backing for a challenging assignment for the mentee.
- Referral agent: The mentor directs the mentee to proper sources to achieve his or her goal and introduces the mentee.
- Role model: The mentor is a senior participant who demonstrates, by example, the traits, performance and contributions that spell success; someone the mentee wants to emulate.

A good mentor has the knowledge, experience and willingness needed to guide the mentee. A good mentor must be accessible to the mentee, must be well-respected among professional peers, and must have professional contacts. A good mentor gives the mentee useful feedback in a constructive and caring manner, serves as a sponsor or advocate for the mentee, fosters the growth and independence of the mentee, and encourages the mentee to develop within his/her own terms.

The mentee must assume the role of one who is committed to learning, who will take responsibility for his or her career development, and one who will enter into an agreement to work with a mentor. The mentee's role includes making the best estimate of his or her current skills and competencies, participating in the style preference and needs assessments, and working with the prospective mentor to achieve a workable utilitarian contract to reach their agreed-upon goals. The mentees must commit to follow through on their action plans including re-addressing things that don't appear to be working well.

A good mentee possesses a positive and enthusiastic attitude toward work and career, a clear willingness to learn from the experience and wisdom of others, and a receptiveness to instruction. A good mentee is willing to work hard, does not expect the mentor to do work that the mentee is capable of doing him/herself, and does not expect to obtain benefits that have not been earned. A good mentee does not expect perfection from others and is willing to accept the limitations as well as the strengths of the mentor.

*Guidelines for Mentors*

A good mentor has the knowledge, experience and willingness to guide a protégé. He or she must also have a good sense of his or her parameters for the relationship. As the more seasoned participant in the relationship, it is up to you to set the tone for the relationship. As you enter into any type of mentoring relationship, you should:

- Set expectations: Tell your mentee how you can—and cannot—help him. If career counselling is to be an aspect of your contribution to the relationship, make sure that he understands that his success depends upon his efforts and that you cannot assure promotion, tenure, grant success, etc., simply by associating with him.
- Set boundaries: Be clear about how much time and energy you are willing to put into the relationship. A good mentor must be accessible to the protégé, but should not be expected to be accessible at all times. Advise the mentee on what areas of career development you feel that you can contribute to. For example, if you feel that you can contribute more in terms of research development, refer the mentee to another potential mentor for assistance in developing teaching skills. It is difficult to know at the beginning of these types of relationships whether or not the relationship will evolve into a friendship or remain relatively collegial. If you expect a mentoring relationship to remain a professional collaboration, communicate that early on in the relationship.
- Set standards: Define the standards of excellence within your areas of expertise. Share knowledge and information about the criteria you and your colleagues use to evaluate. Refer the mentee to specific resources or examples of excellence. Spend time with her analysing and illustrating why those resources and/or examples constitute 'excellence'.

- Provide feedback: When you observe behaviour that you feel is productive or problematic, share your observations with your mentee. Be clear about why you think that particular behaviour was positive or less than positive. When she accomplishes a particular objective, recognize and praise the accomplishment. Use this occasion as an opportunity to work with the mentee to set new goals. The key is to stay involved, listen, assess, observe and adopt the style that fits the situation. Inflexibility stifles growth and may cause the mentor/mentee team to dissolve.

Every organization has employees, who by virtue of their life, career, experience, education and wisdom have the ability to transfer to other people their knowledge, experience and wisdom through the process of mentorship coaching and guiding. A mentor is not a teacher, trainer, counsellor or supervisor, but complements the other roles by guiding the nominee through his/her professional, personal or organizational realities. A mentor builds support props around high potential individuals and makes them more confident and willing to face challenges. Each mentor would be encouraged to take on a few high potential individuals as mentees and LI shall facilitate such a mentoring process.

### Pillar 7—Developmental Assignment

Modern organizations are complex, most often created with different divisions for specialized tasks. Specialists run modern day organizations. While specialization can dramatically improve efficiency, it breeds tunnel vision and an inability to appreciate the role and relevance of other departments. It creates artificial barriers across the organization. In order to move up the ladder, it becomes imperative for every employee to gain hands-on experience in all the key functional areas of the organization. There are high potential people distributed randomly across the organization who are bright, creative and willing to learn and implement new strategies for business development. Working in multiple departments would enable the individual to develop strategic focus.

The developmental assignment pillar aims to create general managers out of specialists who have high potential. Developmental assignment is a special process that takes a leaf from the common sense idea that experience is the best teacher.

Developmental assignment is the process by which high potential individuals are exposed to the different functions of the organization and they generate an appreciation of the activities of key divisions and develop a holistic view of all the components of the system. Developmental assignment can help groom high potential individuals to migrate to new and evolving desks; it helps an organization tap internal talent. It also helps the organization build quality leaders within the group as it embarks upon new businesses in new geographical locations.

While it is advantageous in the long run, but in the short run, any step in the direction of moving and exposing people to other divisions can cause turmoil and disruption in the work flow. Hence, organizations tend to hesitate in implementing any drastic measures to rotate people. Hence, in order to give participants at least a glimpse of hands-on experience, this strategy is adopted in LI. This will, in the long run, lead to a large number of LI nominees gaining insight into the working of other divisions.

Nominees from different division are free to collaborate and form small teams to jointly undertake internal consulting assignments. This would facilitate a collaborative approach. It will also help foster a cooperative climate and will help the nominees understand group processes and real life leadership issues. It will be of particular significance in harnessing complementary skills for synergy.

Since internal consulting facilitates the honing of problem-solving skills, this process can also be used as a launch pad for the developmental approach. This will bring in a greater synergetic linkage amongst the three important pillars—internal consulting, developmental relationship and developmental assignment.

## Pillar 8—Community Empathy

LI aims to support the building a better society. At the corporate level, LI has initiated many steps for building a better country by funding and supporting various activities that need corporate support. In line with LI's vision to build a better world, it will encourage its faculty and nominees to join forces in assisting the needy by way of offering learning opportunities (for example, computer skills, accounting skills and entrepreneurial skills).

The LI faculty shall conduct seminars and debates on issues like energy conservation, renewable sources of energy, preservation of the environment, avoiding wastage, waste recycling, etc.

## Pillar 9—Developmental Assessment

This pillar represents developmental assessment and helps the LI measure the impact of the developmental process and its attendant results. The pillar also envisages rewards and recognition for outstanding performance.

The results of LI would be evident in the form of:

- LI nominees showing improvements in their knowledge and skills.
- LI nominees showing improvements in performance appraisal ratings.
- Lower attrition rate amongst LI nominees.
- Benefits to the organization through internal consulting assignments initiated by LI nominees.
- LI nominees shouldering higher responsibilities through the development of leadership qualities.

The instruments of assessment should also consider the process and the quantitative and qualitative impact of these processes. The most important LI processes which are measurable in terms of quantity and quality are:

- The individual development plans of nominees.
- Leaders Teach series, faculty seminars and knowledge seminars.
- Internal consulting.
- The impact on leadership and succession planning.

## Annexure 1: Development Assessment

*1. IDP and Performance Appraisal*

| | |
|---|---|
| Qualitative | Achievement of goals/change objective. Improvement in performance, evidenced by performance appraisal ratings. |
| Quantitative | Number of submissions, follow-ups and version changes. |

## 2. Leaders Teach Series, Faculty Seminars and Knowledge Seminars

| Qualitative | Course feedback |
| --- | --- |
| | Post-course evaluation of impact of training through instruments |
| Quantitative | Number of programmes held against target |
| | Number of business needs programmes held |
| | Number of LTS held |

## 3. Internal Consulting Impact on Process/Profitability/Product

| Qualitative | Improvement in processes and methods |
| --- | --- |
| | Improvement in profitability |
| | Innovations and development of products and services |
| Quantitative | Number of internal consultancy assignments |

## 4. Impact on Leadership/Succession Planning

| Qualitative | Confidence shown by the LI in advertising for jobs internally |
| --- | --- |
| Quantitative | Number of internal promotions gained by LI nominees |
| | Number of successful certificate holders and grades obtained |

## Annexure 2: Post-Course Evaluation

*Questionnaire for Assessing Impact of Learning—By Supervisor*

| COURSE: | DATE: FROM......TO |
| --- | --- |
| NAME OF PARTICIPANT: | |

In relation to the above-mentioned course attended by your staff member, please rate the post-course performance using the scales mentioned below:

| Key to Ratings | | | | |
| --- | --- | --- | --- | --- |
| A—Excellent | B—Very Good | C—Good | D—Fair | E—Poor |

*(The table may be modified by the faculty conducting the post-course evaluation)*

| Assessment | Grading Before the Course | Grading after the Course |
|---|---|---|
| Level of knowledge/skill/behaviour | | |
| Self-confidence | | |
| Motivation | | |
| Aspiration towards performance | | |
| Working relationship with peers/colleagues | | |
| Teamwork | | |
| Management of time and priorities | | |
| New ideas and innovations | | |
| Ability to accept responsibility | | |
| Overall productivity and effectiveness | | |
| Attitude and behaviour towards customers | | |
| Attitude and behaviour towards colleagues | | |

In what ways was the course effective from your point of view?

| OVERALL ASSESSMENT | GRADING |
|---|---|
| Rate how much improvement you have seen in general performance | |

*Prerequisites to Advise a Company for Establishing a Leadership Institute*

Criteria for a 'Go' or 'No Go' decision

| Parameter | Minimum Required on a Scale of 1-10 | Remarks |
|---|---|---|
| A growing company | 09 | Performance in terms of business and profits for the past three years should always be rising year-on-year |
| Image of the company | 05 | The company should have a positive image amongst the public as one which is above board in all transactions |

| Corporate governance | 08 | The company should be transparent in all dealings and there should be top-below communication on a regular basis |
|---|---|---|
| Outlook of the board | 09 | Board should be positively inclined to set up the institute |
| Growth plan in next **3-5** years *Organization Culture* | 08 | The company should have chalked out ambitious plans for business growth in the next **3-5** years and there should be willingness to grow |
| Top management receptive to new ideas and open to change and innovation *HR Philosophy and Policies* Quality of human resources | 09 | Top management should have a very positive attitude to try out new ideas and innovations Human resources should be of good quality and willing to learn |

## Prerequisites for a Great Leadership Development Programme (LDP)

| On a Scale of 1 to 10 | Don't start | Start but Watch | Start |
|---|---|---|---|
| Top management's understanding of why/what | <6 | 6-8 | >8 |
| Top management's commitment to why/what | | | |
| Middle management's understanding of why/what | | | |
| Middle management's commitment to why/what/ | | | |
| Good rate of growth in the last 3 years | | | |
| Plans for high growth in the next 5 years | | | |
| Open to change and innovation | | | |

| Believes and practises meritocracy | | | |
| --- | --- | --- | --- |
| Demonstrated willingness of the top management to lead by example (for example, Leaders Teach, 360-feedback, IDP, self-assessment and sharing it) | | | |

# NOTES

## Chapter 1

1. Francis Fukuyama (1995). *Trust, the Social Virtues & the Creation of Prosperity*. New York: The Free Press.
2. 'Today, you are the source of power, as the whole world sees,' Mohamed Morsi of the Muslim Brotherhood, after winning Egypt's presidential election, *New York Times*, 25 June 2012.
3. Garry Jacobs and Harlan Cleveland (1999). 'Social Development Theory', 1 November. Available at: www.icpd.org/development_theory/SocialDevTheory.html.
4. Timothy Noah (2012). *The Great Divergence: America's Growing Inequality Crisis and What We Can Do about It*. New York: Bloomsbury Press.
5. Josesph E. Stiglitz (2011). 'Of the 1%, by the 1%, for the 1%', *Vanity Fair*, May.
6. Benjamin Friendman (2012). 'Minding the Gap: Review of *The Great Divergence* by Timothy Noah', The *New York Times*, 27 May.
7. Timothy Noah (2012). *The Great Divergence: America's Growing Inequality Crisis and What We Can Do about It*. New York: Bloomsbury Press.
8. Isabel Ortiz and Mathew Cummins (2011). 'A Rapid Review of Income Distribution in 141 Countries', *Global Inequality: Beyond the Bottom Billion*, UNICEF.
9. 'Income Inequality Doubles in India in 20 Years', *Times of India*, 7 December 2011.
10. 'Poverty in Japan—Shadowy Figures', *The Economist* (Asia print edition), 3 March 2012.
11. Paul Krugman (2012). 'The Great Abdication', *New York Times*, 24 June.
12. Josesph E. Stiglitz (2011). 'Of the 1%, by the 1%, for the 1%', *Vanity Fair*, May.
13. David Brooks (2013). 'The Collective Turn', *New York Times*, 21 January.
14. Ross Douthat (2013). 'A World Without Work', *New York Times* Op-ed column, 23 February.
15. Russell Ackoff (1971). 'Towards a System of Systems Concepts'. *Management Science*, 17(11), pp. 661-67.

## Chapter 2

1. F. Heyligen (1997). 'Occam's Razor', *Principia Cybernetica*, 7 July.
2. Rick Newman (2010). '10 Great Companies That Lost Their Edge: How to Avoid Three Traps that Ensnare even Breakthrough Companies'. U.S. News & World Report, 19 August.
3. *Ibid.*
4. Jim Collins (2009). 'How the Mighty Fall, A Primer on the Warning Signs', *Businessweek*, May.
5. In Chapter 3, I present a model for the 'Rise and fall of Open Systems' (first presented in my dissertation, 'The Creation of New Settings', 1976, UCLA Graduate School of Management). I used the right-hand side of an image of a bell curve to describe the fall of an open system with similar stages and examples.
6. Jim Collins (2009). 'How the Mighty Fall, A Primer on the Warning Signs', *Businessweek*, May.
7. One of the early usages of the term 'transcendence' and the five qualities ascribed as 'pillars' here in the context of leadership was in the PhD dissertation by the author published in 1976 (UCLA Graduate school of Management, 1976, *Creation Of New Settings*, pp. 106–17).
8. Mathematician Somerhoff would have called it 'Directive Correlation'. (Ah! These mathematicians, what jargon, right?) A man goes to the forest at night and lights a candle. Another man goes to the forest and lights a bonfire. The first man accomplishes only one thing—there is a bit of light around the candle, that is all. The second man achieves multiple objectives—there is a lot more light, it provides cosy warmth in the cold night, it keeps wild animals away, it serves as fire for cooking his dinner, and if he is romantic, it will be a beautiful fire under the starry skies. The second strategy is transcendence.
9. Doris Kerns Goodwin (2006). *Team of Rivals*. New York: Simon & Schuster, p. 748.
10. Richard Feynman (1988). 'The Value of Science' from the classic *Feynman: All the Adventures of a Curious Character*.
11. Stephen Carter (1996). *Integrity*. New York: Harper Perennial, p. 7.
12. A mafia don is quoted as saying, 'You be crooked as much as you like, son, but don't ever have those working for you be anything but clean with you. In what you build there is place for only one crook, and that is you. Everyone else toes the line.'
13. For full disclosure, the author needs to share that he was the first Chairman of Infosys in its infancy (1981–85), and then again the Founder-director of Infosys Leadership Institute at Mysore, India (2001–03).
14. In the *Ramayana*, the ancient and sacred Hindu epic, Rama goes hunting in the forest while banished to live in the wilds by his father. He charges his loyal brother, Lakshmana, to look after Sita, his wife. Sometime later, Lakshmana

hears a piteous cry in Rama's voice from deep in the woods. Lakshmana is torn between protecting Sita and responding to his beloved brother's cry. He then decides to rush to his brother, but not before he draws a magic line on the ground in front of their hut. 'Please keep within this *lakshman rekha*,' Lakshmana implores Sita. 'All will be well if you keep within this line, whatever the temptation or provocation.' Then the devoted brother speeds away into the woods. As soon as he is gone, a holy man appears in front of the hut asking for food and alms. Sita brings out the food and tries to give it to the sage, but he was standing beyond the line. She hesitates and he says, 'Daughter, if you are so small-hearted that you do not even want to offer your alms to an old sacred man with respect, and if you wish to throw the food from a distance, then I do not accept your mean gift. Then the sin of refusing to feed a holy man will be on your head. If you wish to honour me, you must come to me and put the food properly into my bowl.' Sita reluctantly agrees and crosses the *lakshman rekha*, and lo and behold, the old man becomes the great demon Ravana who seizes Sita and abducts her away to his kingdom Lanka, thereby precipitating a bloody and terrible war with Rama and his army of monkeys and bears. Since then, *lakshman rekha* has become a metaphor for the limits of ethical action in life. Cross it and you may lose your most precious assets—moral identity, integrity and self-worth.

15. *The Economist* (21 January 2013). 'Leaders without followers', World Economic Forum Report, Davos, Switzerland. Retrieved on 21 April 2014 from http://www.economist.com/blogs/newsbook/2013/01/world-economic-forum-davos?fsrc=scn/tw/te/bl/leaderswithoutfollowers.
16 'To whomever much is given, of him will much be required; and to whom much was entrusted, of him more will be asked', *Luke 12:35–48* (World English Bible).
17 They said (I can't find who now) of Ezra Pound, the great American poet, who also was a supporter of Benito Mussolini of Italy, 'For his poetry give him the Nobel Prize; for his fascism shoot him.' My sentiments precisely towards Mr Churchill—not the shooting part, but you get my drift.
18 Isaiah Berlin (1940). *The Proper Study Of Mankind: An Anthology of Essays on 'Winston Churchill in 1940'*. New York: Farrar, Straus and Giroux, p. 607.
19 Benjamin Nugent (2013). 'The Adulterous Sins of Our Father Figures', *The New York Times*, 2 February.
20 Sir Geoffery Vickers (1968), *Value systems and Social Process*. New York: Basic Books.
21. Buckminster R. Fuller (1975). *Synegistsics: Explorations in the Geometry of thinking*. New York: Macmillan.
22 Bill Bryson (2003). *A Short History of Nearly Everything*. New York: Broadway Books, p. 19.
23 Charles Knight (1992). 'Emerson Electric: Consistent Profits, Consistently', *Harvard Business Review*.

## Chapter 3

1. Meadows et al. (1972). *The Limits to Growth.* New York: p. 24.
2. James G. Miller (1965). 'Living systems: Basic Concepts', *Behavioral Scientist,* 10(3), pp. 193-237.
3. Negentropy, also known as negative entropy or syntropy or extropy or entaxy, of a living system is the entropy that it exports to keep its own entropy low; it lies at the intersection of entropy and life. The concept and phrase, 'negative entropy', was introduced by Erwin Schrödinger in his 1944 popular-science book, *What is Life?* Later, Léon Brillouin shortened the phrase to *negentropy*, to express it in a more 'positive' way: a living system imports negentropy and stores it. In a note to *What is Life?* Schrödinger explained his use of this phrase: '[...] if I had been catering for them [physicists] alone I should have let the discussion turn on free energy instead. It is the more familiar notion in this context. But this highly technical term seemed linguistically too near to energy to make the average reader alive to the contrast between the two things.'
4. Philip Slater (1974). *Earthwalk.* New York: Anchor.
5. Geoffrey Vickers (1968). *Value Systems and Social Process.* New York: Basic Books, p 83.
6. D.A. Schön (1973). *Beyond the Stable State: Public and Private Learning in a Changing Society.* Harmondsworth: Penguin Books.
7. Lewis Thomas (1974). *Lives of a Cell: Notes of a Biology Watcher.* London: Penguin Books, p. 118.
8. Arthur Koestler (1969). 'Act of Creation' and 'Literature and the Law of Diminishing Returns', *Encounter.* London: Penguin Books.
9. D.A. Schön (1971). *Beyond the Stable State.* New York: Random House.
10. James March and Herbert Simon (1958). *Organizations.* New York: Wiley, p. 190.
11. D.A. Schön (1971). *Beyond the Stable State.* New York: Random House.
12. *Ibid.*
13. Arthur Koestler (1969). 'Act of Creation' and 'Literature and the Law of Diminishing Returns', *Encounter.* London: Penguin Books.
14. Alfred North Whitehead (1933). *Adventures of Ideas.* New York: Free Press, p. 203.

## Chapter 4

1. An object at rest will remain at rest unless acted up on by an unbalanced force. An object in motion continues in motion with the same speed and in the same direction unless acted upon by an unbalanced force. This law is often called 'the law of inertia'. What does this mean? This means that there is a natural tendency of objects to keep on doing what they are doing. All

objects resist changes in their state of motion. In the absence of an unbalanced force, an object in motion will maintain in this state of motion.
2   T.E. Weckowicz (1989). *Ludwig von Bertalanffy (1901-1972): A Pioneer of General Systems Theory*. Working paper, February, p. 2.
3   'Ludwig Von Bertalaffy', *Wikipedia. Accessed in* September 2014.
4   M.K. Smith (2001, 2011). 'D.A. Schön: Learning, Reflection and Change', *The Encyclopaedia of Informal Education*. Available at: www.infed.org/thinkers/et-Schön.htm, accessed on 12 April 2013.
5   D.A. Schön (1973). *Beyond the Stable State. Public and Private Learning in a Changing Society*. Harmondsworth: Penguin.
6   *Ibid*.
7   *Ibid*.
8   *Ibid*.
9   *Ibid*.
10  *Ibid*, p. 166.
11  *Ibid*.
12  Elting E. Morison (1966). 'Gunfire at Sea: A Case Study of Innovation', in *Men, Machines, and Modern Times*. Cambridge, MA: The MIT Press, pp. 17-44.
13  *Ibid*.
14  *Ibid*.
15  Steven R. Rayner (1996). *Megatraps: The Team Killers*. Rayner and Associates.
16  *Ibid*.
17  D.A. Schön (1973). *Beyond the Stable State: Public and Private Learning in a Changing Society*. Harmondsworth: Penguin.
18  Steven R. Rayner (1996). *Megatraps: The Team Killers*. Rayner and Associates.
19  F.E. Emery and E.L. Trist (1965). *The Causal Texture of Organizational Environments*. London: Tavistock Publications.
20  R.L. Ackoff (1971). 'Towards a System of Systems Concept,' *Management Science*, 17(11).
21  Tom Wolfe (1968). *The Pump House Gang*. New York: Farras, Straus and Giroux.
22  Louis Smith and Pat Keith (1971). *Anatomy of an Educational Innovation*. New York: John Wiley.
23  F. Emery and E. Trist (1965). 'The Causal Texture of Organizational Environments', *Human Relations*, 18(1) pp. 21-32.
24  *Ibid*, p. 2.
25  *Ibid*.
26  Geoffrey Vickers (1968). *Value Systems and Social Process*. New York: Basic Books, pp. 77-78.
27  *Ibid*, pp. 79-80.
28  Chris Argyris and D.A. Schön (1978). 'Organizational Learning: A Theory of Action Perspective', pp. 22–23; also see Gregory Bateson, Don D. Jackson,

Jay Haley and John Weak land (1956). 'Toward a Theory of Schizophrenia', *Behavioral Science,* 1(4), pp. 251–54.

29  Atul Gawande (2009). *The Checklist Manifesto.* London: Picador, pp. 18-19.
30  Anthony Bianco and Pamela L. Moore (2001). 'Xerox: The Downfall', *Businessweek,* 4 March.
31  Joe Flower (1993). 'We Can Do Better: An Interview with Robert Camp', *The Healthcare Forum Journal,* January-February 36(1).
32  Andrea Nagy Smith (2009). 'What Was Polaroid Thinking?' *Yale Insights,* November.
33  *Ibid.*
34  *Ibid.*
35  Peter Senge (1990). *The Fifth Discipline: The Art and Practice of Learning Organizations.* New York: Random House.
36  *Harvard Business Review* (January 1992). 'Emerson Electric: Consistent Profits, Consistently', Charles F. Knight. Retrieved on 21 April 2014 from http://hbr.org/1992/01/emerson-electric-consistent-profits-consistently/ar/7.
37  Frank Boles, Mary Janzen and Richard Popp (1981). 'Descriptive Inventory for the Bowman Dairy Company Records'. Chicago Historical Society.
38  *Ibid.*
39  *Ibid.*
40  'The History of the Can: An Interactive Timeline'. Can Manufacturers Institute. Available at http://www.cancentral.com/can-stats/history-of-the-can.
41  'A Time for Innovation', Can Manufacturers Institute. Available at http://www.cancentral.com/can-stats/history-of-the-can/time-innovation.
42  G.K. Jayaram (1976). 'Open Systems Planning', in W.G. Bennis et al. (eds), *The Planning of Change* (3rd edition). New York: Holt, Reinhart and Winston, pp. 275-283.
43  For full disclosure, the author provided consultation services to CEMEX in their 18 factories in Mexico during the 1990s.
44  D.A. Schön (1971). *Beyond the Stable State.* New York: Random House, p. 56.
45  The definition of change may be modified during this transformation journey, but that is 'par for the course' of a holistic, systemic change under conditions of VUCAI. In fact, one must get suspicious about the learning ability of the change system if the definition does not change to a little or large extent, qualitatively and quantitatively.
46  Doris Kearns Goodwin (2005). *Team of Rivals: The Political Genius of Abraham Lincoln.* New York: Simon & Schuster.
47  'Xerox Corp's Turnaround Strategy', *ICMR Case Studies Collection,* 2004. Available at http://www.icmrindia.org/casestudies/catalogue/Business%20Strategy2/Xerox%20Corp%20Turnaround%20Strategy.htm.
48  *Ibid.*
49  Joshua M. Plotnik, Frans B.M. de Waal and Diana Reiss (2006). 'Self Recognition

in an Asian Elephant', *Proceedings of the National Academy of Sciences of the United States*, 30 October.
50  'The Science: Publications', *Think Elephants International Website*. Available at http://thinkelephants.org/pages/ow_elephants_think.html.
51  *Ibid.*
52  *Ibid.*
53  'Elephant Leadership'. *Coaching Through Wilderness,* 14 January 2013. Available at http://wamvengatraining.com/teambuilding-leadership-course/.
54  Lesley Evans Ogden (2014). 'What Elephants Can Teach Us about the Importance of Female Leadership', *New Scientist*, Issue 2950.

# Chapter 5

1  Judith Silver (2001). 'Movie Day at the Supreme Court "I Know It When I See It": A History of the Definition of Obscenity'. Available at: Coollawyer.com.
2  L.G. Valiant (1984). 'A Theory of the Learnable', *Communications of the ACM, Artificial Intelligence and Language Processing,* 27(11).
3  Susan S. Stratton, Lisa H. Wootton and Dorothy I. Mitstifer (2000). 'Self-Managed Mentoring', Kappa Omicron Nu (KON) Honor Society. Available at http://www.kon.org/mentoring/.
4  J. E. Blackwell (1989). 'Mentoring: an action strategy for increasing minority faculty', *Academe,* 75(5), pp. 8-14.

## ACKNOWLEDGMENTS

For an autodidact, a book is a mother, a mirror, a brother, a lover... A good book is sometimes a refuge from reality, at other times a return to harsh reality, but always—an ideal friend. They only give and ask nothing in return.

I knew this as a compulsive reader but have come to know that it is even truer for a compulsive writer.

To me, writing a book is an act of affection towards the life one has lived and a lustful invitation to the life that lies ahead. Such a creation can only happen when those who care for you are willing to listen to you. In my life, people who have been gracious enough to have given their time and mind in bringing out this book are the following:

My wife, Minny (Mrinalini) Jayaram, who has been hearing about this book for more than thirty years, so often that she could have written it herself. Her affection and care has sustained me through the white-water-rafting life we have lived. Our children, Athmeya—the philosopher and Amshula—the justice crusader, are my close friends and also my stern critics. Athmeya read and critiqued most of this book in the midst of his dissertation. This book owes a lot to him. Amshula, for her part, has heard me speak about the book with grace, good humor and critical intelligence. I hope she likes it.

A special phase of my life, and the life of ILID, our organization, had begun about the same time I had started writing on 'how to help an elephant make a U-turn'. This phase became a laboratory for the testing of ideas mentioned in this book and helped me learn, once again, the lessons that I had learnt in the past four decades of work. I owe a lot to those who helped me create Project PUPIL, a free online tutoring program for poor kids in India and the US, with grant funds form the US project subsidizing our Indian school initiatives. There are four leaders of global stature—S.D. Shibulal, Kris Gopalakrishnan, N.R. Narayana Murthy and Bill Gates—who, especially, supported my idea. Today, the project is in its second year, and is serving 2,000 poor kids in the US and India, and will serve many more thousands in the years to come.

A special thank you to the friend, one of the most remarkable leaders I have known, N.R. Narayana Murthy, for being with me since 38 years and supporting my many adventures to 'do good' in the world.

To all the leaders who graciously consented to be interviewed by me for two hours or more, I am very grateful. The list of these good leaders is in the book, but I must absolve them of any responsibility for the contents of my views. I plucked and picked flowers from the gardens they laid out and made garlands out of them, whether for good or worse, you be the judge.

Devapriyo Ghosh, thanks for reading the book thoroughly. You were brilliant in your understanding, providing the most valuable insights.

Vijay Mahajan, friend and adopted brother, one of the most brilliant do-gooders, a great leader and a great human being. Your encouragement was invaluable to me in this process. I express my gratitude to Naved Ahmad and Dharen Chadda for their thoughtful critique in the early stages of the book.

Steve Jobs was a fan of a journal called *Whole Earth Catalog* from its inception in the 1970s, round about the same time when the core concepts of this book began its journey. I thank the systems, theorists and practitioners of the esoteric art of transformation for letting me learn their science, art and craft.

The poem below is the distilled wisdom of the generation that dared to dream:

> *beware of whole systemitis*
> *it's the loneliness awareness,*
> *Imagine you are a nearsighted, bucktoothed, kid, doing sunflower seeds,*
> *and somebody comes along and puts eyeglasses on you,*
> *holds up a mirror,*
> *then takes you up a hilltop at night*
> *points up at the little winks out there*
> *and tells you they aren't little winks at all,*

*but great big flashes,*
*a long way away,*
*then asks you if you want some more sunflower seeds.*

*you want to throw away the eyeglasses, but it is too late,*
*you are stuck,*
*you have seen it,*
*you are little,*
*alone,*
*puny,*
*except...*
*except for a few soft flannel thoughts,*
*and a belief that there are others like you,*
*brothers like you,*
*and that a sunflower seed*
*is a whole system too.*

*Whole Earth Catalog,* 5 May 1974, p. 5